IMAGES
of America

NEWTON COUNTY

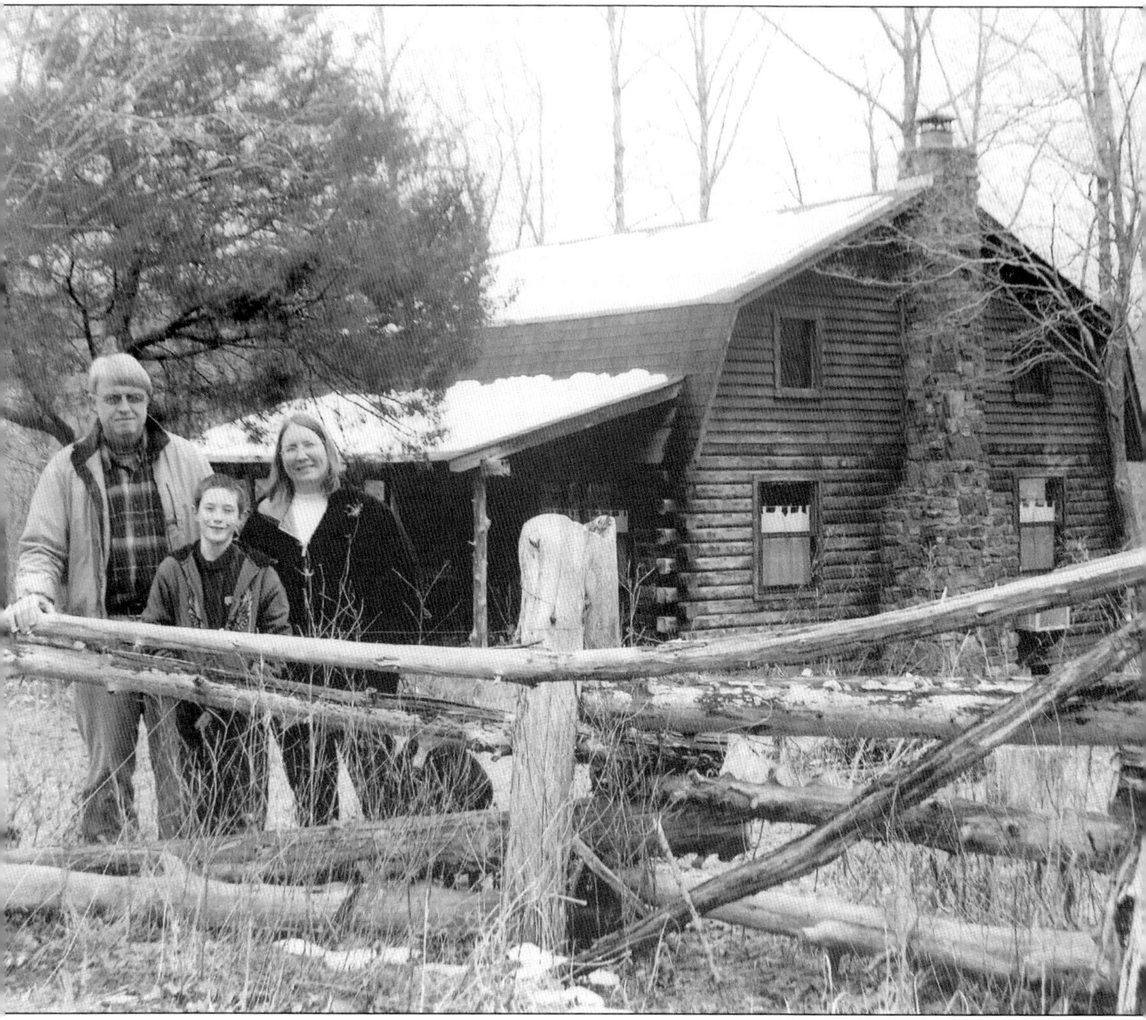

The authors and their son J.D. are photographed in front of their log cabin, located above Spider Branch east of Jasper. Log cabins are a part of the fabric of the heritage of Newton County, Arkansas, and are prized today by not only the authors but others in the county.

ON THE COVER: The Buffalo River has been a favorite for swimmers since the first settlers arrived in the early 1800s. The swimmers were photographed at the Little Buffalo River, a tributary of the main Buffalo River, at what is today Jasper's Bradley Park. The photograph is from around 1920, an era of modest swimming attire for men and women alike.

IMAGES
of America

NEWTON COUNTY

Ray and Diane Hanley with the
Newton County Historical Society

ARCADIA
PUBLISHING

ISBN 978-0-7385-9431-6

Published by Arcadia Publishing
Charleston, South Carolina

Printed in the United States of America

Library of Congress Control Number: 2012940082

For all general information, please contact Arcadia Publishing:
Telephone 843-853-2070
Fax 843-853-0044
E-mail sales@arcadiapublishing.com
For customer service and orders:
Toll-Free 1-888-313-2665

Visit us on the Internet at www.arcadiapublishing.com

We dedicate this book, in equal parts, to those who have strived to capture and preserve the history of Newton County and to those who have worked tirelessly to protect the magnificent gifts of creation found in nature that make the area such a special place.

Contents

Acknowledgments		6
Introduction		7
1.	Life and Commerce around the Jasper Courthouse Square	9
2.	The Timeless Buffalo and the Nature that Surrounds It	31
3.	Working Hard to Earn a Living from a Rocky Land	45
4.	Hardship and Perseverance in the 1930s	55
5.	Hamlets and Crossroads	69
6.	Teaching and Preaching in Schools and Churches of Newton County	79
7.	Bygone Tourist Attractions	93
8.	Scenic Highway 7	105
9.	Faces of Newton County	117

Acknowledgments

This book has been possible only because of help from a number of people, both within and outside of Newton County. Major thanks go to Donna Dodson of the Newton County Historical Society for invaluable help locating photographs and for her scores of e-mails to help with research and editing. Thanks to the rest of the Newton County Historical Society for endorsing the project. Thanks to Jennifer Tapp of the Newton County Library for giving access to the archived photographs previously assembled by Lois Landrum. Thanks also to Marie Demeroukas of the Shiloh Museum at Springdale for help on the 1930s chapter; to Geoffery Stark of the University of Arkansas Special Collections for access to Dr. Neil Compton's Buffalo River photographs; to Lytle James for photographs of the "search for Haley"; to Robert Cole of the Newton County Historical Society and of Ozark Realty in Jasper (whom anyone searching for their own piece of Newton County should call); to Cathy Bain for scanning help, and to Ray Scott Photography of Little Rock (www.rayscottphotos.com) for providing a great photograph of a majestic elk. A very special thanks goes to Arcadia Publishing for seeing the potential in putting this work into print.

Photograph credits are as follows: Newton County Historical Society noted by NCHS; Newton County Library by NCL; others as delineated in text; where not noted, photographs are from the authors' collection. The quotations and photographs throughout the fourth chapter are from Ernest and Opal Nicholson.

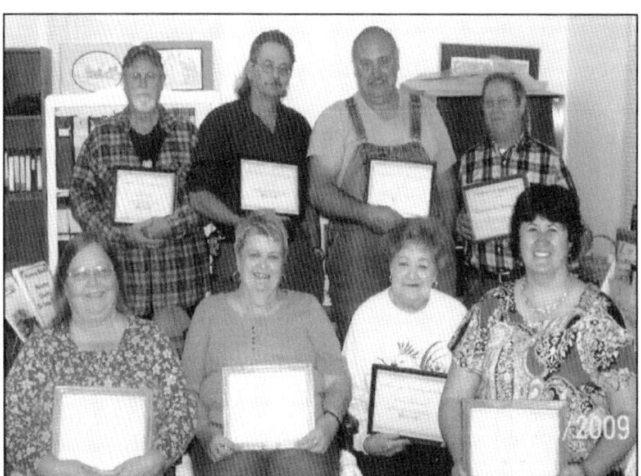

The Board of the Newton County Historical Society, since the organization was founded in the early 1950s, has worked tirelessly to capture and preserve the history of the county. Pictured in 2010 are board members, from left to right, (first row) Sharon Pierce, board vice president Rhonda Teter, Barbara Carpenter, and Yalonda Martin; (second row) James Robert Campbell, Robert Cole, Darrell Martin and board president Thomas Niswonger. Sharon Pierce has since resigned, and Bill Perry has replaced her.

Introduction

Our family started coming to Newton County, Arkansas, over 30 years ago to backpack the trails of the Upper Buffalo River Wilderness Area that traversed perhaps the most rugged, scenic landscape in the central United States. We hiked first as a young newlywed couple and later with our young daughters, who grew up sleeping on the ground in the winter and wading in cold mountain streams on the way to the best campsites.

In the winter of 2010, having reached an age when it was not as appealing to sleep on the ground in all manner of weather, we bought a log cabin and 57 acres of mountainside above Spider Branch east of Jasper. As our stake in Newton County grew, we turned our interest to capturing the remarkable history of the area in a book, a project embraced by the staff at Arcadia Publishing. We chose to reach out to the Newton County Historical Society as collaborators on this project; this group's help has proven invaluable.

The history of Newton County is both long and fascinating, a history going back thousands of years. When the first pioneers of European descent began to arrive after 1800, they found that tribes such as the Cherokee, Choctaw, Fox, Kickapoo, and Osage either lived in the area or came there to hunt.

The town of Jasper first appeared on maps in 1840, two years before Newton County was created in 1842, having been carved out from Carroll County. The county was probably named to honor Thomas W. Newton, who would be elected to Congress in 1842. The origin of Jasper as a name is uncertain, but a popular legend is that John M. Ross picked the name by comparing the characteristics of a rock formation in the area to that of jasper, one of the 12 precious stones referred to in the Book of Revelation.

The peace and prosperity of Newton County was interrupted by the Civil War, when the Union army burned Jasper to the ground while searching for Confederate guerrilla leader John Cecil. The area recovered quickly after the war, as Jasper became a boomtown with local sawmills employing hundreds of men. Oak timber was turned into barrel staves, and the cedar that lined the Buffalo was harvested to make pencils. By 1900, Newton County recorded a population of 12,538 people.

The people and hills of Newton County came to wider notice during the Great Depression, when the Federal Writers Project commissioned otherwise unemployed writers to go into the remote areas of the state. The resulting book, *Arkansas: A Guide to the State*, offered the outsiders' observations of the county. These visiting writers found a people who, by measures of the outside world might have been poor, yet maintained pride and self-sufficiency centered on their families, churches, and hard work. In 1941, when the book was published, the population of Jasper was 412, about 50 less than it is today.

As observed in *Arkansas: A Guide to the State*, "Though most of the Ozarks are low and gently rounded, these fall away in breath-taking descents and present wide views of tumbled forests that fade into a blue haze. Because of the sharp angles of the terrain the farmer usually cultivates only the top of a hill." The Writers Project authors, working at the end of the Great Depression, took note of the remoteness of the area and how it influenced residents' self-sufficiency: "Such typical pioneer contrivances as rail fences, and horse troughs made from half a hollow log, bespeak of the isolation that the mountains have forced upon inhabitants of this region." The writers, who had lived in distant cities where their food had come from grocery stores, marveled at the Newton County residents' independence in putting food on their tables. They stated, "The cultivated plots in this rugged area are planted in corn, vegetables and feed crop, and farmers are nearly independent of the outside world for their food. Attics are packed with canned and dried peaches and apples, strings of dried peppers, beans, onions, and home-cured salt pork."

The writers went to some length to describe the inhabitants as rough, somewhat uncouth, and definitely of an earlier time in speech and dress. The descriptions, once published, helped perpetuate the "hillbilly image" that both the Ozarks and Arkansas as a whole have long felt to be unfair not just in 1941, when the book came out, but also for many years after that. The struggle to cast aside the "hillbilly" image would remain with Newton County and all of Arkansas for years to come, in part because of radio comedians like Bob Burns and the duo of Lum and Abner.

During the Great Depression and World War II, an exodus from the Ozarks began, as people moved off the land to seek better jobs in other states. The US government began to acquire cutover timberland; old homesteads, some along remote, uncut valleys and canyons, became part of the expanding Ozark National Forest. By the 1940s, the Buffalo River and the Newton County scenery were starting to be noticed by people well beyond the borders of Arkansas. *National Geographic* did an article on the area in 1945; *Time* magazine did a 1961 feature on camping and used pictures of the Buffalo River to illustrate the story. Yet by 1965, the area had fewer than half the population that had been present in 1900.

Today, Newton County is the recreational hub for the upper portions of the Buffalo National River, the nation's first such designated stream. Threatened with dams from the 1930s, it appeared that the beautiful Buffalo, lined with soaring limestone bluffs, would suffer the fate of many of the other rivers in the Ozark region—to be submerged beneath vast impoundments of water. The creation of the National River came about amidst considerable controversy for the US government would have to take over land by eminent domain and would place use restrictions on other parcels that had been in some families for generations. While some area residents favored the dams and resulting impoundments, in a county where good jobs were scarce, the majority of residents simply desired to keep the river and the land the way it was, with no dams and also with no federal takeover to create a National River. The creation of the National River, however, was sealed with the support of the Arkansas congressional delegation and with that of Gov. Orval Faubus, himself a native of neighboring Madison County. On March 1, 1972, the 100th anniversary of the creation of Yellowstone National Park, President Nixon signed the legislation. The Buffalo National River consists of 132 miles of free-flowing river, bordered by some 95,000 acres of designated wilderness land. Although many residents would have preferred a different outcome to the battle over the Buffalo, both Jasper and Newton County have been able to successfully market the natural wonders of the river and surrounding park. In February 2012, the *Newton County Times* reported that the previous year had seen tourism bring $11 million into the county, a considerable sum for such a rural area.

As of the 2010 census, the county seat of Jasper is home to 466 people, while Newton County as a whole lists just over 8,000 residents. The area hosts thousands of canoeists, hikers, bikers, and sightseers year-round. On behalf of the authors and the Newton County Historical Society, it is hoped that this book will allow some of those visitors to take home a bit of the history of this beautiful place.

One

Life and Commerce around the Jasper Courthouse Square

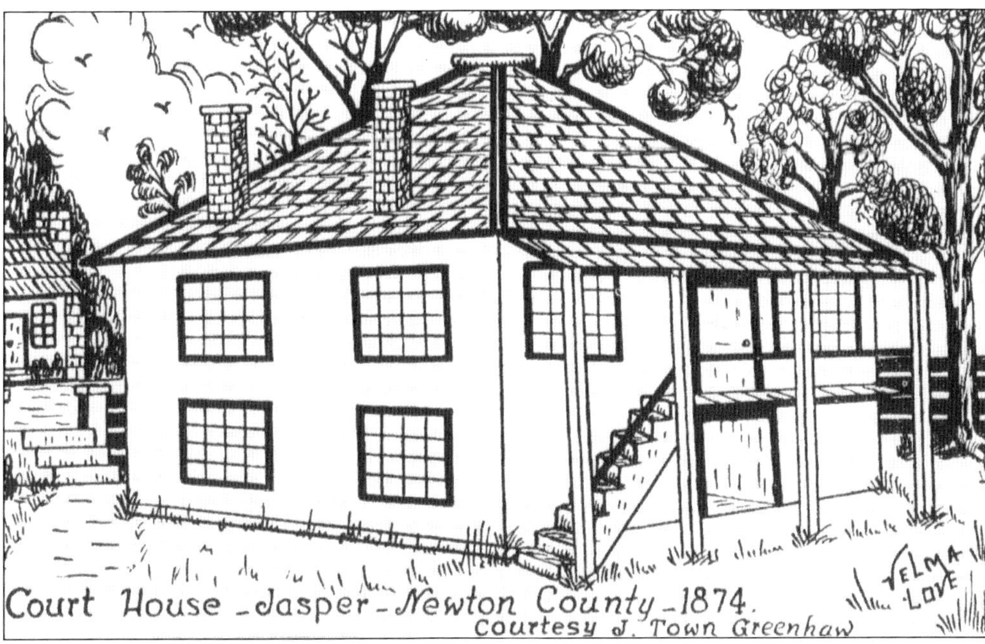

The first non-log courthouse for Newton County was constructed by Robbie Hobbs in 1872, using rocks hauled from the Little Buffalo River. The walls were 10 inches thick and plastered with mortar made from burned, crushed limestone mixed with sand. The surface was finished and marked to look like cut stone. A curious lady discovered she could dig through the surface with a fingernail and soon incited the population against the builder, Hobbs, who had promised a building that would last forever. Local lore states that an angry group of citizens took Hobbs to nearby Dog Hollow and cut his throat. His building, however, would stand for several more years, actually requiring dynamite to remove it for a replacement courthouse.

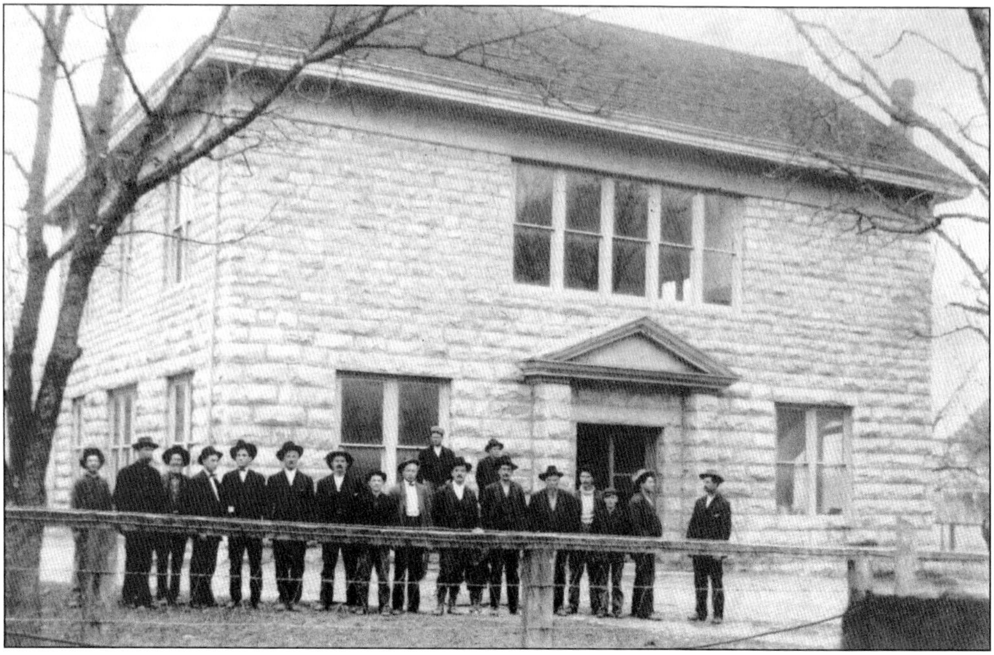

A new courthouse, along with a jail across the street, was erected in 1902 for a total of $9,200. Among the men posed before the new building are, from left to right, Ike Moss, Jess O'Neal, Joe Morgan, Walter Smith, Wilburn Moore, W.W. Moore, Bill Green, Garrett Brasel, Charley Smith, Judge Spears, Ben McFerrin, Lester Davis, Sam Hudson, John Brasel, Dick O'Neal, Argie Cecil, Dee Snow, and Fred Boomer. Some of these men were descendants of pioneer families. (NCHS.)

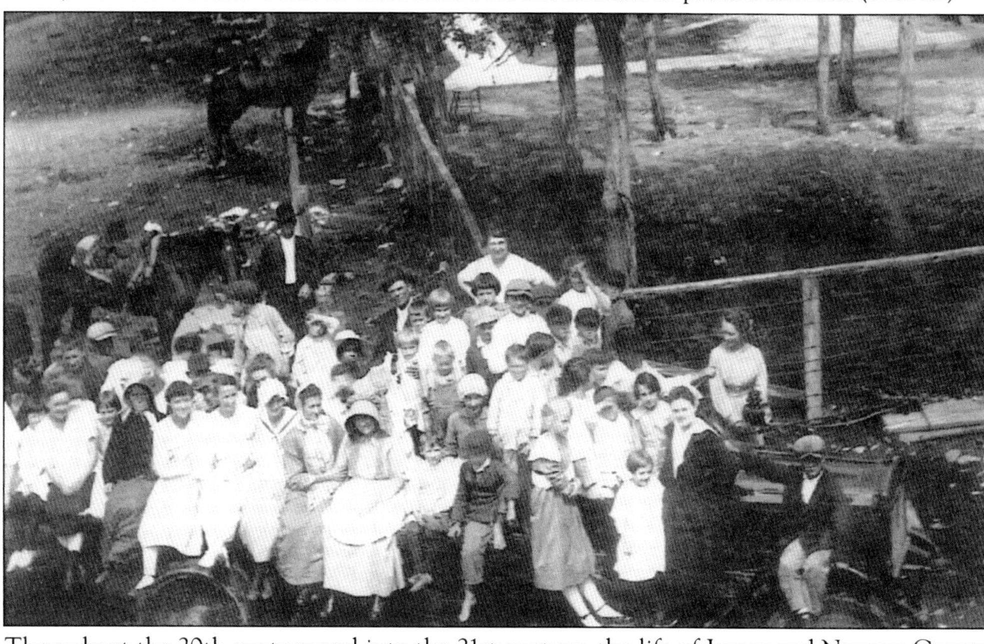

Throughout the 20th century and into the 21st century, the life of Jasper and Newton County revolved around events and everyday commerce in the historic square. Seen here in 1916, taken from atop a building, a crowd of mostly women and children has gathered at the edge of the courthouse lawn, with some seated on a shiny new truck. (NCL.)

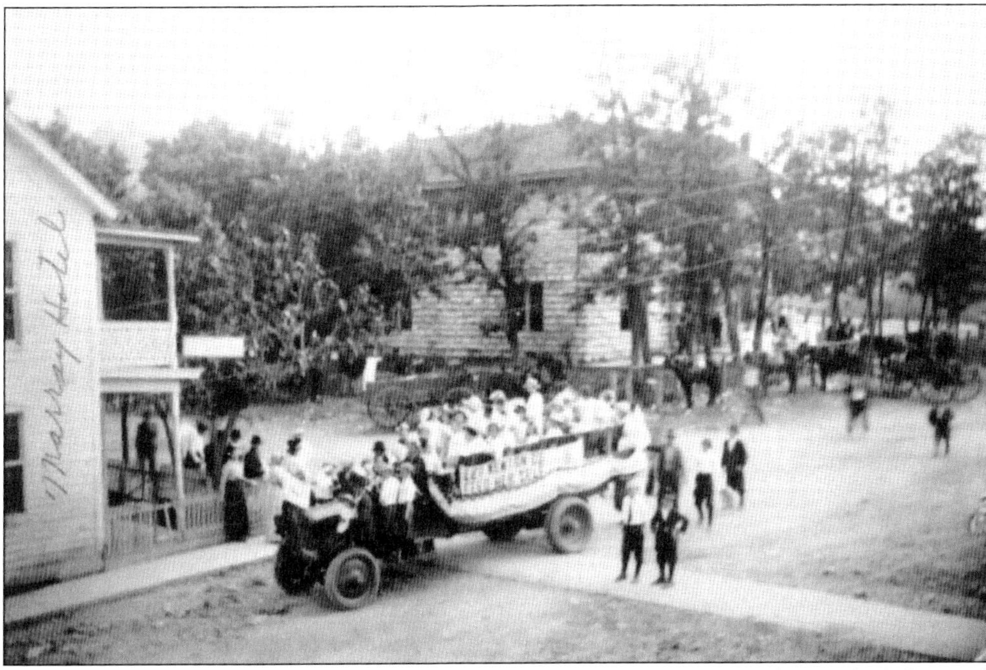

The first Newton County Fair Parade passed the courthouse in 1916. The truck, laden with young people, bore a banner that proclaimed, "Let Newton County Feed Herself." The Murray Hotel is just to the left on the unpaved square. The truck was reported to be one of the first trucks brought to Newton County and was used to haul ore from the Panther Creek Mine to the railroad at Harrison. (NCL.)

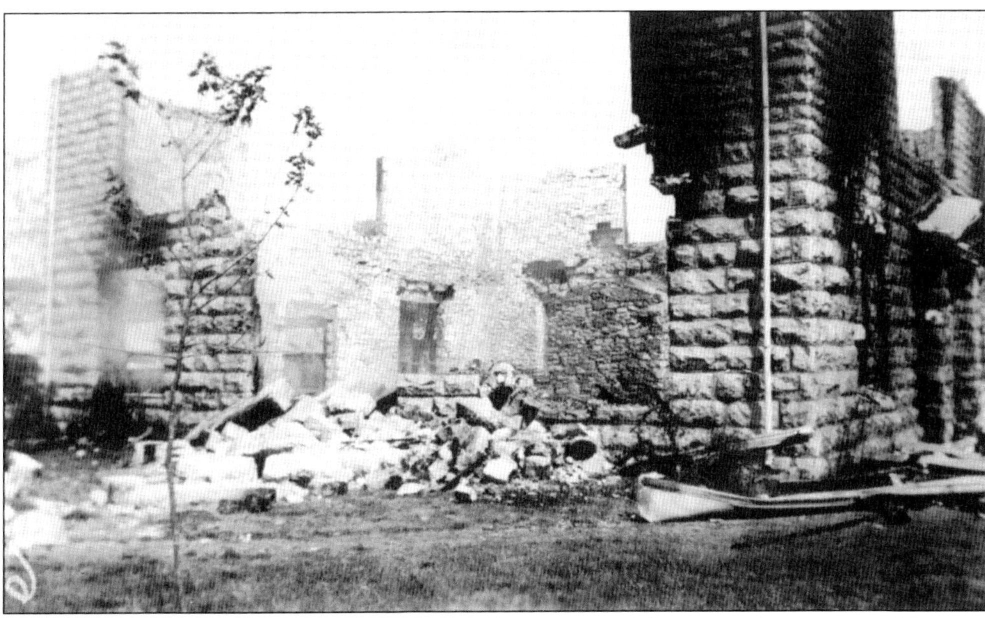

The 1902 courthouse was destroyed by fire in 1938, a fire widely rumored to be arson. However, no one was ever tried or convicted of the suspected act. Soon, attention turned to building a new courthouse. (NCL.)

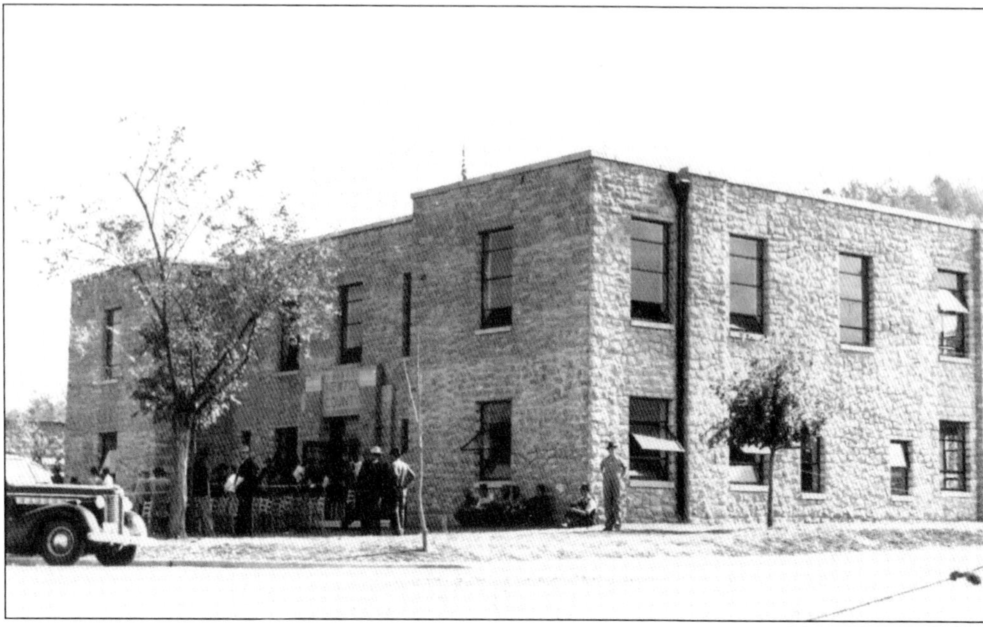

The new courthouse was a WPA project, completed in 1942. It was designed to be fireproof, as it was built of limestone quarried from the bed of the Little Buffalo River and supplied with concrete floors. The residents of Newton County were taking no more chances. The building still serves today as the focal center of the town square and is on the National Register of Historic Places. (NCL.)

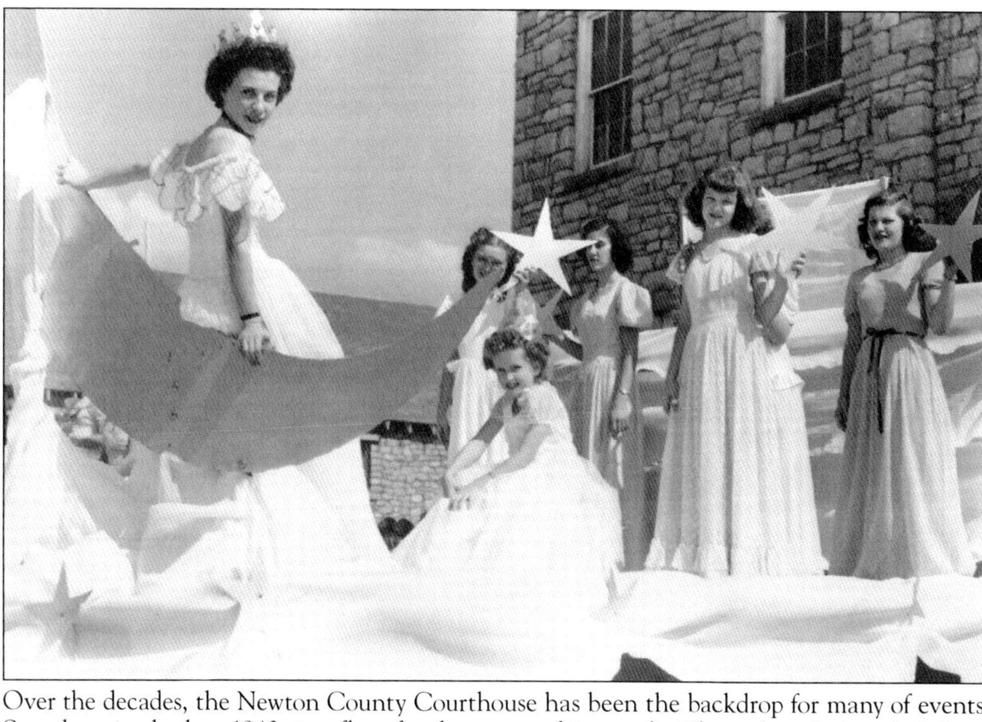

Over the decades, the Newton County Courthouse has been the backdrop for many of events. Seen here in the late 1940s is a float for the county fair parade. The only girl identified, Jerry Lynn Reynolds, is sitting second from the left. (NCL.)

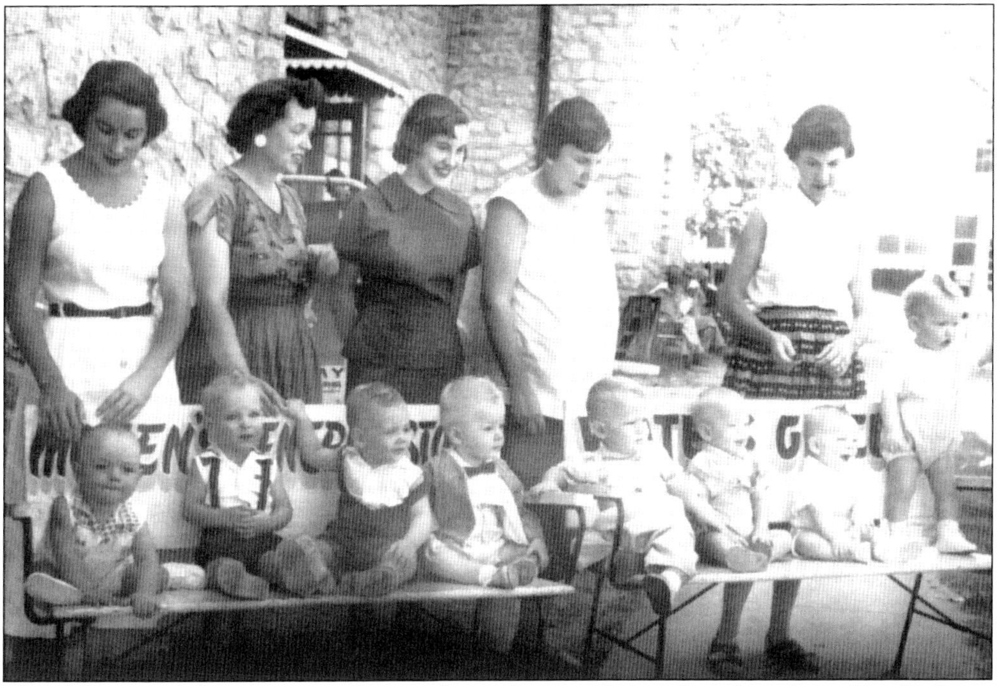

The 1960s saw a baby contest on the courthouse lawn, with proud mothers dressed in the finery of the day and posed behind their well-groomed toddlers. (NCL.)

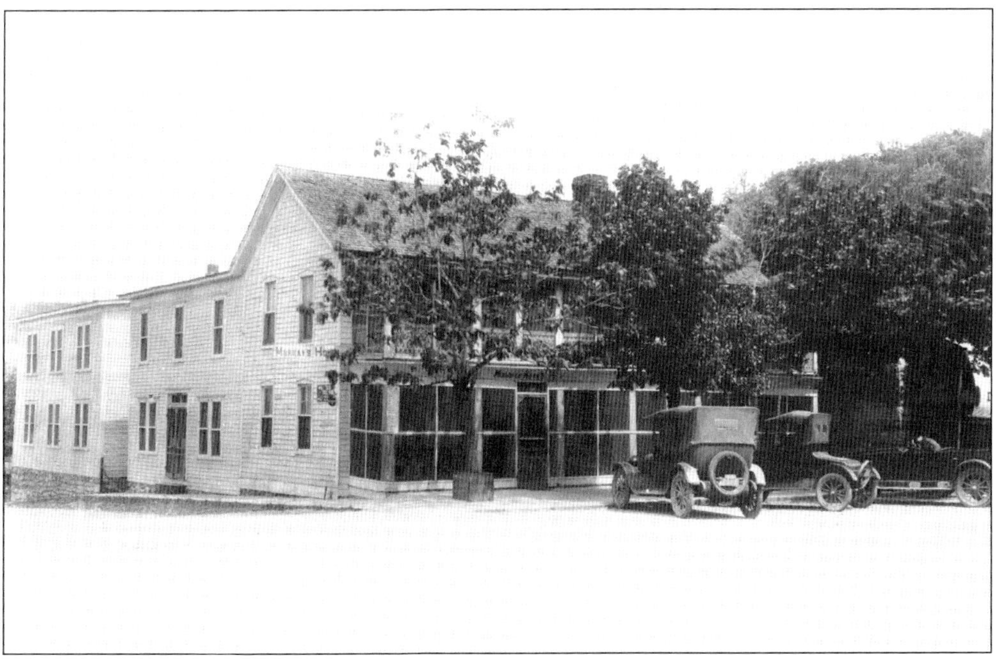

Shown around 1920, the rambling, wooden Murray Hotel, located across Spring Street from the Newton County Courthouse, hosted tourists and traveling salesmen for many years before being razed. At the time of this photograph, a room would have cost less than $2, with meals for perhaps 25¢ to 50¢.

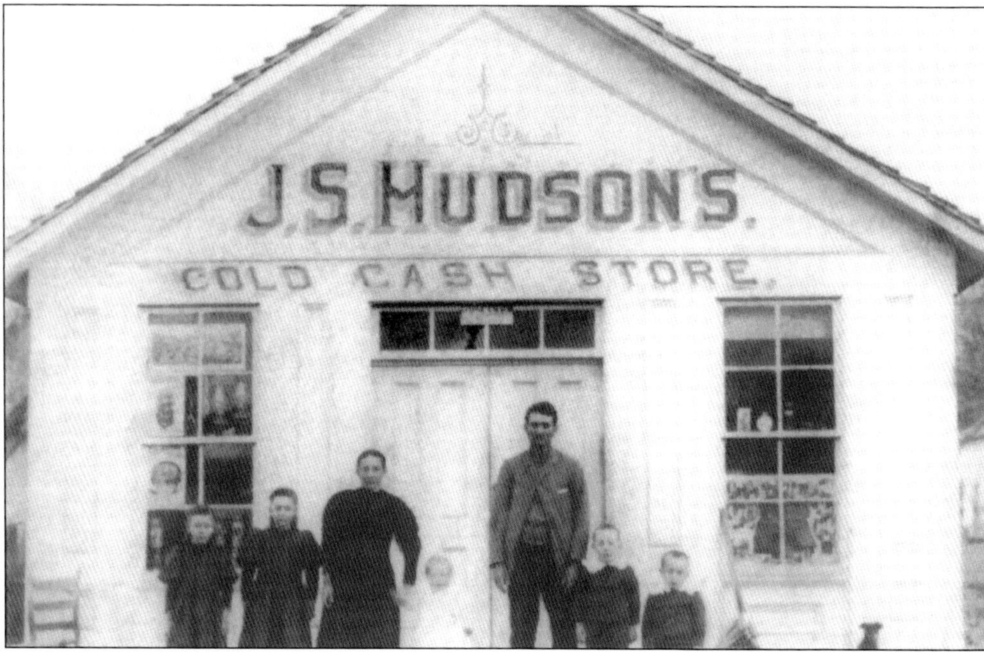

Visitors strolling the Jasper Courthouse Square today might stop to use the ATM at the Bank of the Ozarks (formerly the Newton County Bank), found across Church Street from the courthouse. In 1910, the same location was home to J.S. Hudson's Cold Cash Store, meaning he did not sell on credit. The building was torn down in 1964 to be replaced by a sturdy bank building. (NCL.)

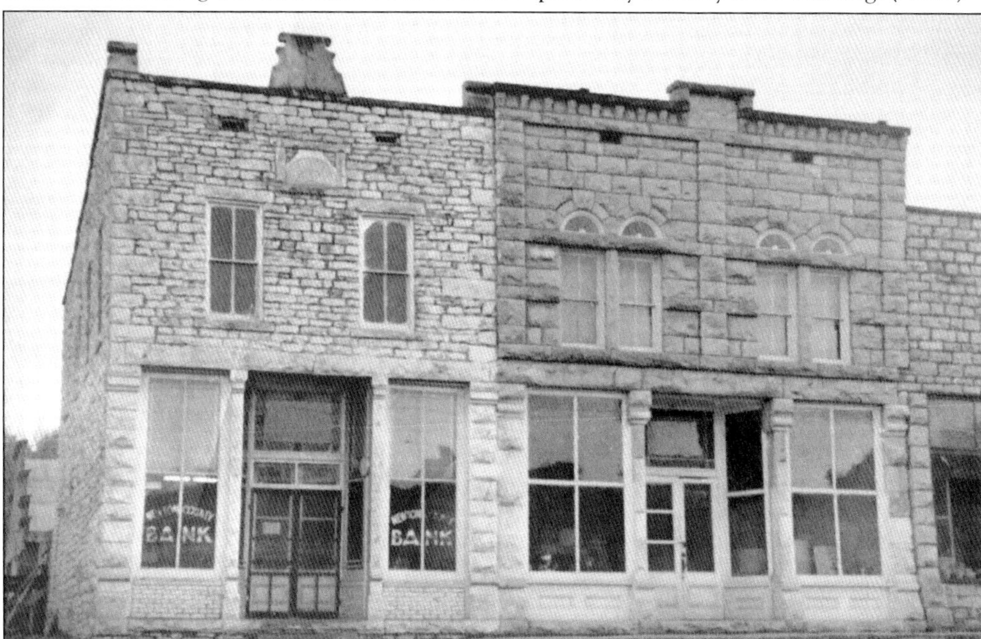

The B.F. Ruble Building was erected at the corner of Stone and Church Streets in 1894 and was built of native materials. For most of the 20th century, the building was home to the Newton County Bank. In 1903, Ben F. Ruble, who served as county clerk and later as a state legislator, also built in 1903 the Ruble Building seen next-door in this early view. (NCHS.)

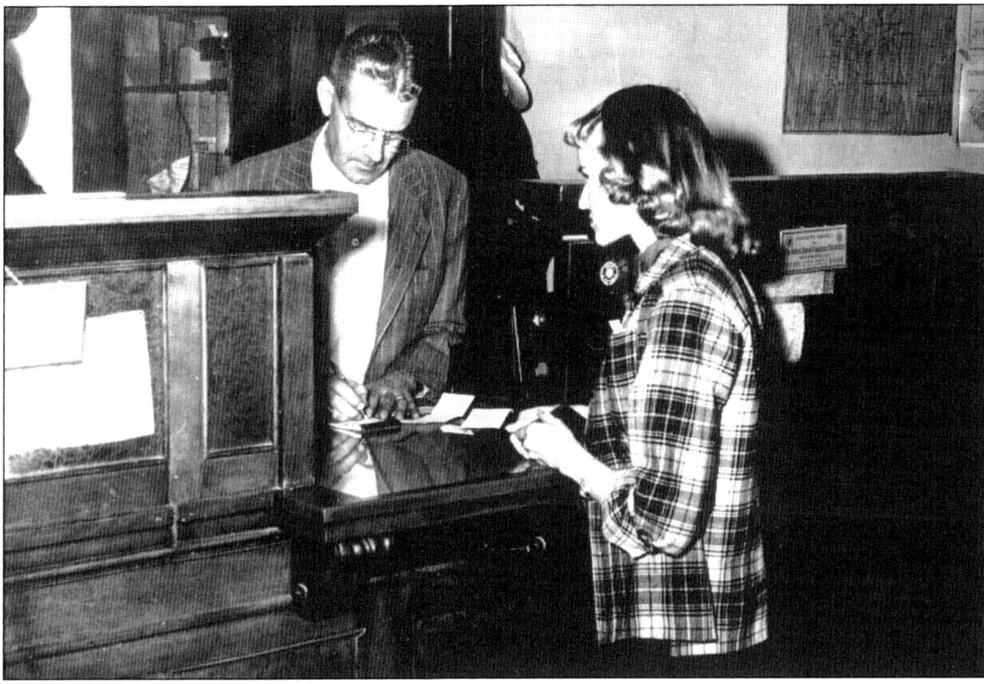

Around 1950, Lawrence Nance of the Newton County Bank was photographed filling out a transaction for a young lady. In 1927, while Nance's father, Sam L. Nance, was on duty, men who had declared the bank "easy pickings" robbed it. They got away with some $6,000, but Ed Foreman, "Blackie" Monroe, Joe Martin, and Sandy McGehee were all captured within a few days. Dee Brown, who later became a world-renowned writer, was also arrested at the time on suspicion of having committed the robbery, though he was released within a short time. Sam L. Nance served at the bank from 1904 until 1946. (NCL.)

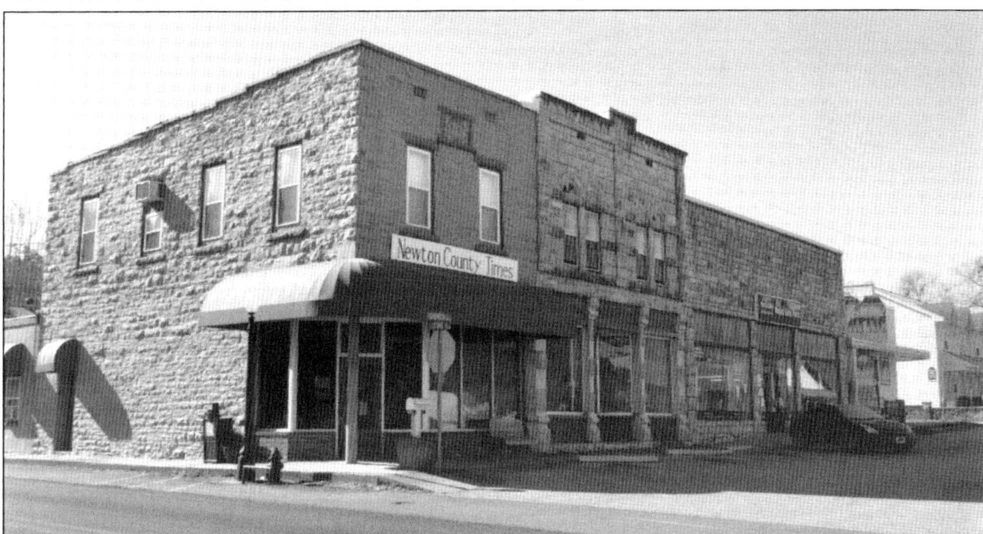

The Ruble Building was the former home of the Newton County Bank, which had moved to a new building by the time this 2011 photograph was taken. The 1894 B.F. Ruble Building is now the proudly restored home of the *Newton County Times*. (Photograph by Ray Hanley.)

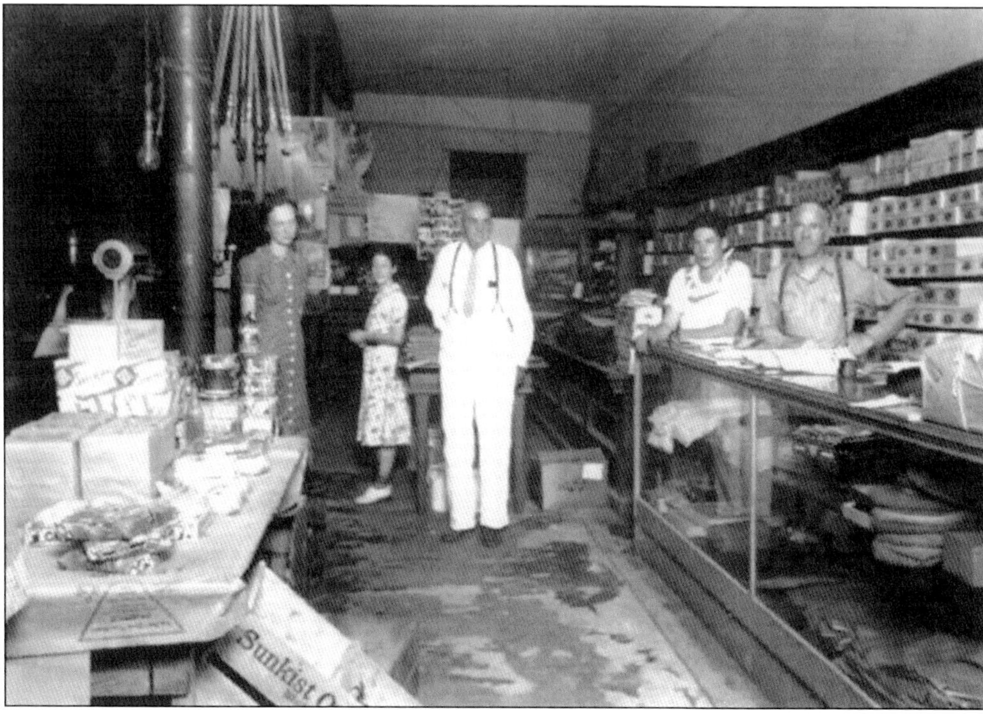

In the 1920s, John M. Phillips's general store was located in a turn-of-the-century stone building at the corner of Court and Stone Streets. The store was also home to the Jasper Post Office; its window was located in the back of the store. (NCL.)

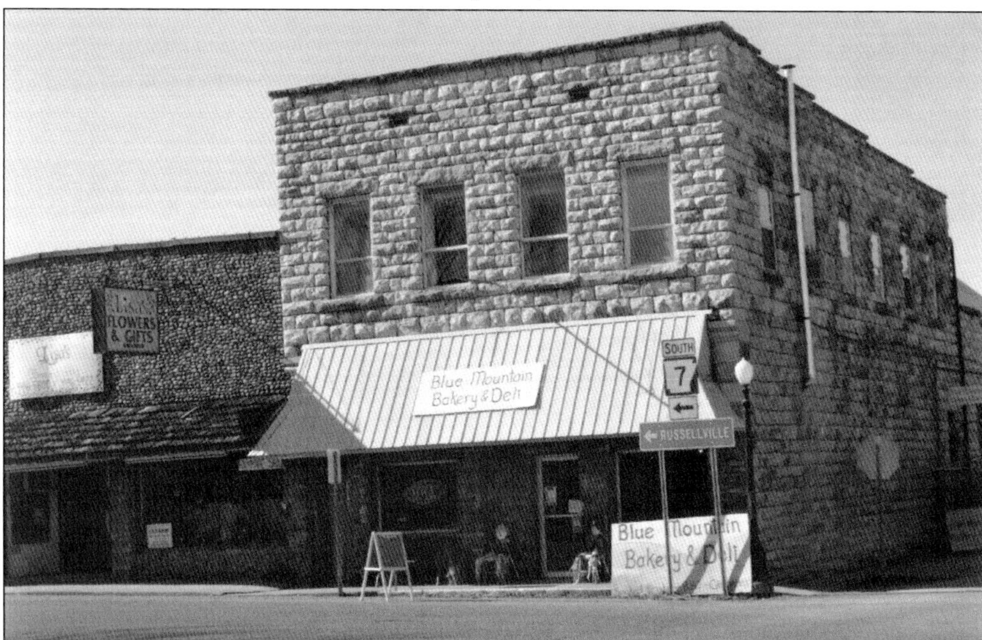

This former Phillips general store was restored in 2011 to become home to the Blue Mountain Bakery and Deli. The bakery relocated to Jasper from its former home in the Pope County community of Pelsor. (Photograph by Ray Hanley.)

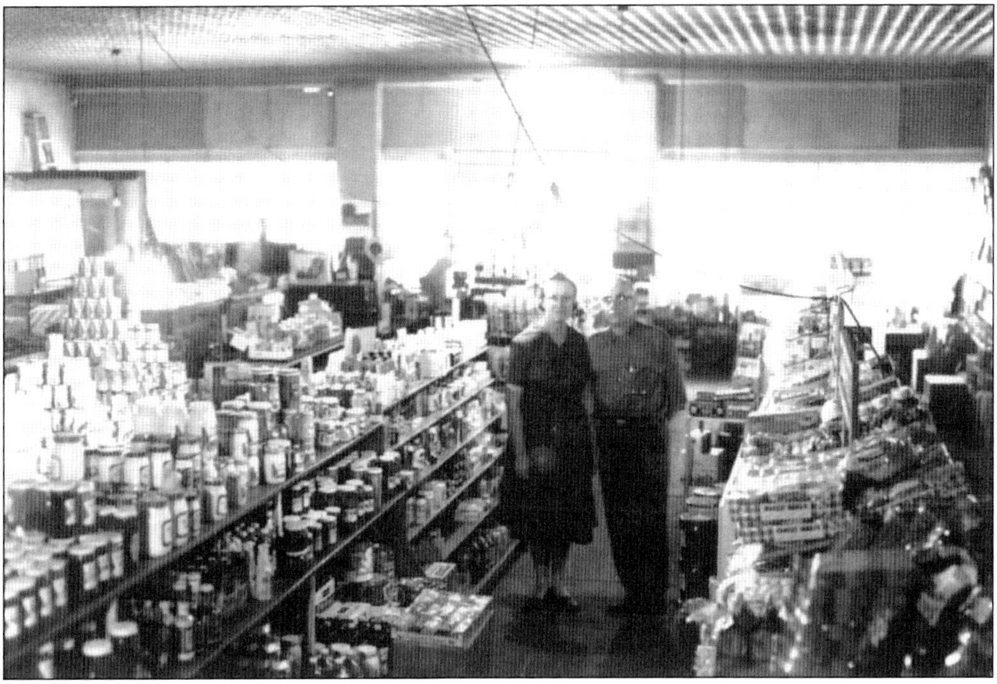

The building to the left of the old Phillips store building was once home to Obie and Dewey Spencer's general store. The couple is pictured amid their well-stocked shelves around 1956. Prior to the coming of the large supermarkets, such stores were common fixtures in small towns. Today, the building is home to a gift shop. (NCL.)

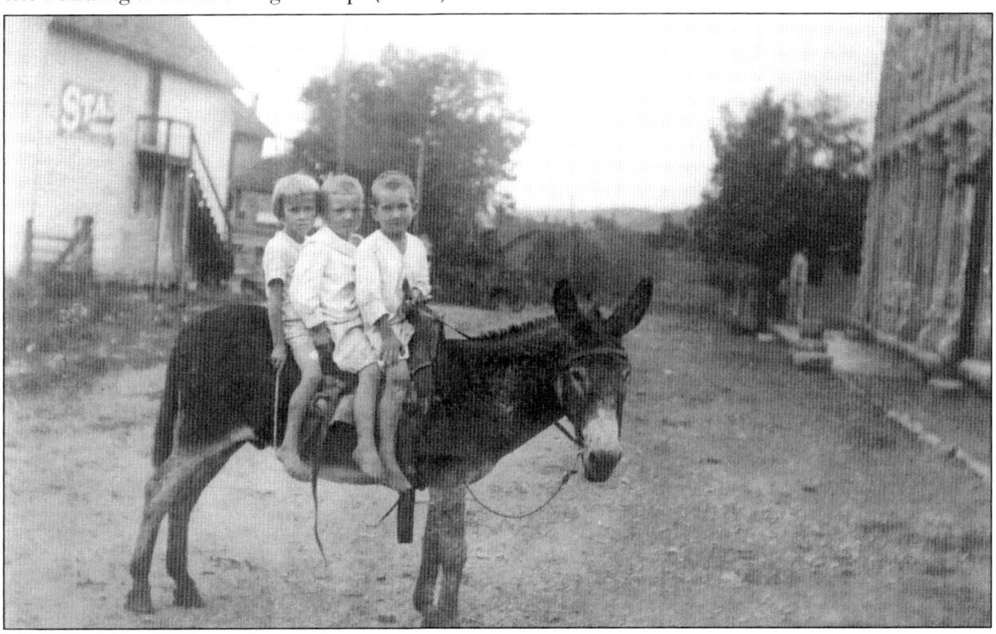

The commerce of the Jasper Courthouse Square often included the bare feet of children looking for amusement and perhaps a penny candy at the general store. "Bronco busters" Frank Bower, Fred Braswell, and Remmel Mayo posed atop a burro on the town's dirt street around 1915. The building just to the right houses the *Newton County Times* today. (NCL.)

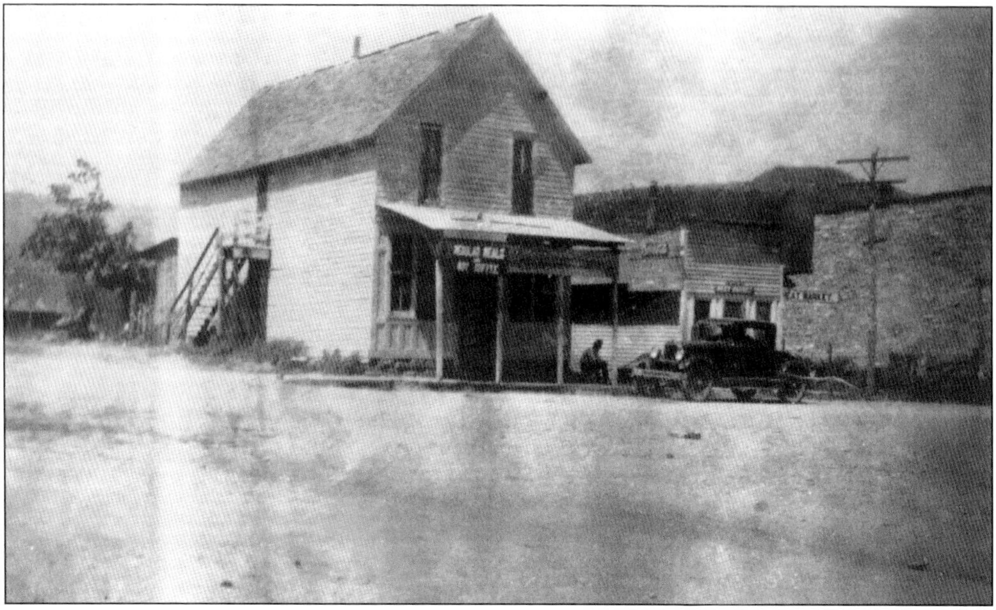

Not all the historic buildings around the square have survived, as in the case of this wood frame diner and later grocery on the west side of the square. Seen here around 1925, the building's sign advertised "regular meals and hot coffee." The automobile parked in front may have brought a hungry patron. (NCL.)

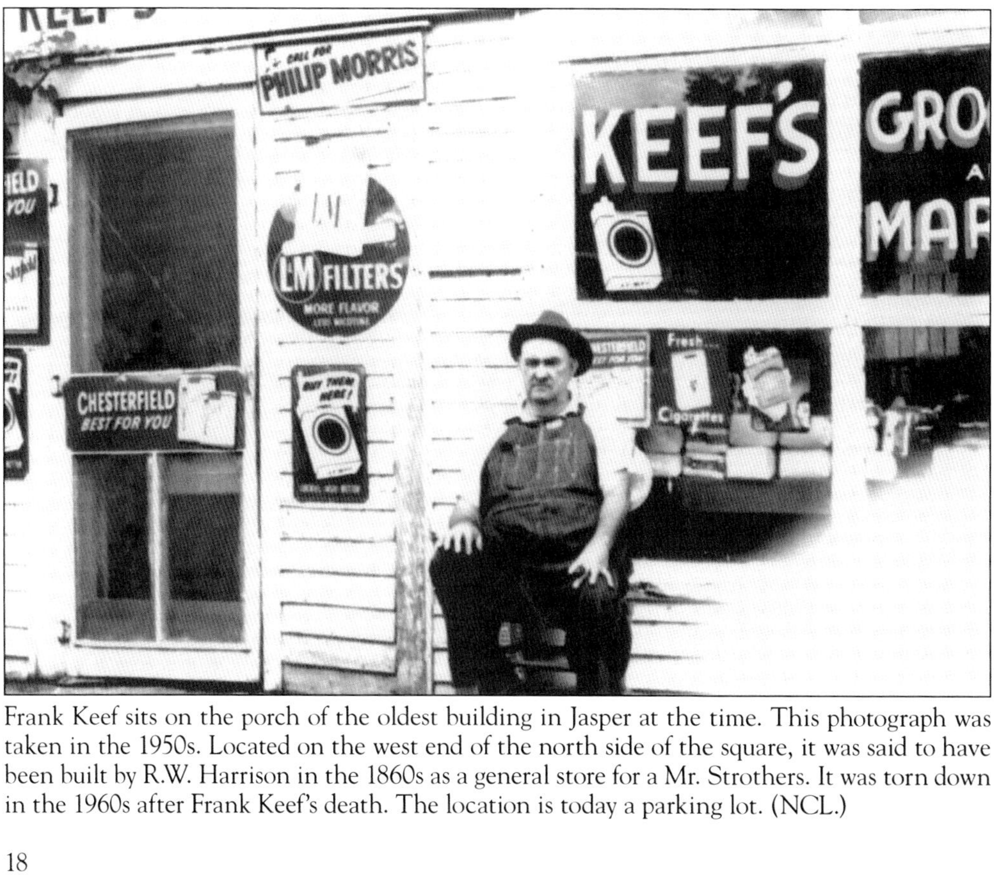

Frank Keef sits on the porch of the oldest building in Jasper at the time. This photograph was taken in the 1950s. Located on the west end of the north side of the square, it was said to have been built by R.W. Harrison in the 1860s as a general store for a Mr. Strothers. It was torn down in the 1960s after Frank Keef's death. The location is today a parking lot. (NCL.)

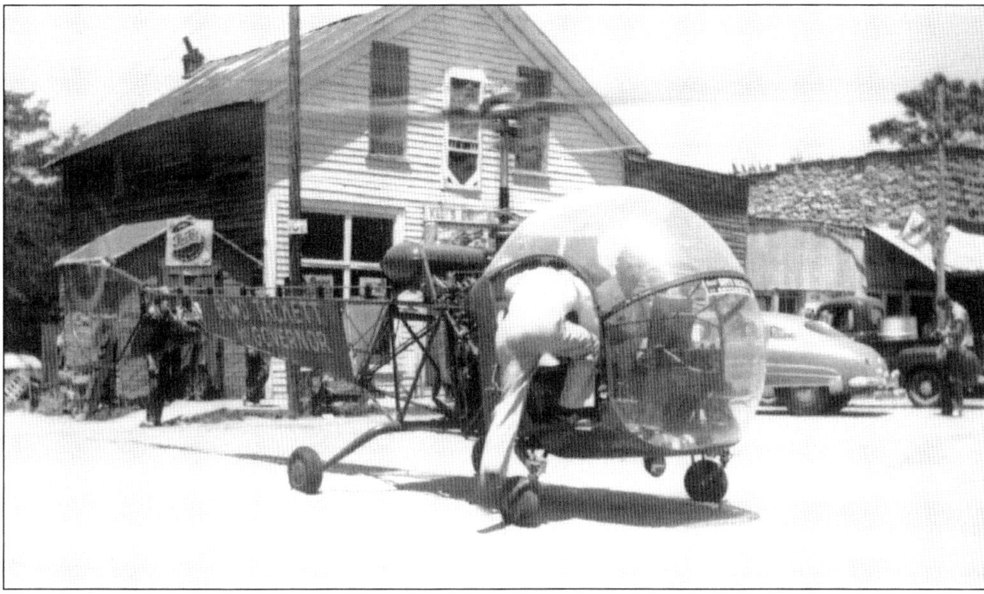

Frank Keef's perch from his store gave him a close-up view of Jasper events over the years. In 1952, Boyd Tackett, former congressman and former state police commissioner, was running for governor. He landed a helicopter bearing his name on the square in front of Keef's store. The tactic was to no avail for Tackett lost the race for the Democratic nomination to Orval Faubus. (NCL.)

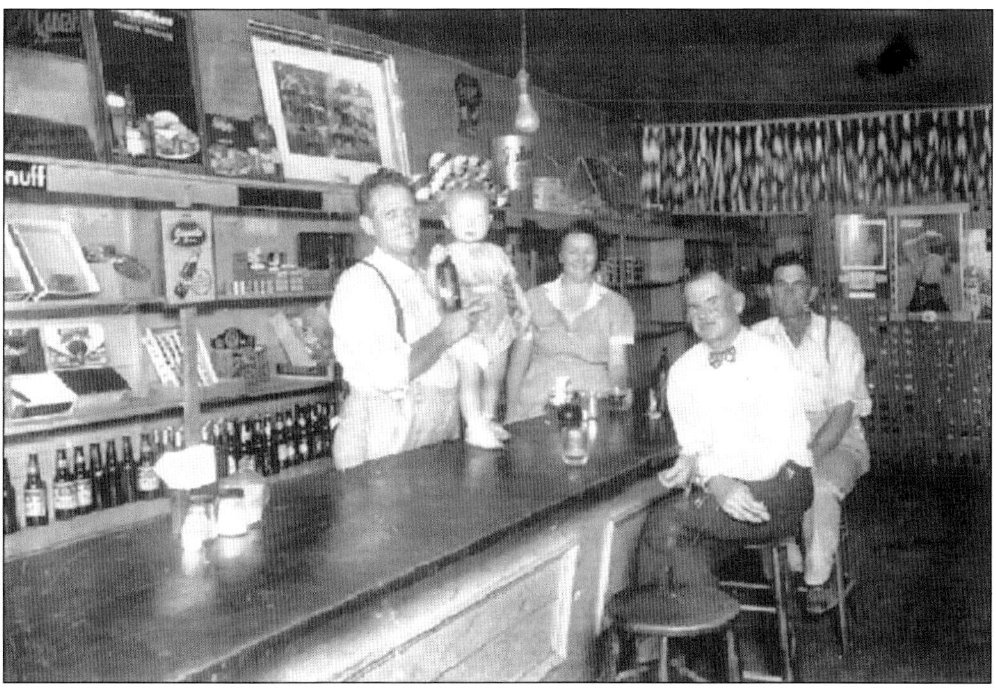

Jesse Hefley, standing behind the counter in this photograph, was born in 1895, likely around Mount Judea. Hefley went into the cafe business, in a building on the site of what had been J.S. Hudson's Cold Cash Store (see page 14). Pictured here around 1940, the cafe sold Budweiser beer in what was then a wet Newton County. Today, Newton County is dry, so no alcohol may be legally sold. The site of the cafe is today occupied by Bank of the Ozarks.

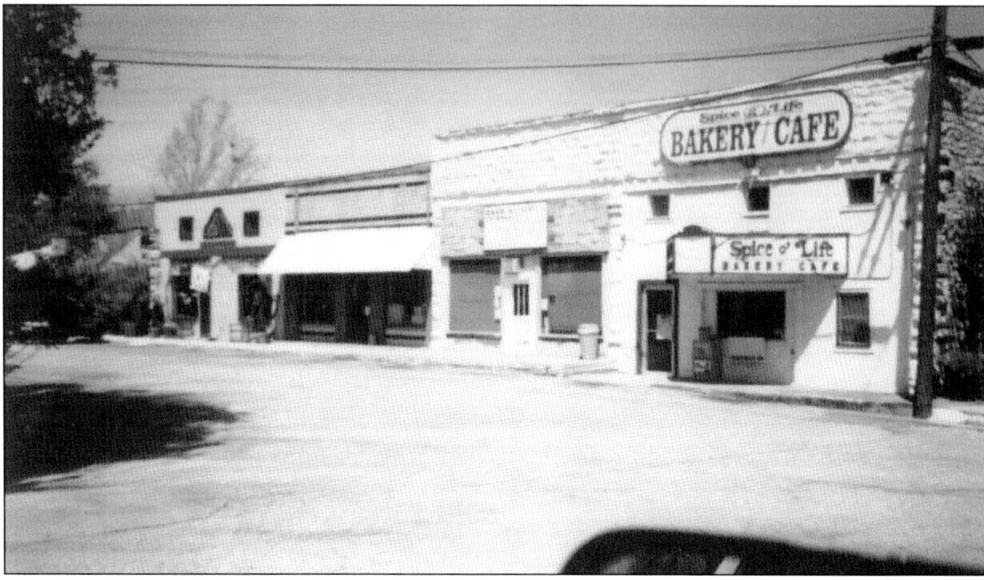

The corner of Church and Spring Streets was anchored for many years by a movie theater. First called the Gilbert, it was renamed the Buffalo in 1952 under new owner Don Jones. Since the screen went dark for the final time in the 1970s, the building has served as a bakery and even as a church. It was sold in 2012 to a local nonprofit organization for use to promote Newton County people, its music, and culture. (NCL.)

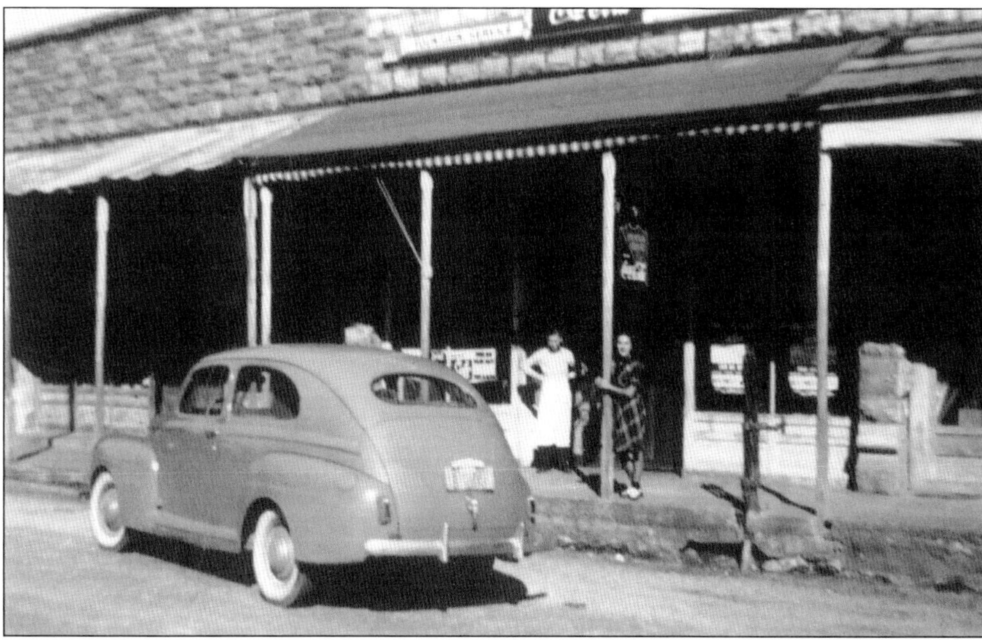

The row of buildings next to the old theater once served as the drugstore of Rufus Arbaugh, and later as Thurman's Rexall Drugs. The Murray Hotel (see page 13) once stood at the far end of the block, but has been gone for many years. The building with the triangular window in the photograph above is now occupied by Spring Street Arts. To the right of that is the chamber of commerce, and displays for sale are of a wide variety of handmade crafts from the artists of Newton County. (NCL.)

Carl Reeves is pictured in front of his dry goods store in the 1950s. The brick building has also been home to the Jasper Mercantile but today serves as overflow seating for the Ozark Cafe.

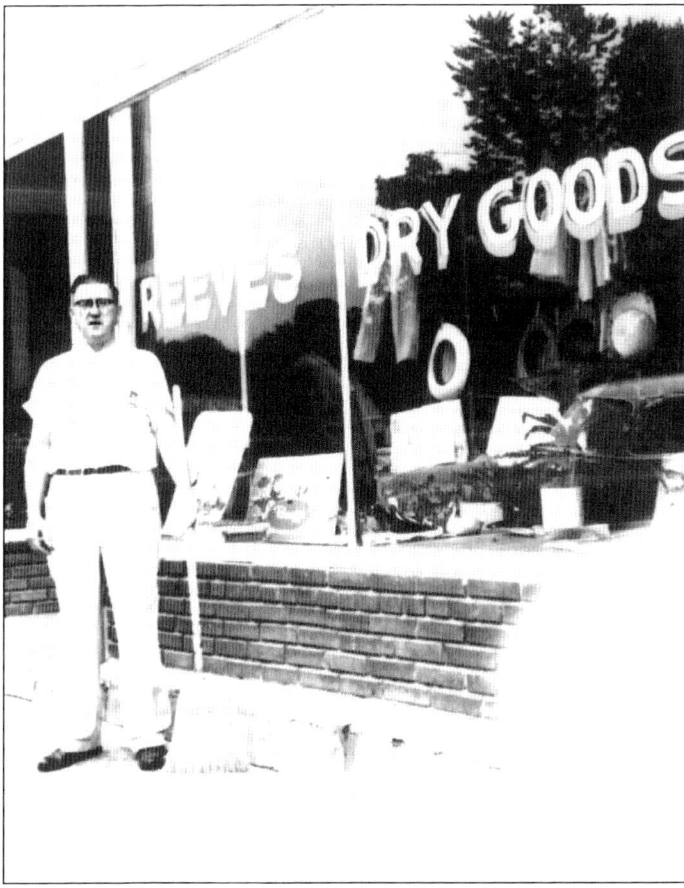

Pearl's Cafe was owned by Pearl and Walter Brasel. When this postcard was made, their phone number listed on the back was "25." It also advertised "refrigerated air condition, fine home cooked food, located in the most scenic part of the Ozarks on scenic Hwy. 7."

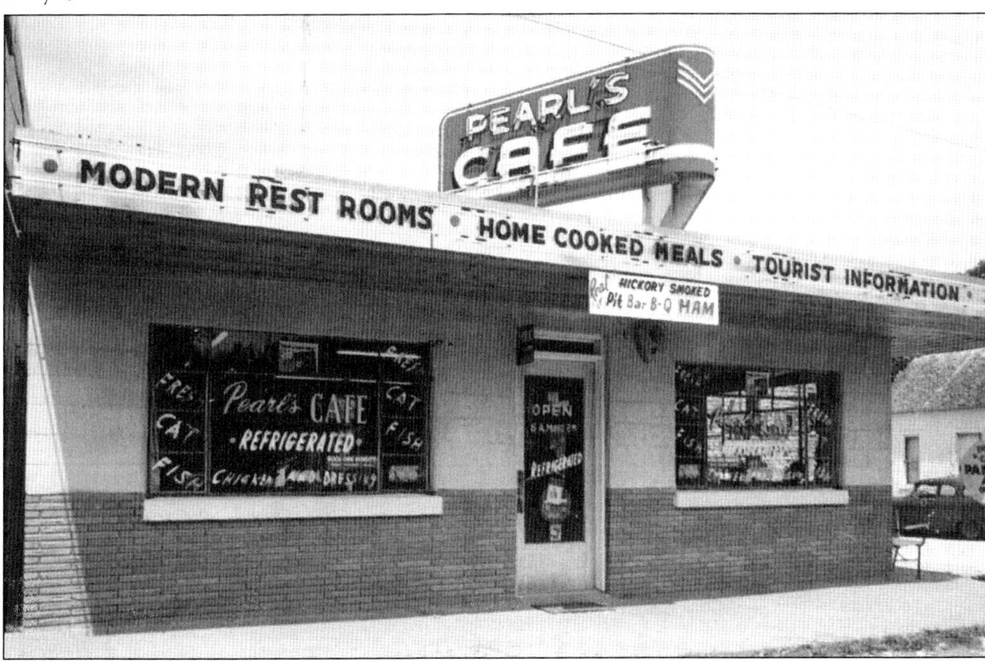

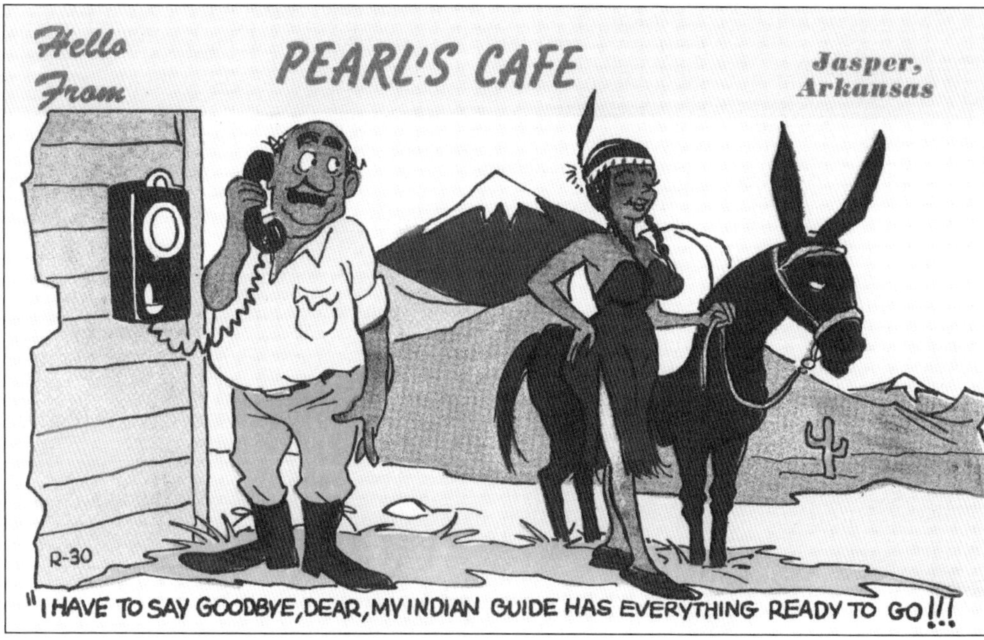

Catering to tourists, Pearl's Cafe sold a series of generic comic postcards that were unrelated to the actual locale. Politically incorrect by today's standards, many such cards were mailed to distant parts of the United States.

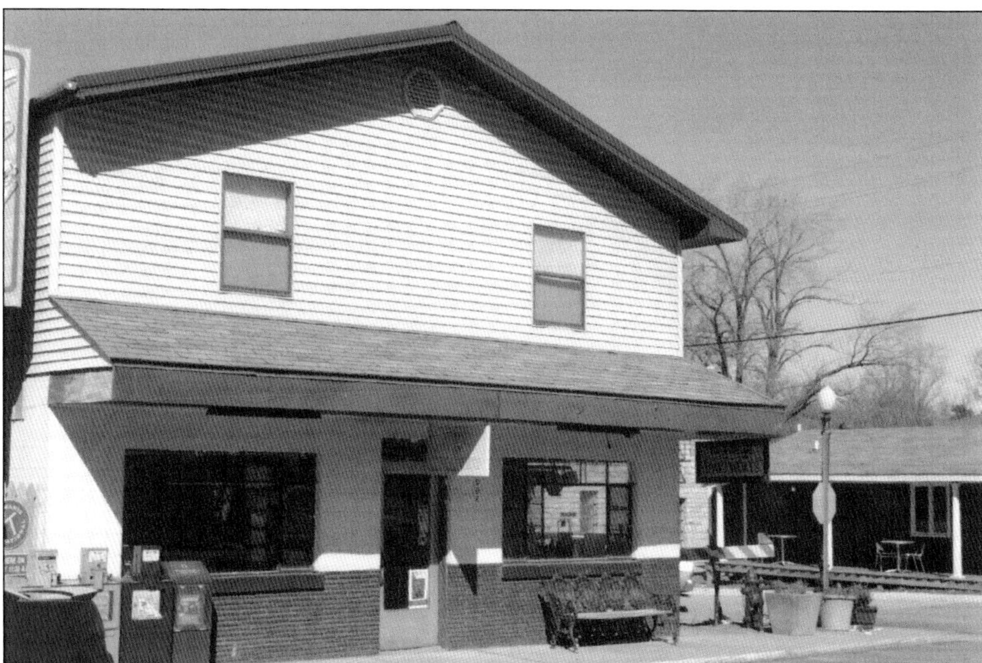

By the 1980s, Pearl's Cafe had faded into dining history, and a second floor for apartments had been added. The lower space has housed a variety of gift shops and other enterprises in recent years.

Shown in the 1930s, the best-known business in Jasper is surely the Ozark Cafe, which has been serving hungry diners since 1909. When it first opened it served in potluck style, with meals costing a mere 25¢. In a century of business, the Ozark Cafe has had 11 different owners. (NCL.)

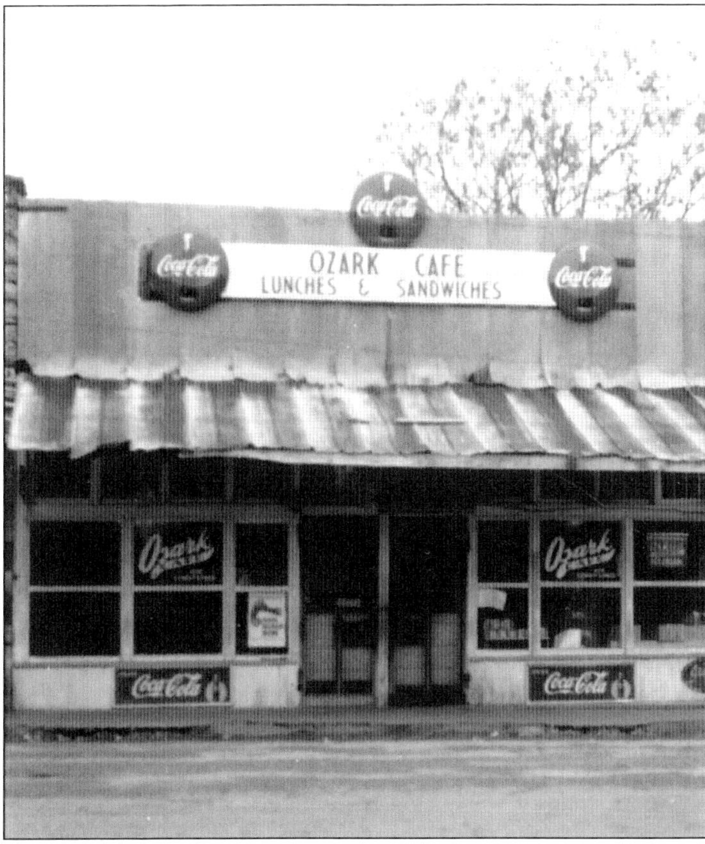

By the 1940s, the owners of the Ozark Cafe had fixed up the front of the building, removing the awning and replacing the rusty tin facing of the 1930s with a coat of white paint. Court Street, also the path of Highway 7, had not yet been paved. (NCL.)

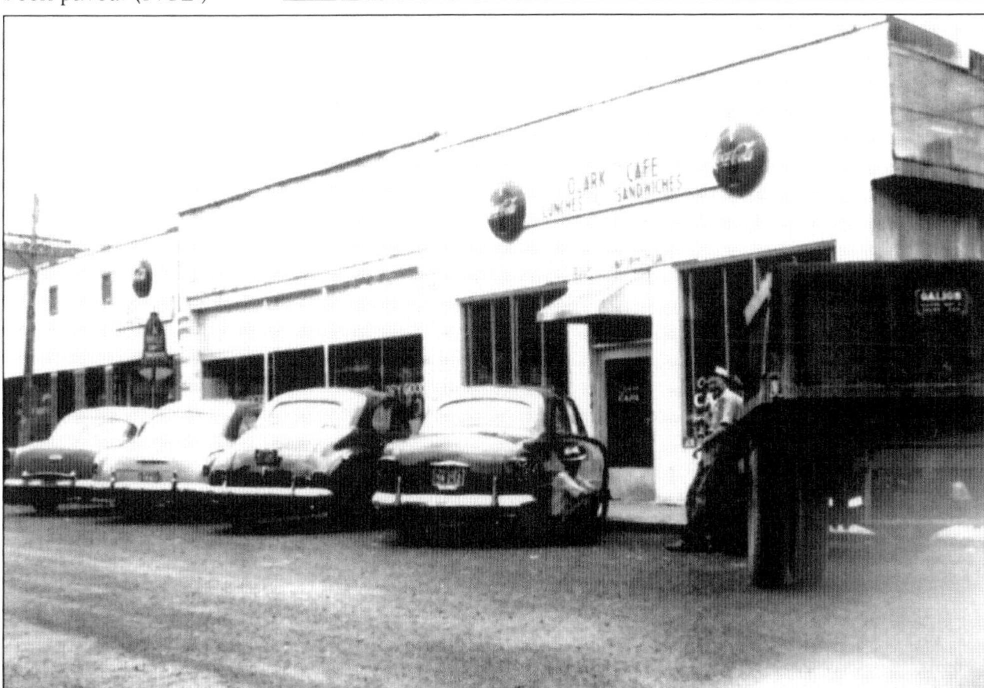

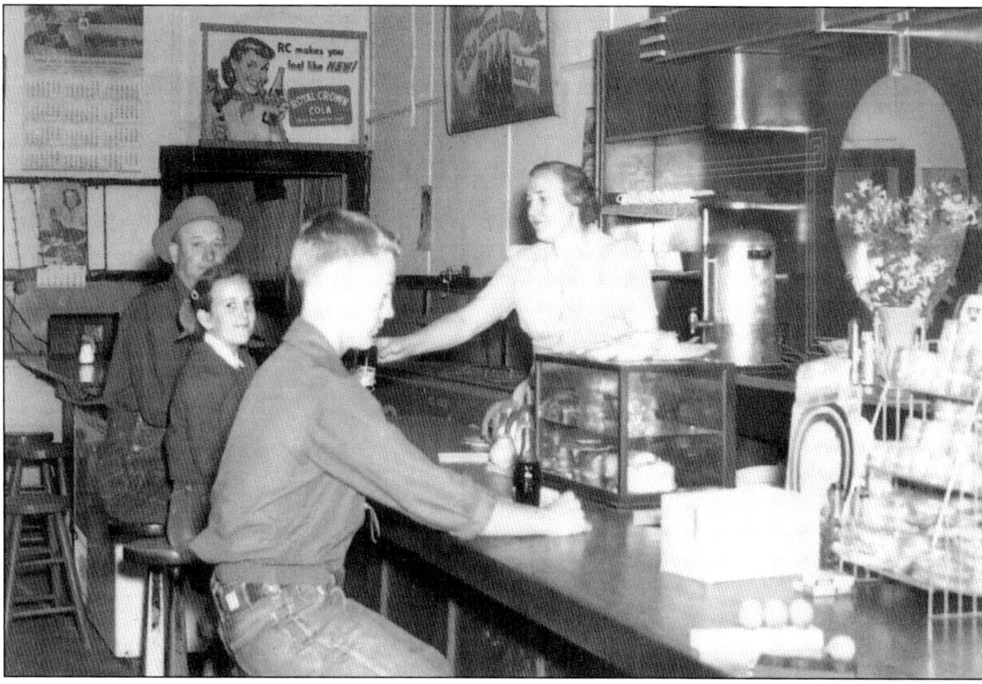

By the 1950s, the Ozark Cafe's bar stools and counter were a favorite perch for youngsters to enjoy a treat and for adults to visit over the counter with the waitresses. Pictured on the bar stools from left to right are former sheriff and county judge Roy Raulston, Brenda Upton, and Billy Dale Brasel. The waitress is Elsie Upton. Note the RC Cola sign in the background. (NCL.)

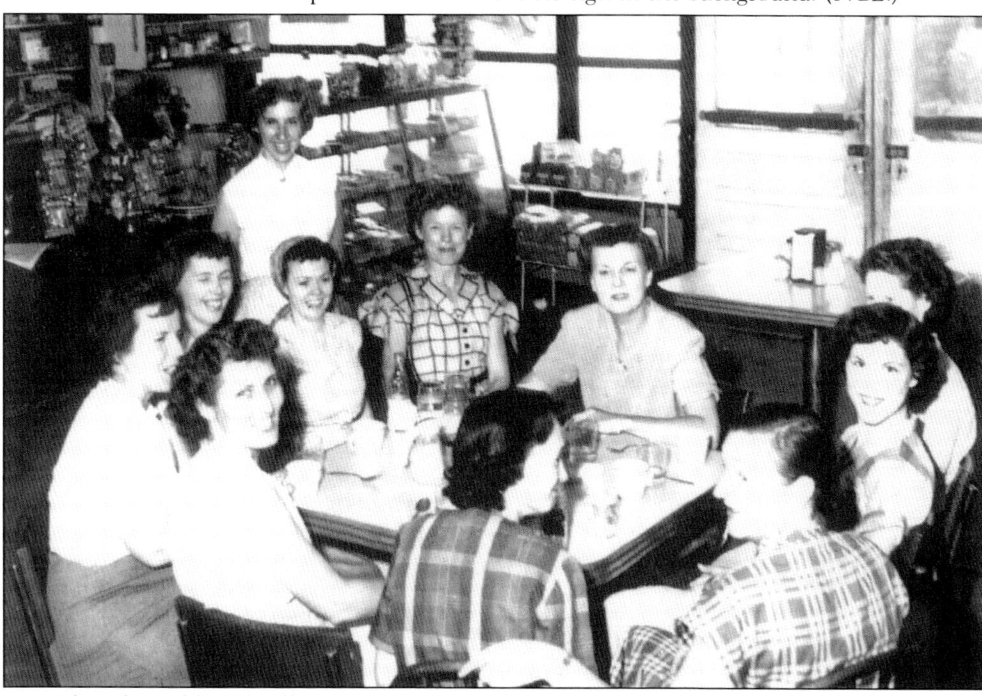

Many friends could, and still can, fit around the tables of the Ozark Cafe. The photographer did not capture the names of the women obviously having a good time over their coffee. (NCL.)

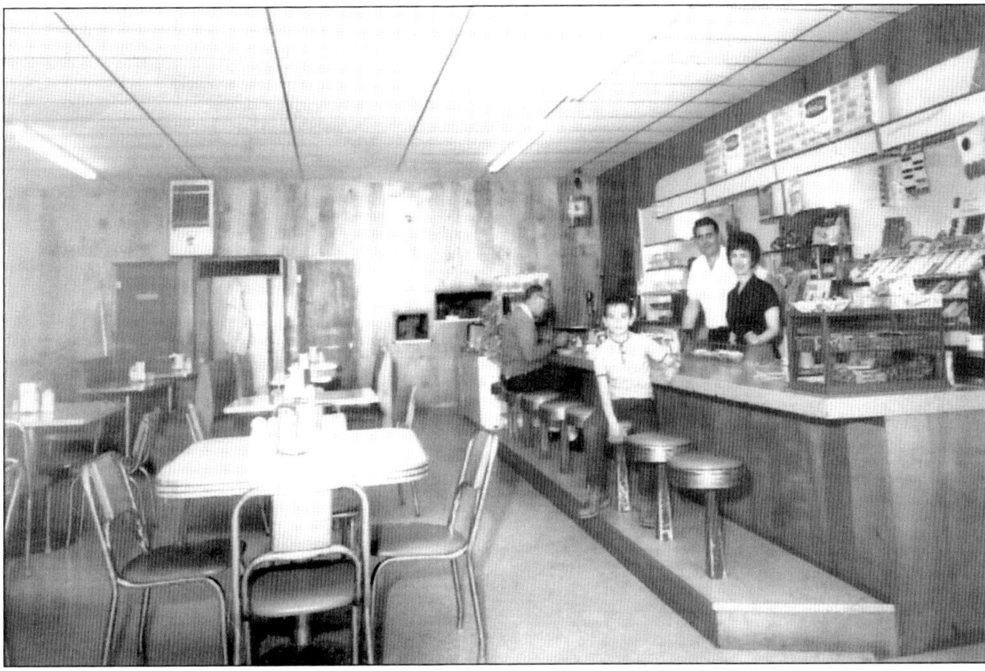

Around 1955, the crowds were gone, but Curly and Sue Mock were posed behind the counter with a young customer. The 2012 photograph below reflects the remarkable restoration done by owner Tim Ray, who studied photographs from the early years of the Ozark Cafe so that he could restore the look of the 1930s and 1940s. (NCL.)

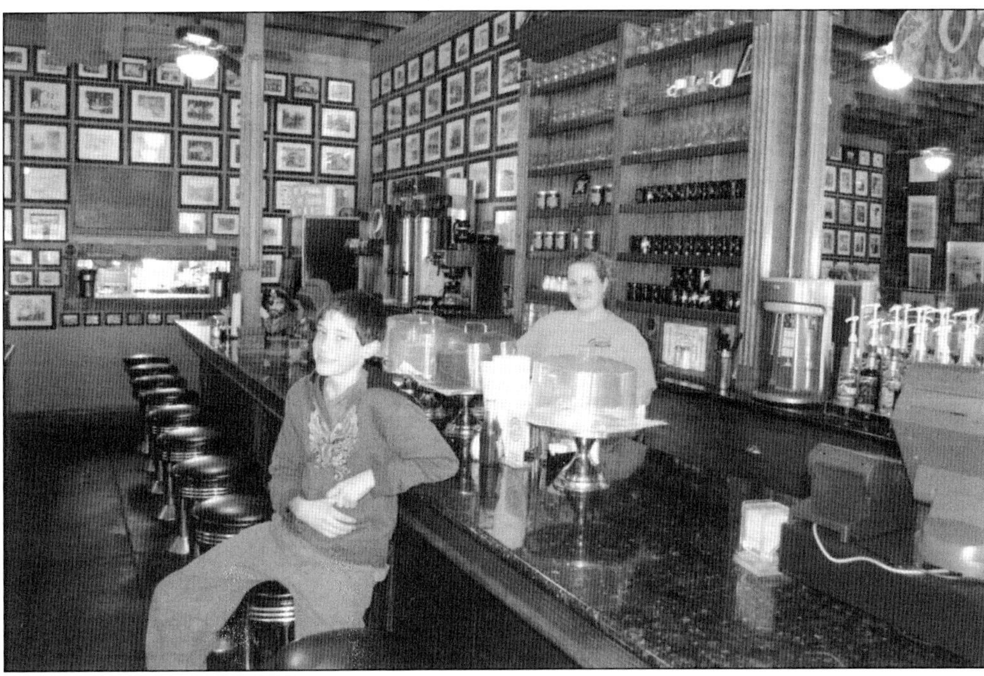

Fast forward from the above photograph to more than a half century to 2012. The authors' son, J.D. Hanley, is posed on a similar stool to that used in 1955 and is being served by waitress Rebeka Cook, who stands where Sue Mock had paused decades earlier.

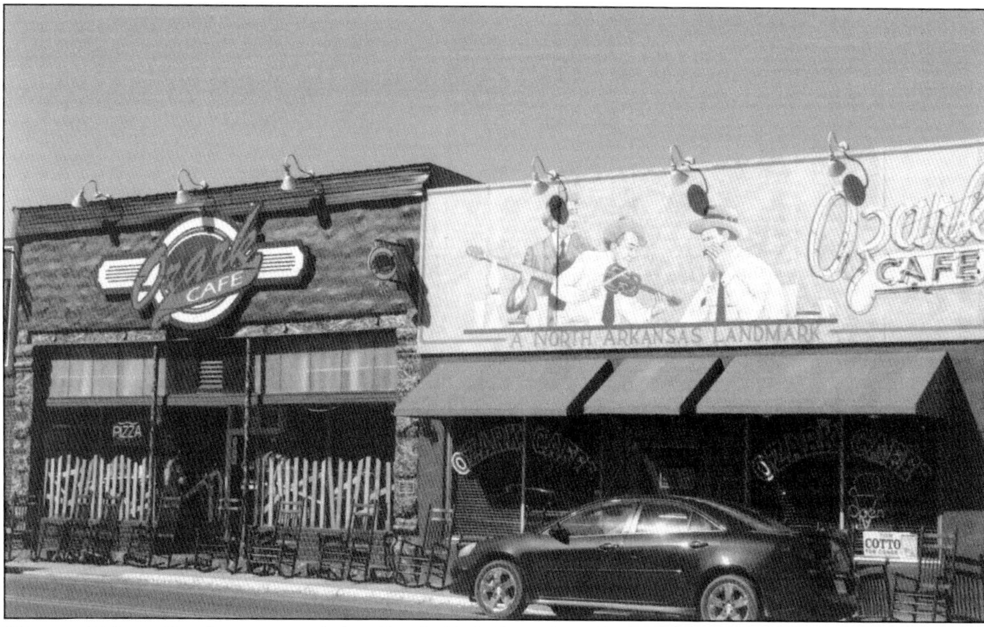

Tim and Mona Ray have owned the Ozark Cafe for a decade. In addition to restoring the interior, they expanded into the adjoining building for much-needed overflow dining space. It was selected by *New York* magazine as the Arkansas representative for the top 50 "Foodie Destinations" in the United States. Live music can be enjoyed on some Saturday nights, often from the local group Jazzper.

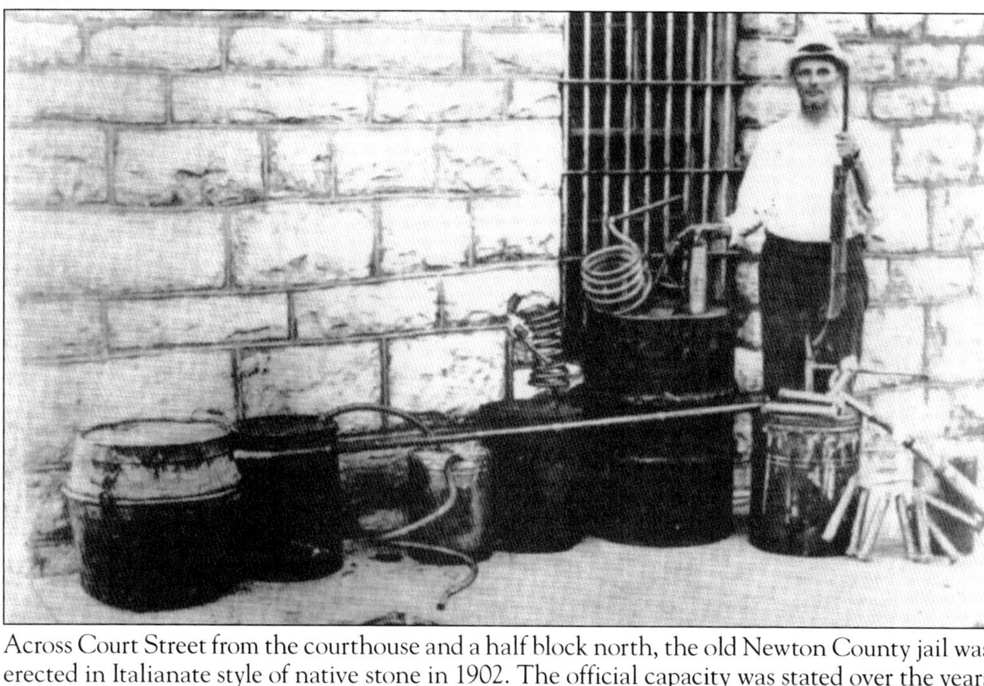

Across Court Street from the courthouse and a half block north, the old Newton County jail was erected in Italianate style of native stone in 1902. The official capacity was stated over the years as four inmates. Presumably, this included the bootleggers whom Sheriff G.F. Carlton arrested in 1921. He posed here by the jail with the confiscated moonshine still. Carlton would later serve as an internal revenue officer and a schoolteacher. (NCL.)

The sturdy jail still stands, although not to house prisoners. It is now the Newton County Food Room, run by local nonprofit organizations. A new, modern jail is being constructed to mirror modern law enforcement facilities. It will house the Newton County Sheriff's offices as well as prisoners. J.D. Hanley, then age 12, posed before the old jail in 2010.

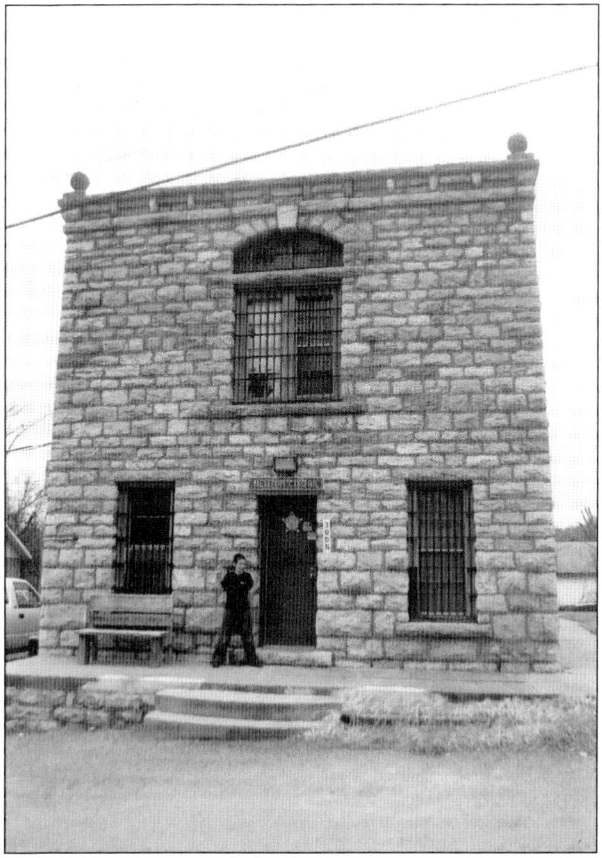

Some of the most noteworthy buildings on the edges of the Jasper Courthouse Square are the work of Charles Gould Jones, who started building from native stone in the 1930s. He is pictured here building a retaining wall on Town Branch, found on the edge of town. Charles Gould Jones was born in 1887 and died in 1972; he is buried in the Jasper Cemetery. (NCL.)

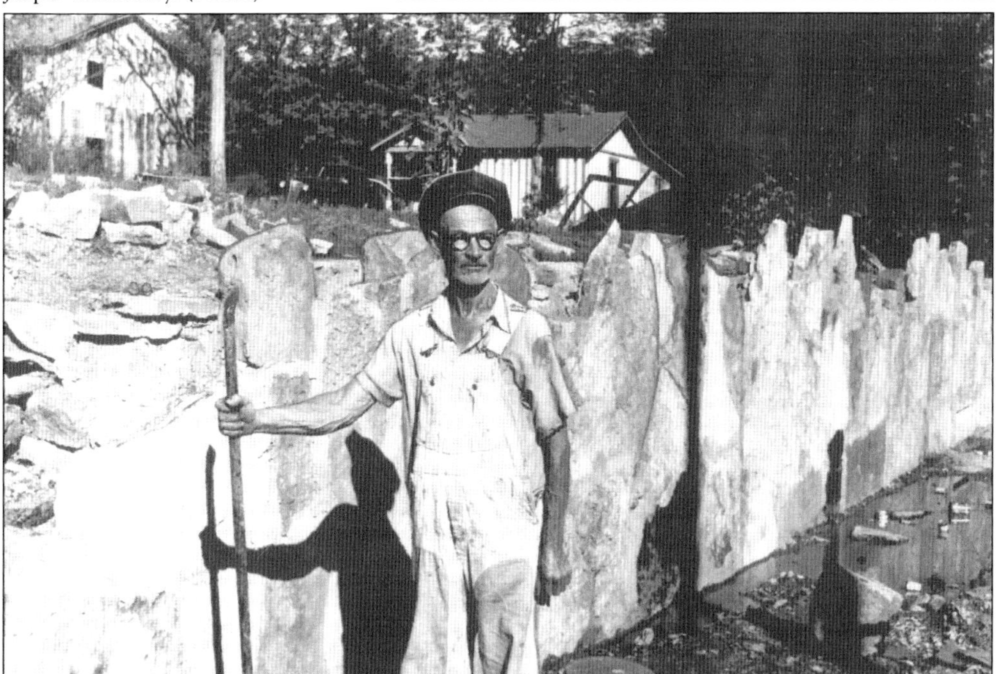

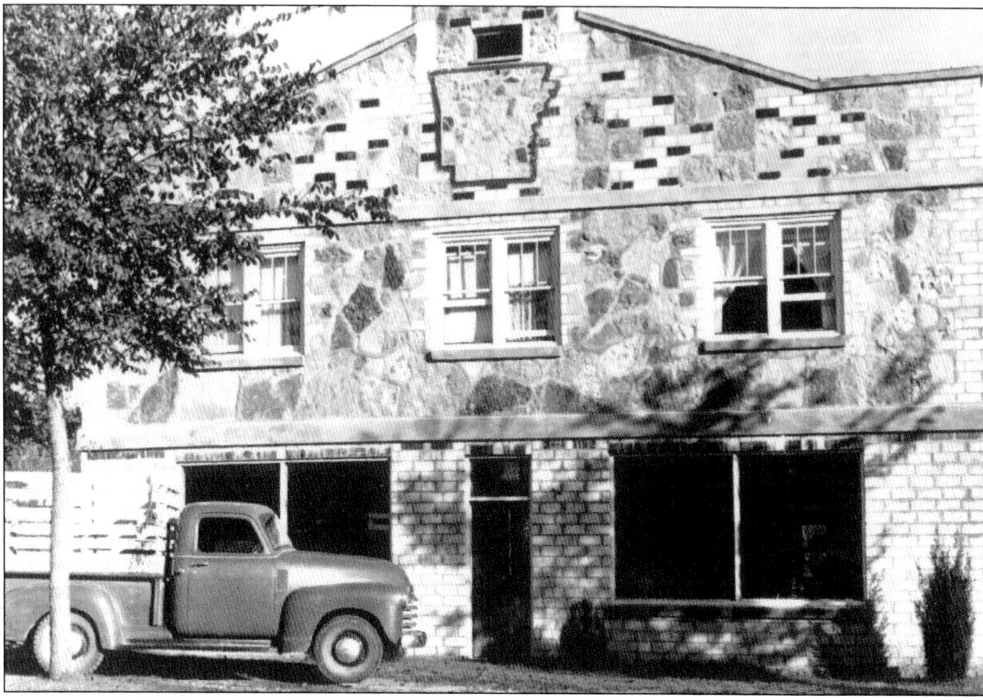

One of Charles Gould Jones's most artistic works is the Arkansas House hotel, built in 1933. The structure is noted for the unique blending of brick and native rock across the face and on the corners of the building. Pictured above around 1950, the outline of Arkansas at the top is a trademark of Jones's work. Seen below in 2012, the Arkansas House hotel is still hosting guests some 75 years after its construction. (Above, NCL.)

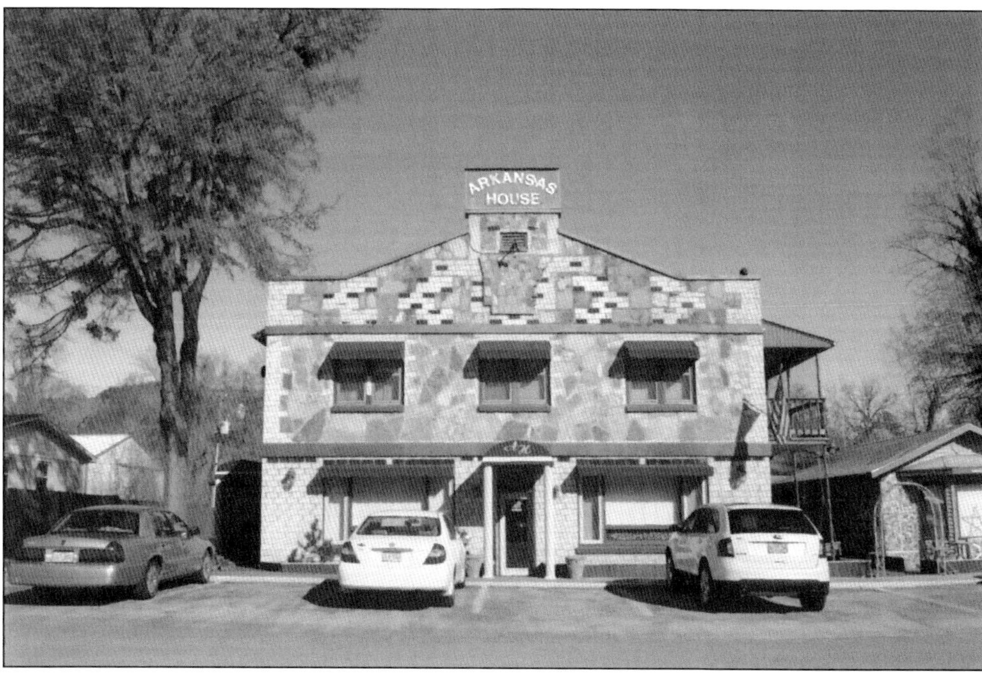

Early in his career, Jones built a large, fully functioning waterwheel on the north edge of Jasper, beside the gravel path of State Highway 7. (NCL.)

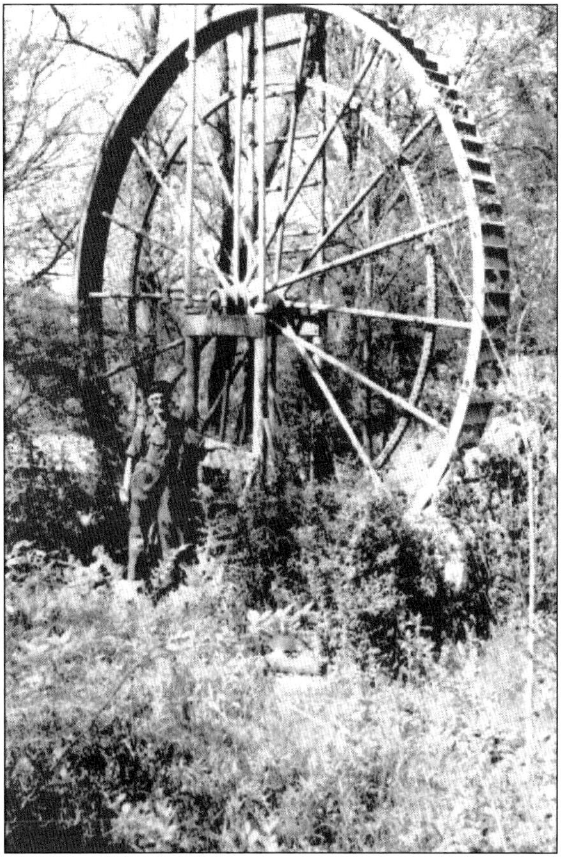

Jones later built the Dairy Diner near his waterwheel. The site would later become the Boardwalk Cafe, after fire destroyed Jones's original building. Seen in this 2012 photograph, the cafe is one of the state's first organic dining establishments. Among other delicacies, it serves buffalo burgers in its location next to the Arkansas House hotel.

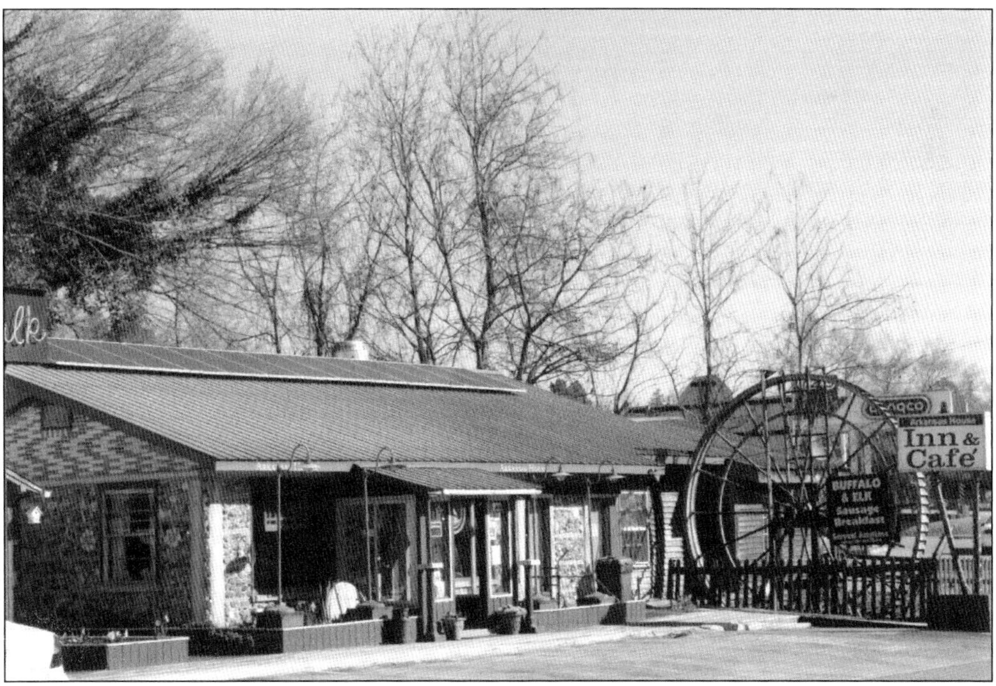

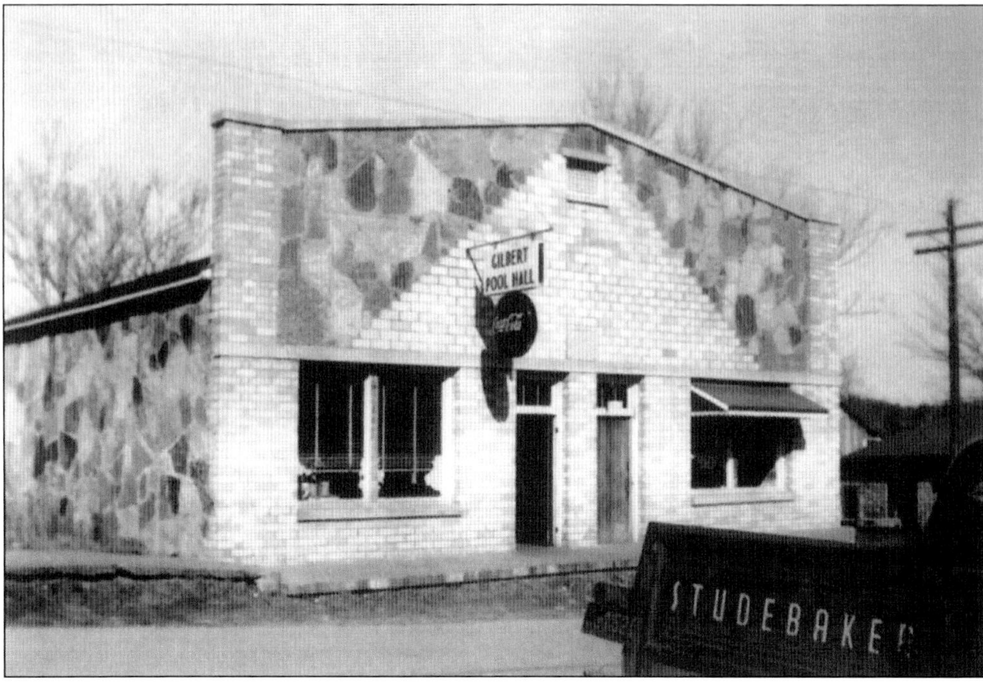

Seen around 1950, the building housing the Gilbert Pool Hall was another of Gould Jones's signature works, blending brick and native stone into symmetrical patterns. Today, the former pool hall is home to one of the frequent stops for visitors to Jasper, Emma's Museum of Junk. The eclectic mix of merchandise, antiques, and collectibles is ever changing and fun for all ages. A Florida tourist wrote on the shop's website, "You will make a worthwhile friend in Emma. She is witty, honest & generous, fair minded; that's a worthwhile friend." (Above, NCL; below, photograph by Ray Hanley.)

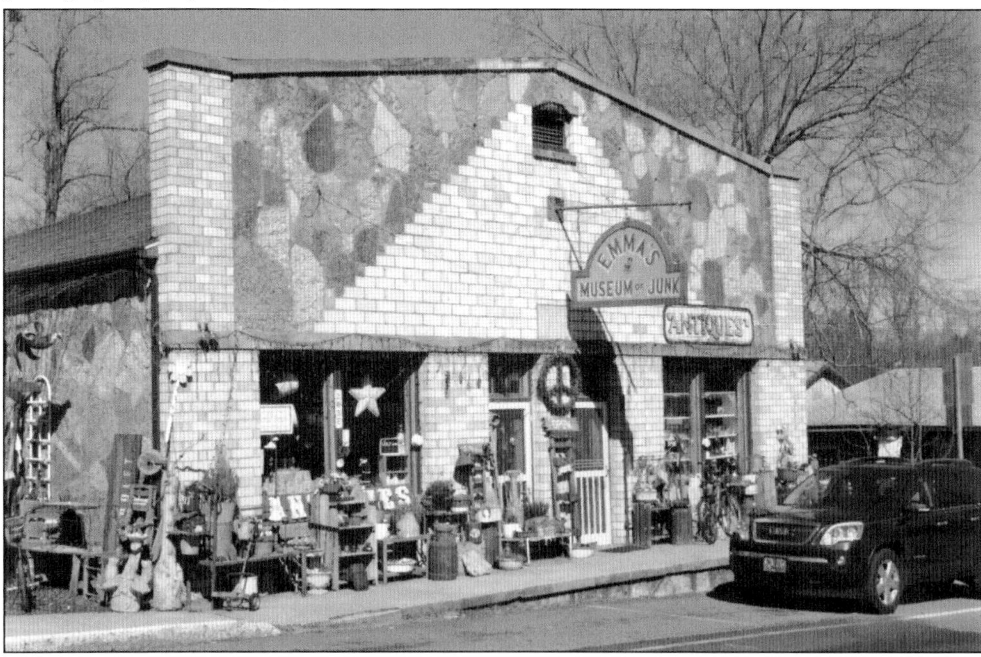

Two

The Timeless Buffalo and the Nature that Surrounds It

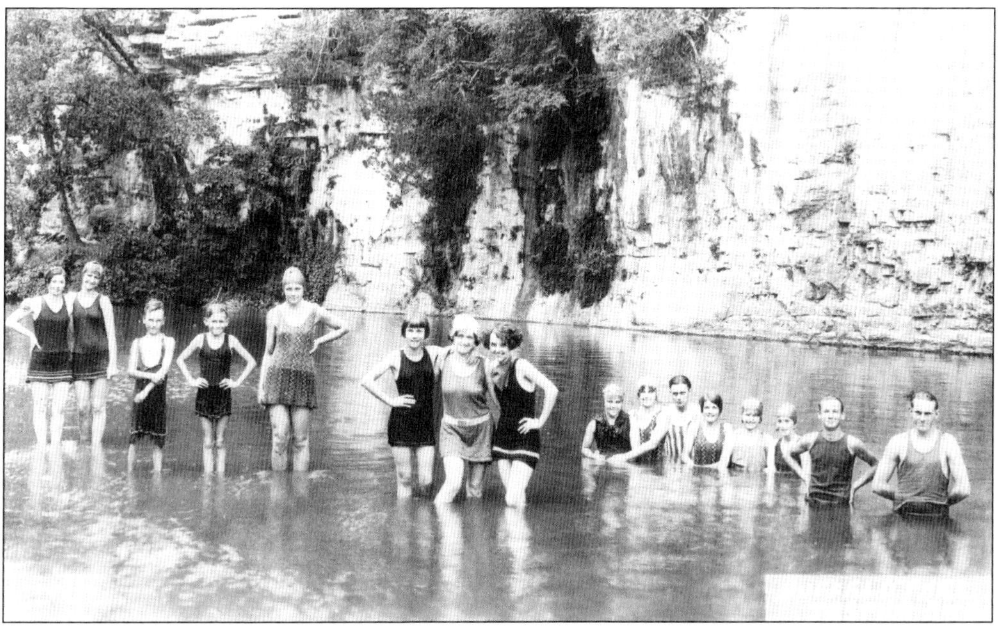

The Buffalo River, rising in the Boston Mountains of western Arkansas, flows for 135 miles, through the heart of Newton County, before meeting the White River at Buffalo City in Baxter County. The majestic river and its smaller tributaries drew many of the early settlers to the area. The river first appeared on maps in 1807. Today, the entire course of the river and some of the surrounding land is the Buffalo National River, a part of the National Park System. Shown around 1930, the Little Buffalo River, a tributary stream, has been a wonderful place to experience for generations and remains so today.

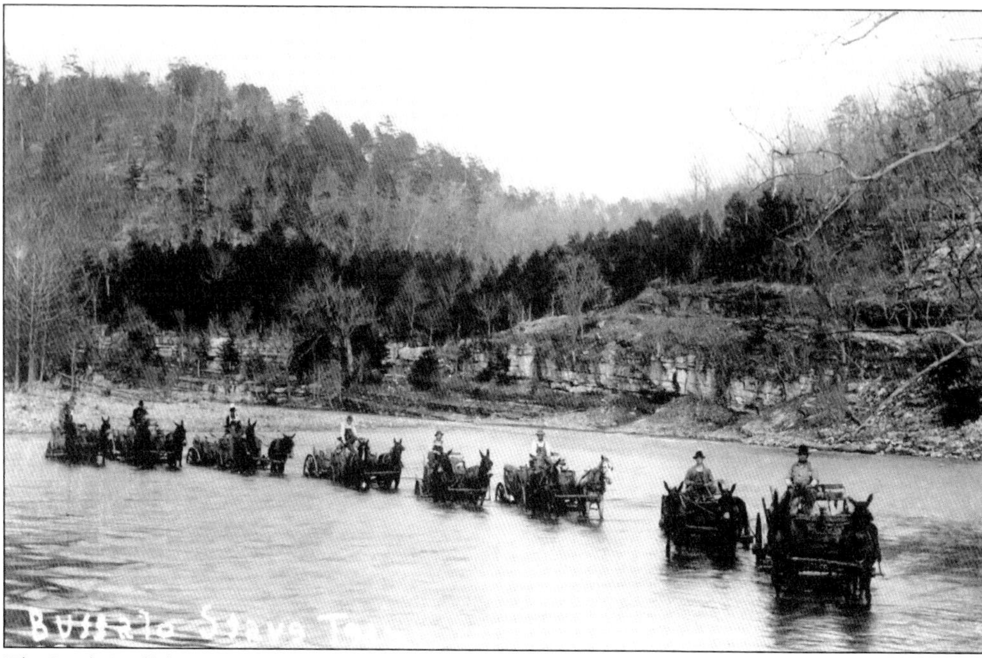

The Little Buffalo River, the largest of the tributaries of the Big Buffalo, flows through the present city limits of Jasper. A century ago, the river, at times almost dry and at others a raging torrent, represented an obstacle to be crossed for both commerce and recreation needs. Pictured around 1900, wagons haul the white oak staves used to make barrels that stored all manner of products, ranging from whiskey to apples.

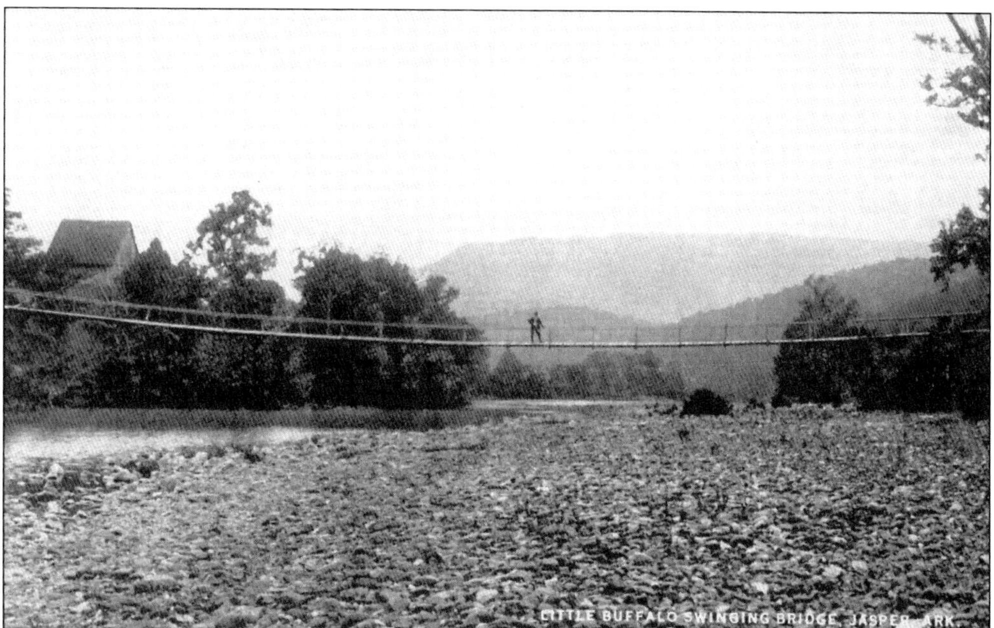

Upstream from Jasper a bit, the local community erected a swinging pedestrian bridge that allowed people to come into town when the river could not be otherwise forded or when it was just more fun to walk the swinging bridge, as seen here around 1915.

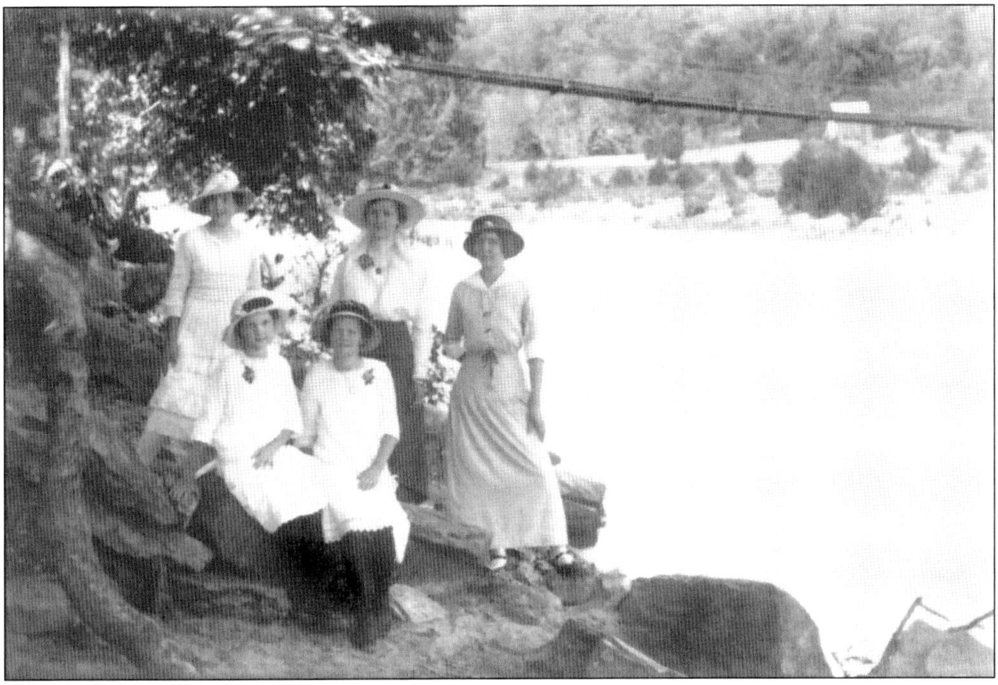

Even those not brave enough to cross the bridge liked to pose with it in the background, as did these young ladies around 1920. Names on the photograph included Eileen, Franki Mae, Agnes, and Ardella Braswell. (NCL.)

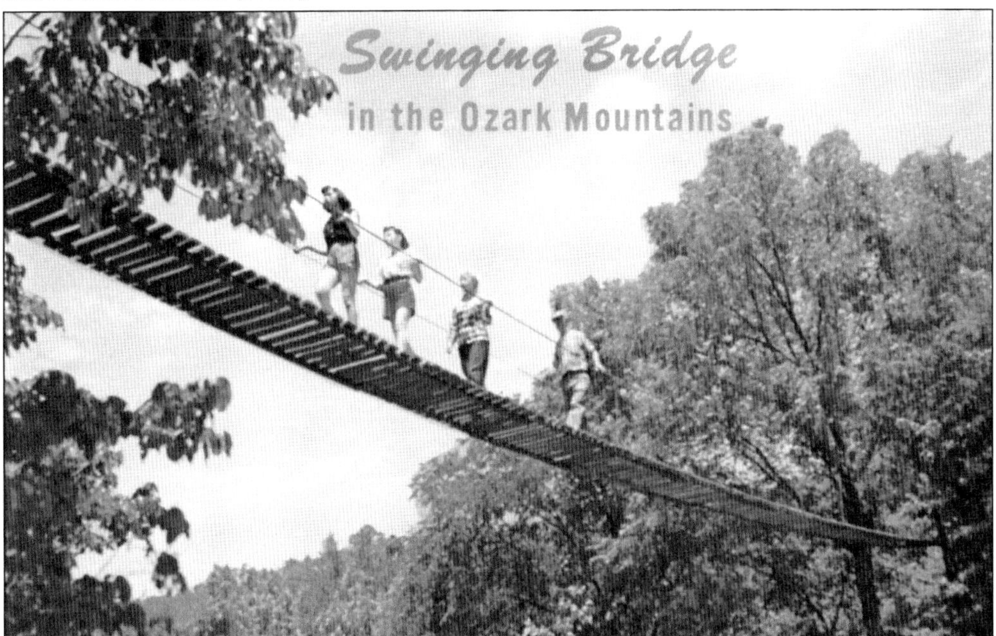

The pedestrian bridge that had been washed away a number of times by floods was rebuilt by the WPA. It was used well into the 1950s, as seen here. From left to right are Mildred Phillips, Mary Brasel, and Mr. and Mrs. Roy Birdwell. The bridge has been gone now for many years, as a modern bridge precluded the necessity to replace it after later floods.

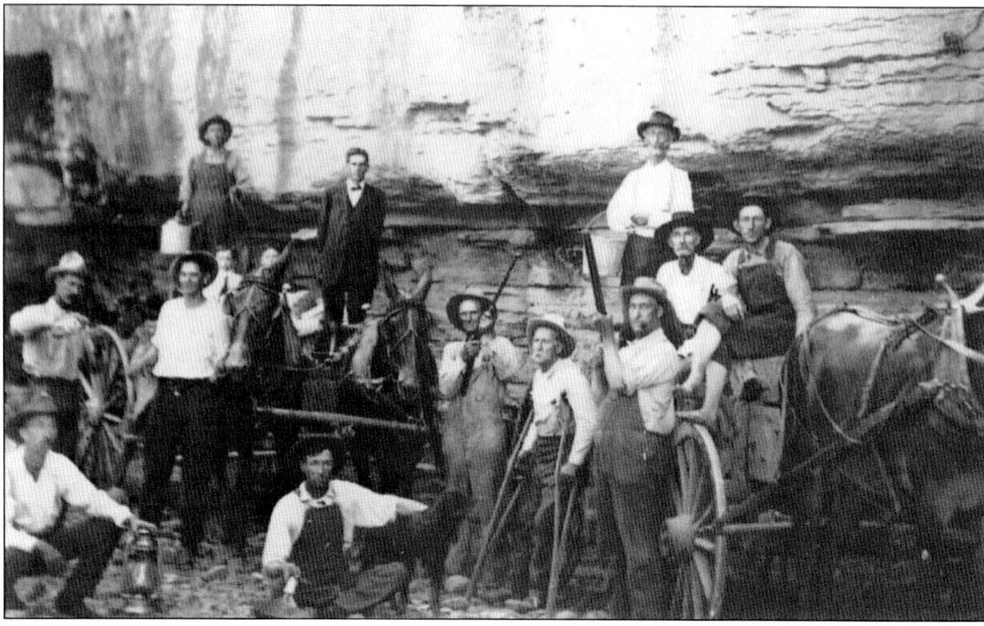

Over the decades, the bed of the Little Buffalo River has provided building stone for the courthouse and other structures, as well as much recreation. See here around 1910 is a group of men camped out upstream from Jasper, having gone on their expedition with mule-drawn wagons. (NCL.)

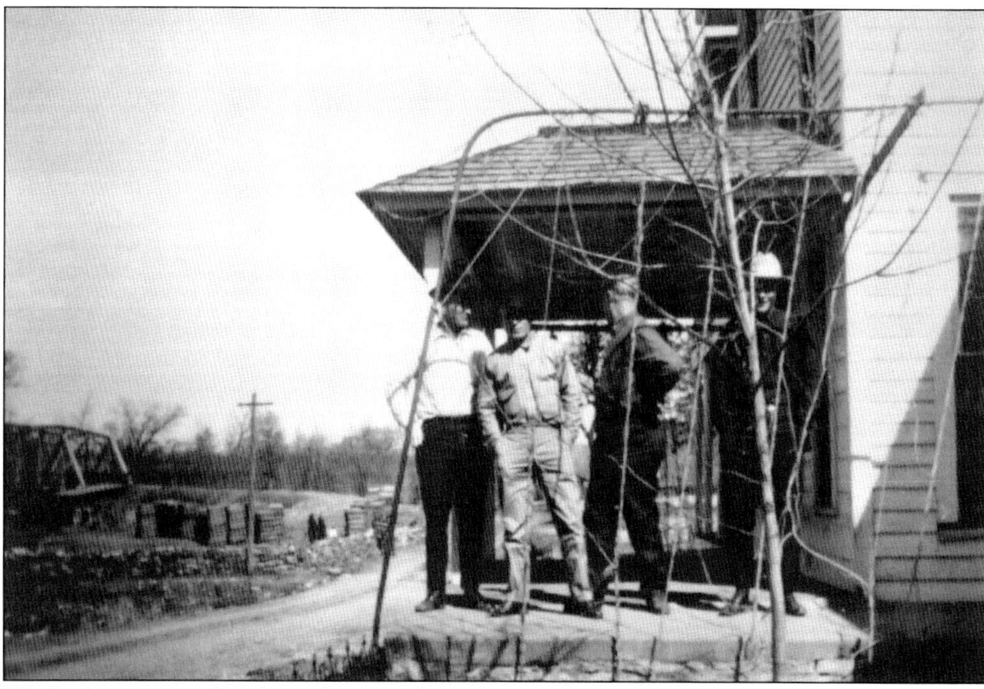

While the paving of Highway 7 was still 30 years in the future, the coming of the automobile to Jasper and Newton County necessitated a more sturdy bridge that would allow passage out of Jasper north toward Harrison. In 1925, an iron bridge, seen at far left in this photograph, was nearing completion over the Little Buffalo. Some of the construction crew posed on the porch of the Commercial Hotel. (NCHS.)

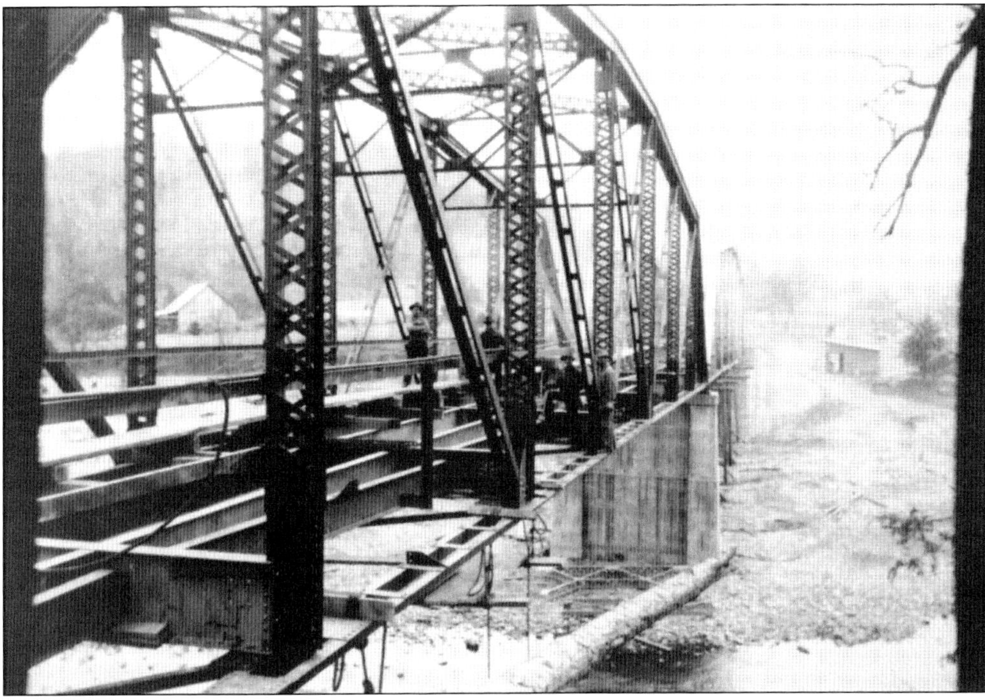

The new iron bridge brought construction jobs to Jasper as well as the promise of more travelers. Knowing they could cross the river regardless of the weather, tourists would be more likely to traverse the still-muddy gravel roads toward Russellville and points further south. Also, local commerce would no longer be brought to a halt by the rising river levels. (NCHS.)

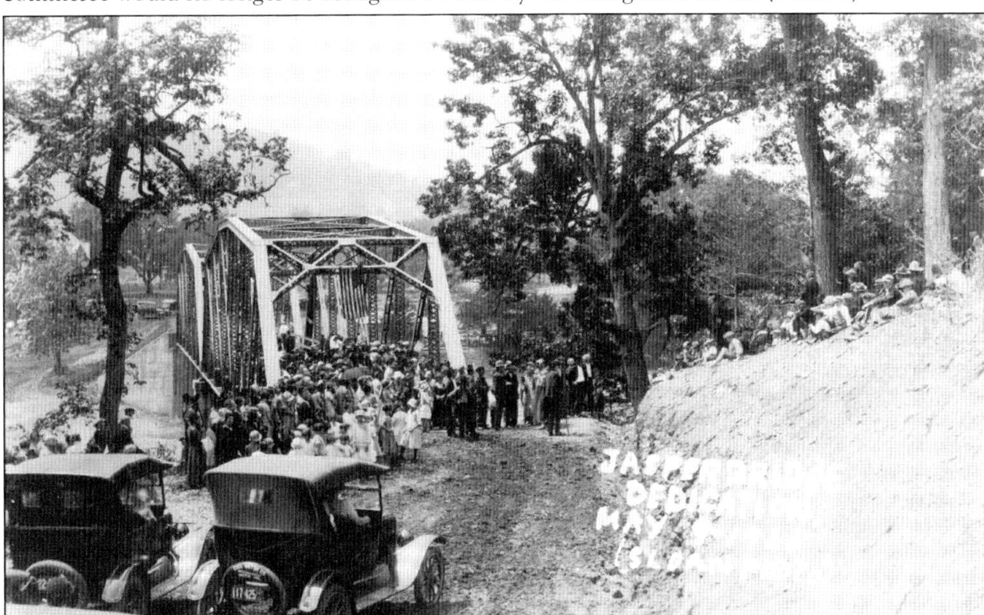

The dedication of the new bridge at the edge of Jasper drew a crowd on May 9, 1925. Children are seen seated up on the high bank, observing the speeches from a distance. The bridge would be replaced 50 years later by the concrete span that still carries traffic today.

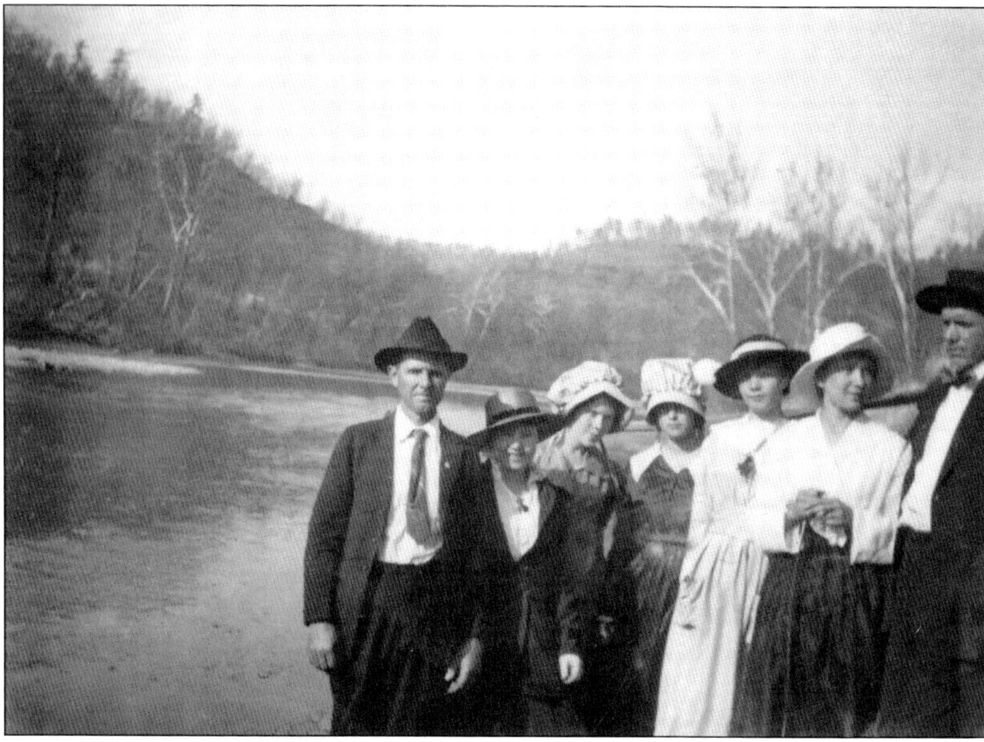

School and church groups, like this one in 1910, often came to the Buffalo River on outings. The photograph was taken by C.E. Wilson. (NCL.)

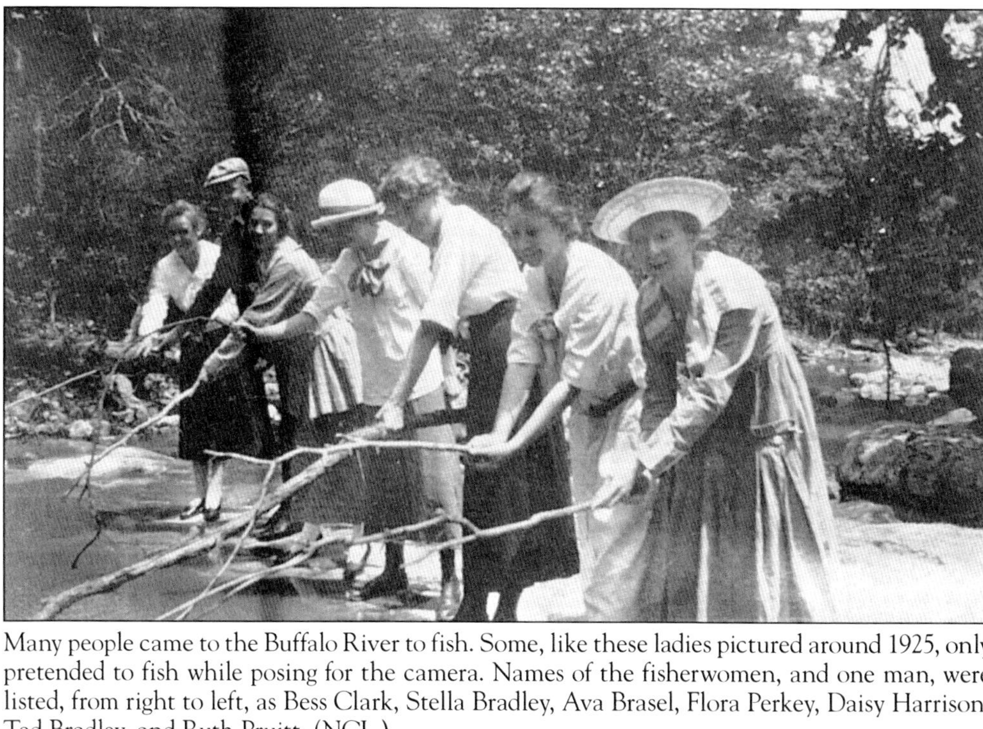

Many people came to the Buffalo River to fish. Some, like these ladies pictured around 1925, only pretended to fish while posing for the camera. Names of the fisherwomen, and one man, were listed, from right to left, as Bess Clark, Stella Bradley, Ava Brasel, Flora Perkey, Daisy Harrison, Ted Bradley, and Ruth Pruitt. (NCL.)

All along the scenic Buffalo River are hidden canyons, soaring bluffs, and waterfalls tucked away on creeks feeding the river. One of these many waterfalls was the backdrop for this c. 1920 postcard.

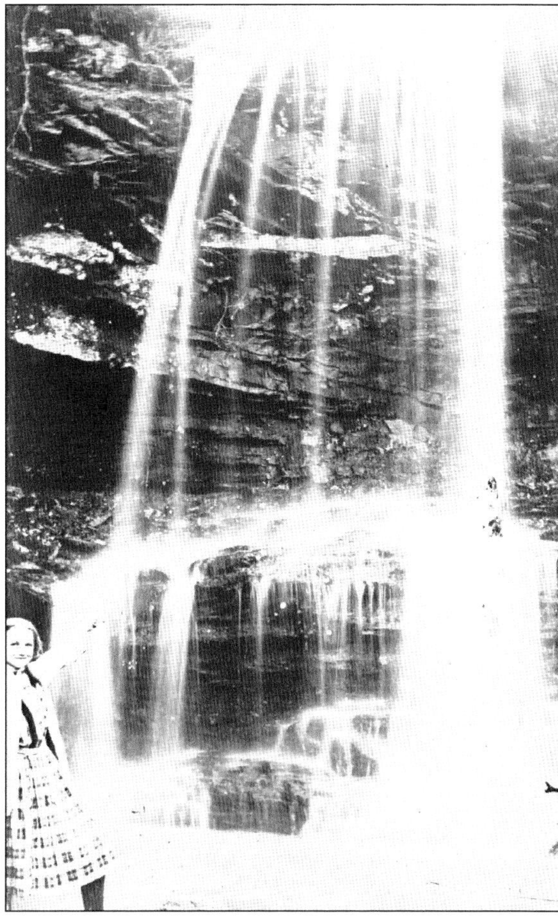

An iron, wood-floor wagon bridge was built in the Carver community, several miles downstream from Jasper, around 1916. P.T. Carver had founded the village that bore his name. He operated the post office, country store, blacksmith shop, gristmill, sawmill, sorghum mill, and a farm. The new bridge helped him and other farmers in communities around Carver get their goods to customers in Jasper and Harrison. (NCL.)

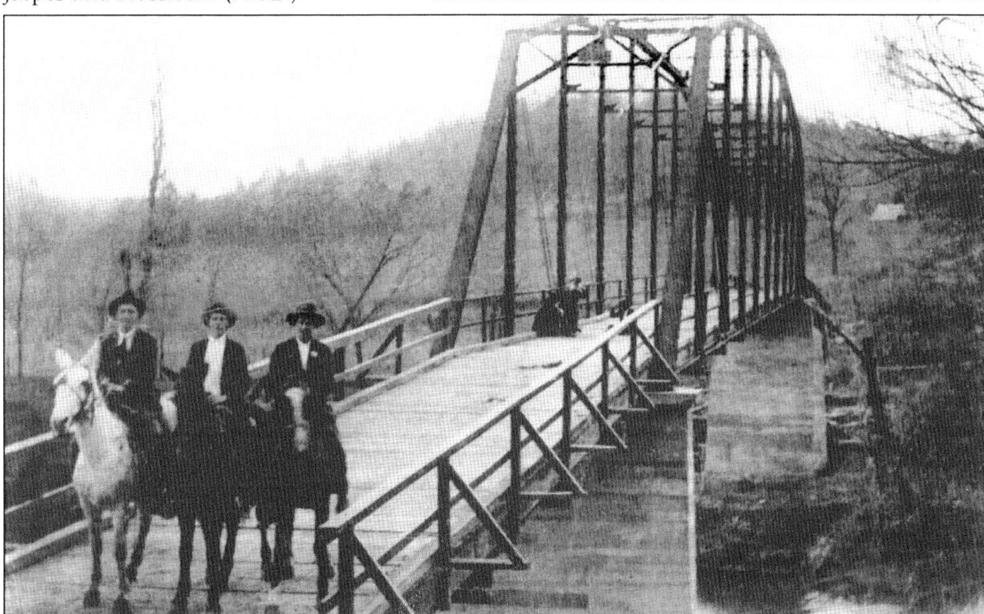

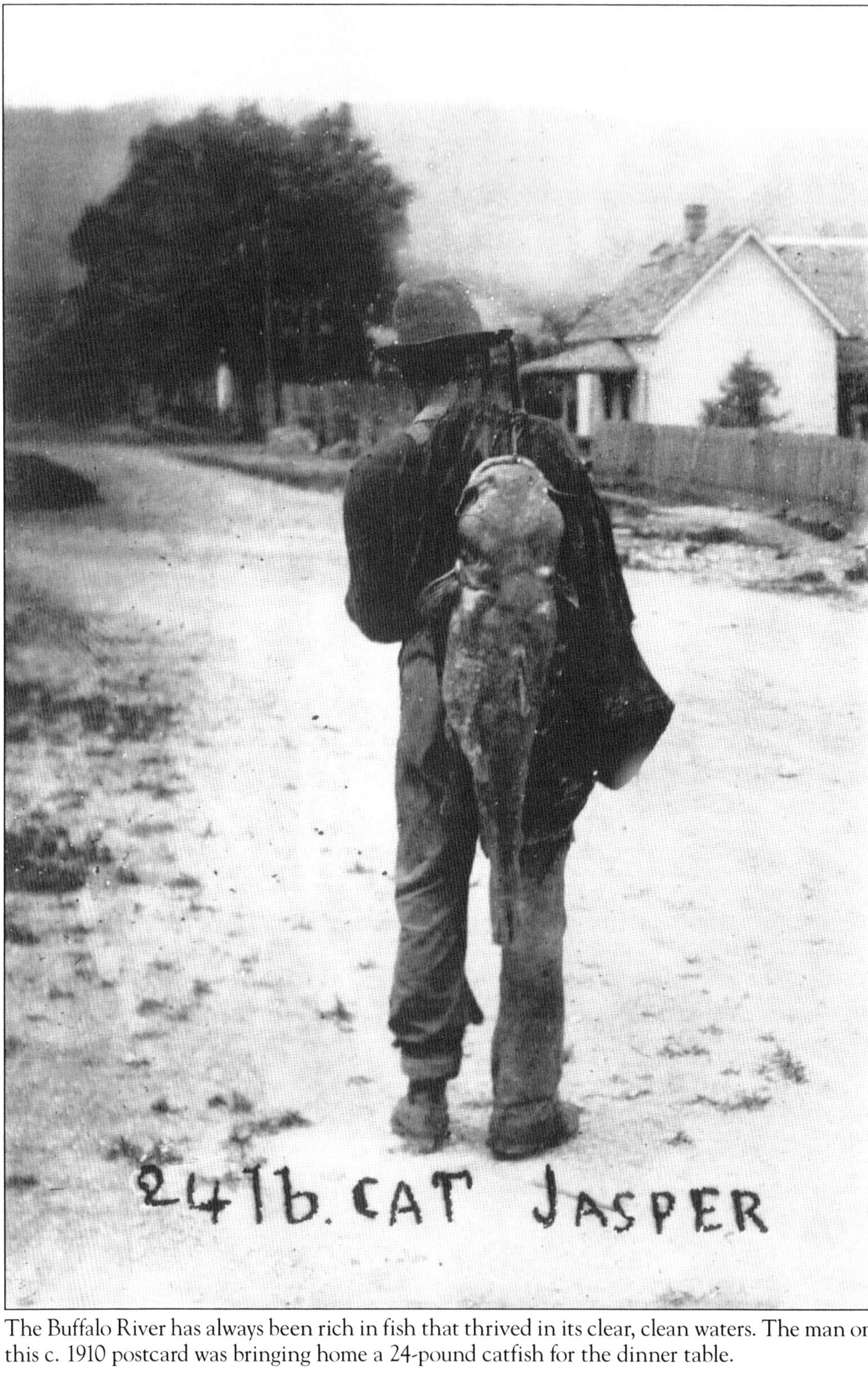

The Buffalo River has always been rich in fish that thrived in its clear, clean waters. The man on this c. 1910 postcard was bringing home a 24-pound catfish for the dinner table.

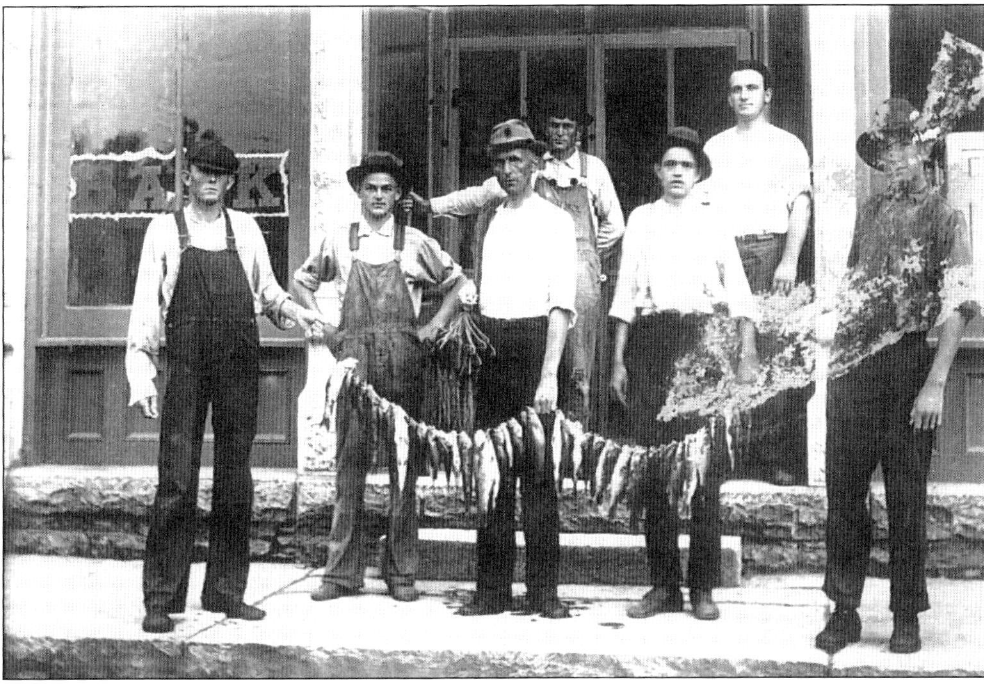

In 1913, these men were proud enough of their catch of small mouth bass that they showed off their haul in front of the bank in Jasper. Names on the photograph were Wilburn Moore, Thurman Sharpensteen, James Murray, Austin Harrison, Harry Clark, Vol Harrison, and Hugh Pruitt. (NCL.)

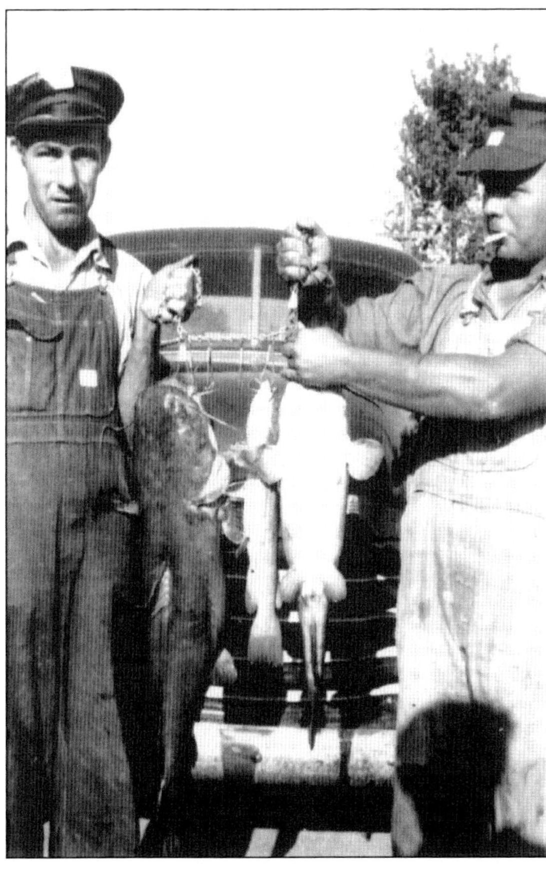

Strong men flexed their muscles to hold up this catch of catfish from the Buffalo River in Jasper around 1950. (NCL.)

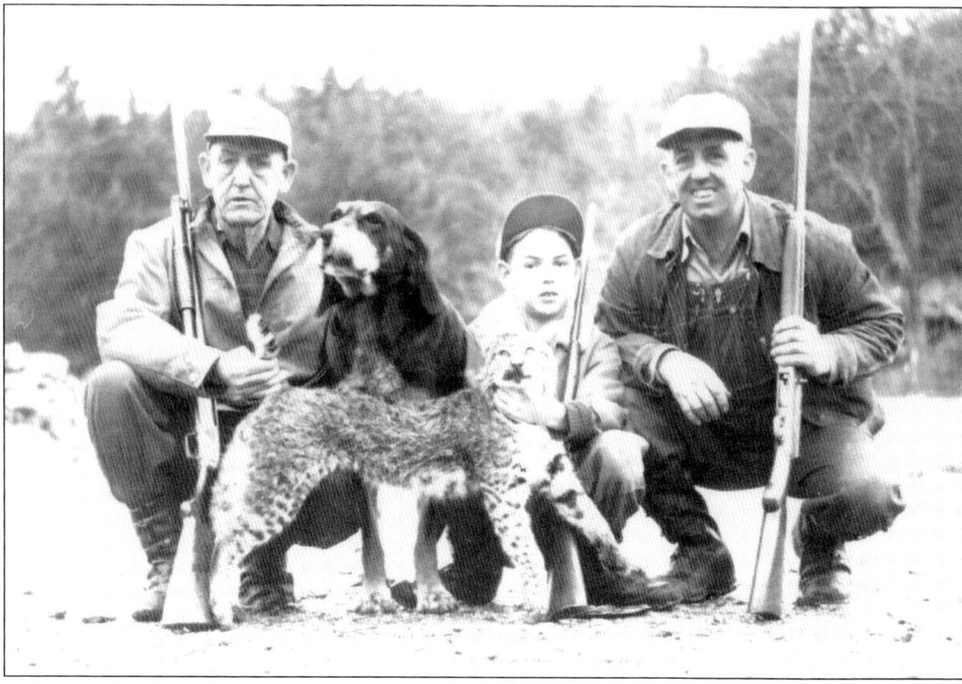

Fishing aside, the wilderness that surrounded the Buffalo River has always been a draw for hunters. On the banks of the river in the 1950s, young Gene Waters (center) posed with his father Veatle (right) and Uncle Dason (left), showing off a bobcat they had killed earlier in the day, likely with the tracking help of the unnamed dog. (NCL.)

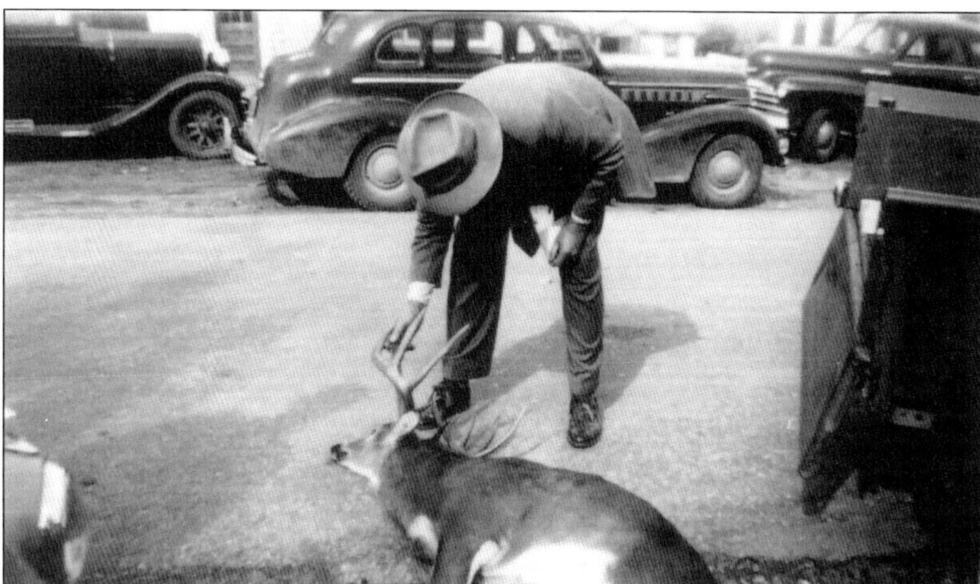

Deer hunting has always been popular in Newton County. Due to good management of the resource by the Arkansas Game and Fish Commission, it remains so today. Seen here was the first deer of the 1951 season, checked by Eugene Eddings at the Jasper check station in front of the Commercial Hotel. (NCL.)

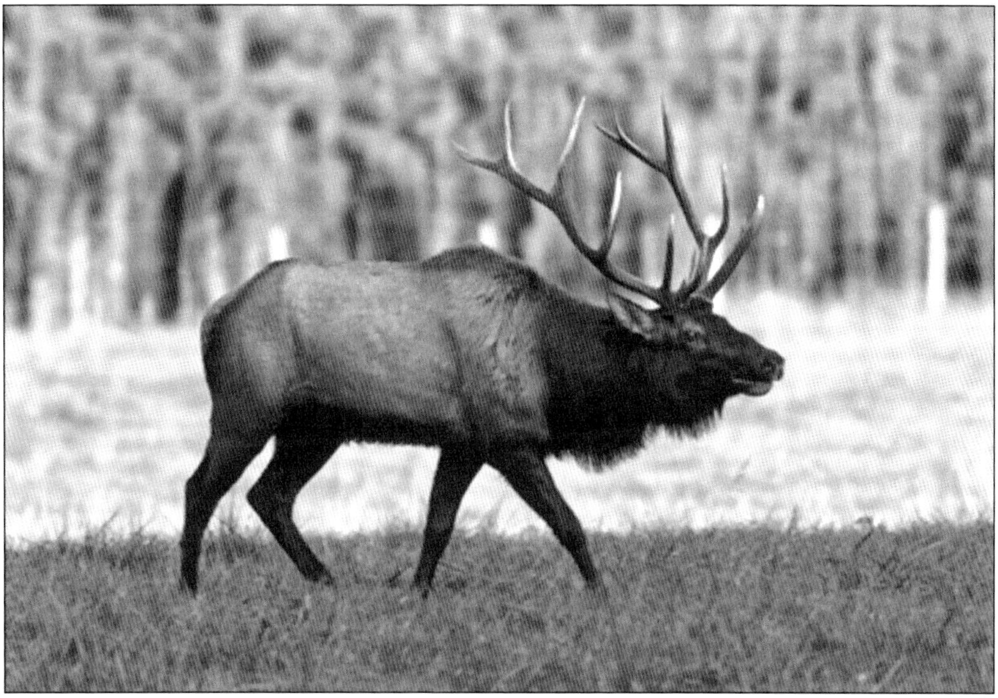

Today, Newton County bills itself as the "Elk Capital of Arkansas," and for good reason. Elk had originally been native to the area but were killed off by the early settlers. The Arkansas Game and Fish Commission imported elk from Colorado beginning in 1981, releasing them around the upper portions of the Buffalo River. Local farmers used their own equipment to help haul the animals from Colorado and deposit them into the backcountry. The herds thrived, making possible a limited hunting season for the animals that can weigh 600 to 1,000 pounds. (Courtesy of Ray Scott of Little Rock.)

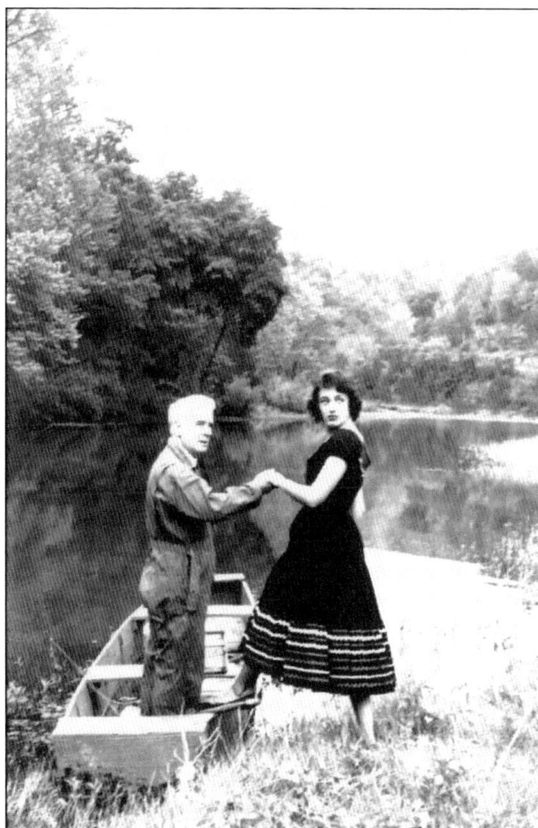

As other rivers in the Ozark region were being dammed, some of the enterprising people of Newton County realized that a favorite sport was being lost to these vast impoundments. Float fishing by johnboat, which locals had enjoyed for years, needed some immediate promotion. In the 1950s, former Arkansas governor Francis Cherry and former Miss Arkansas, Joyce Reed, stepped up to demonstrate the activity to the wider population. (NCL.)

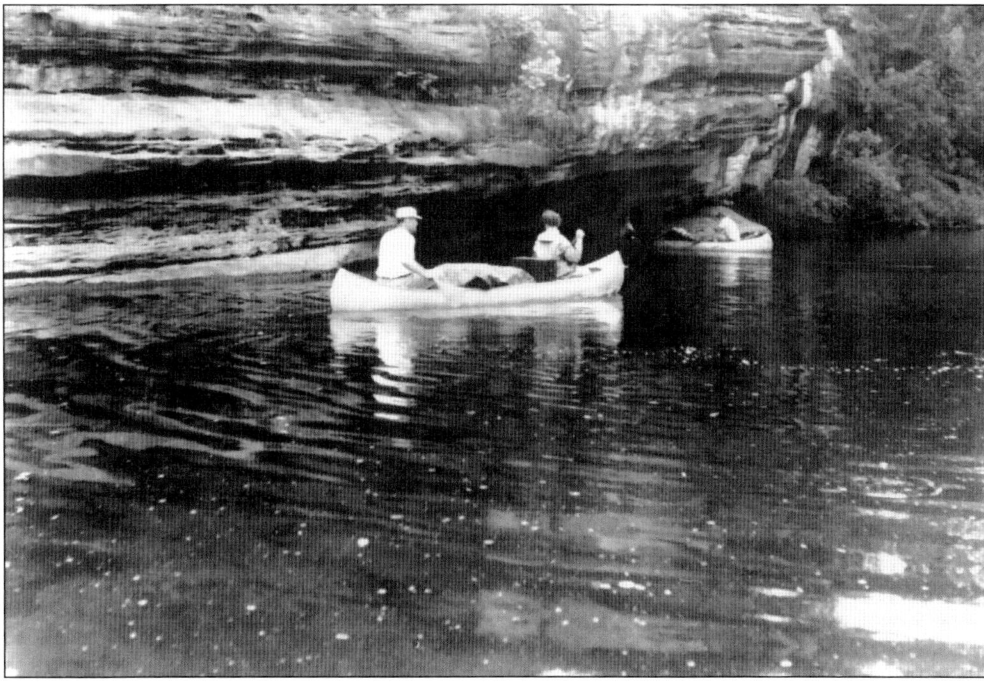

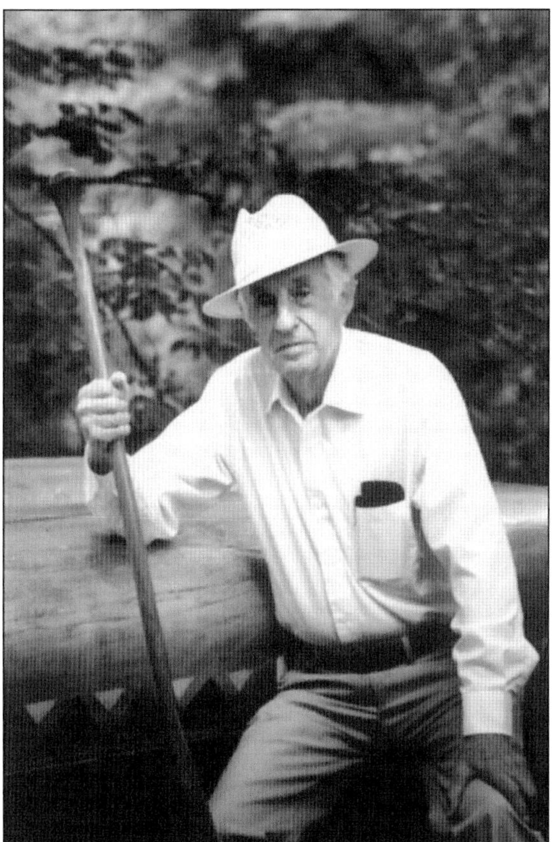

Even more than fishing or hunting, it would be the public's discovery of the joy of floating a canoe down the Buffalo River that would ultimately defeat plans to dam the river. More and more people began to come to the Buffalo River, supporting the new canoe-rental businesses. (NCL.)

The growing number of canoeists began to lobby against the two dams planned by the US Army Corps of Engineers. The Ozark Society was formed for the primary purpose of preventing these dams. The group, led by Bentonville physician Dr. Neil Compton, became a major force in swinging public and political opinion toward the cause of preserving the Buffalo as a free-flowing stream. Dr. Compton is seen here next to a canoe on the Buffalo. He died in 1999 at the age of 87; some of his ashes were put into the Buffalo River. (Courtesy of the University of Arkansas Special Collections.)

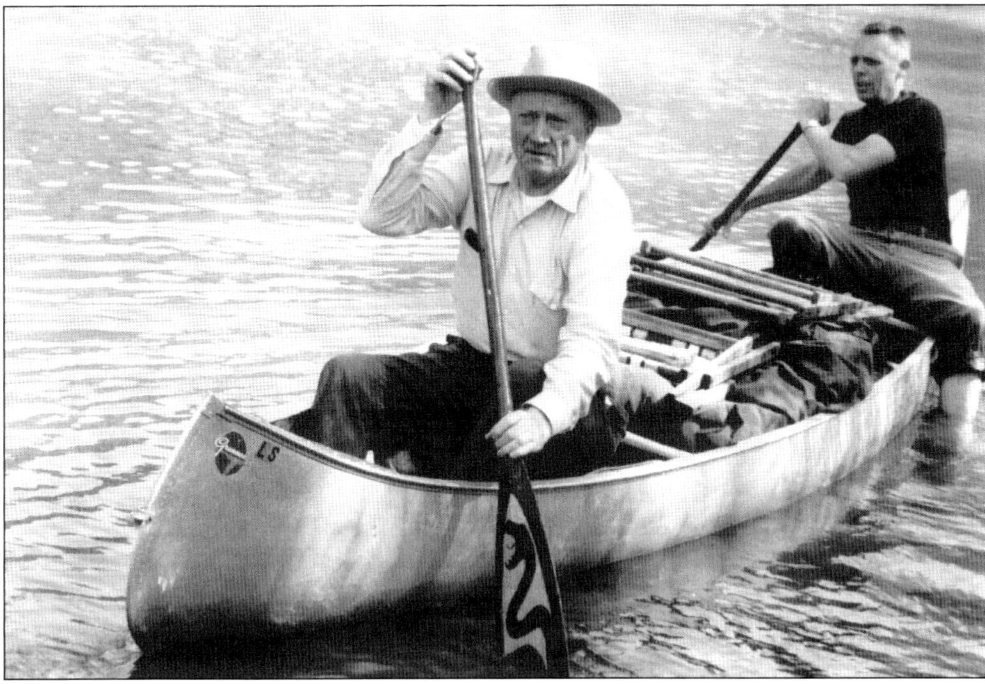

At the invitation of Dr. Neil Compton and the Ozark Society, US Supreme Court Justice William O. Douglas came to float the Buffalo River in 1962, putting in at the low-water bridge at Ponca. Judge Douglas would serve a record 36 years on the high court, writing more opinions and more dissents than any other Supreme Court judge in history. The publicity associated with his trip and his opposition to damming the Buffalo River helped win over others to that cause. (Courtesy of the University of Arkansas Special Collections.)

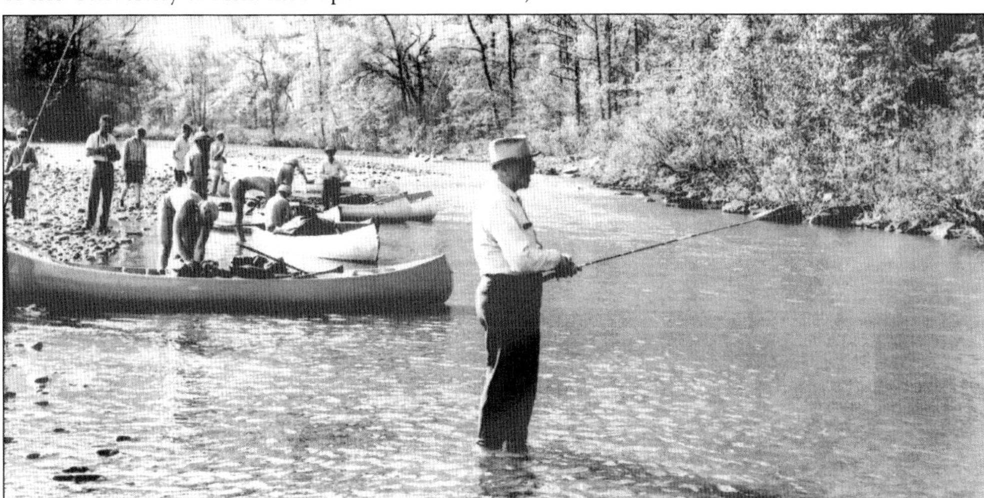

The soaring bluffs of the Buffalo River would never see the river's water rising behind a dam. Congress passed a bill, which President Nixon signed in 1972, designating the Buffalo as a National River and making it a part of the National Park system. Over the four decades since that time, countless thousands from around the world have floated by the Steel Creek section of the river where Supreme Court Justice William O. Douglas was fishing in 1962. (Courtesy of the University of Arkansas Special Collections.)

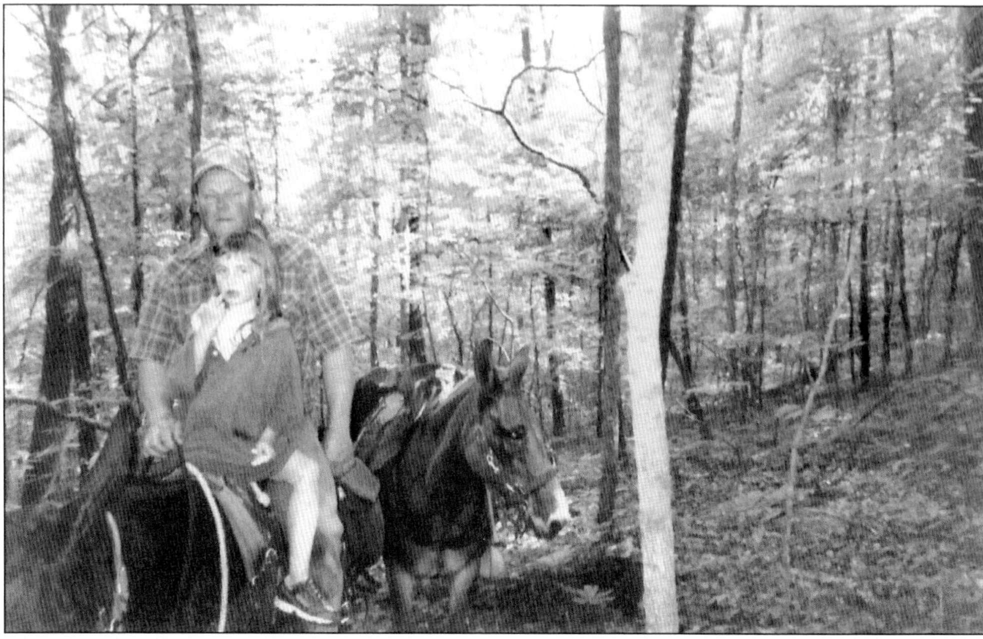

The rugged wilderness around the Hawksbill Crag area (long known locally as Whitaker's Point) was the backdrop for modern-day heroism in April 2001. While her family was visiting the scenic overlook, six-year-old Haley Zega wandered off and disappeared in the rugged woods. As the search progressed into a second day, the professional rescue personnel began to doubt that anyone would find the child. Newton County grandfathers Lytle James and William Jeff Villines thought otherwise. They rode their mules, Copper and Big Momma, into the rugged backcountry, intent on finding the lost child. After Haley had spent three days and two nights alone, scared, and hungry, she was found by the two men and transported safely home. Shown above, Haley rides out of the canyon on Villines's mule. Shown below, Lytle James gives Haley the first food she has eaten since the ordeal began. The two men refused the offered reward, saying getting Haley safely home was reward enough. (Courtesy of Lytle James.)

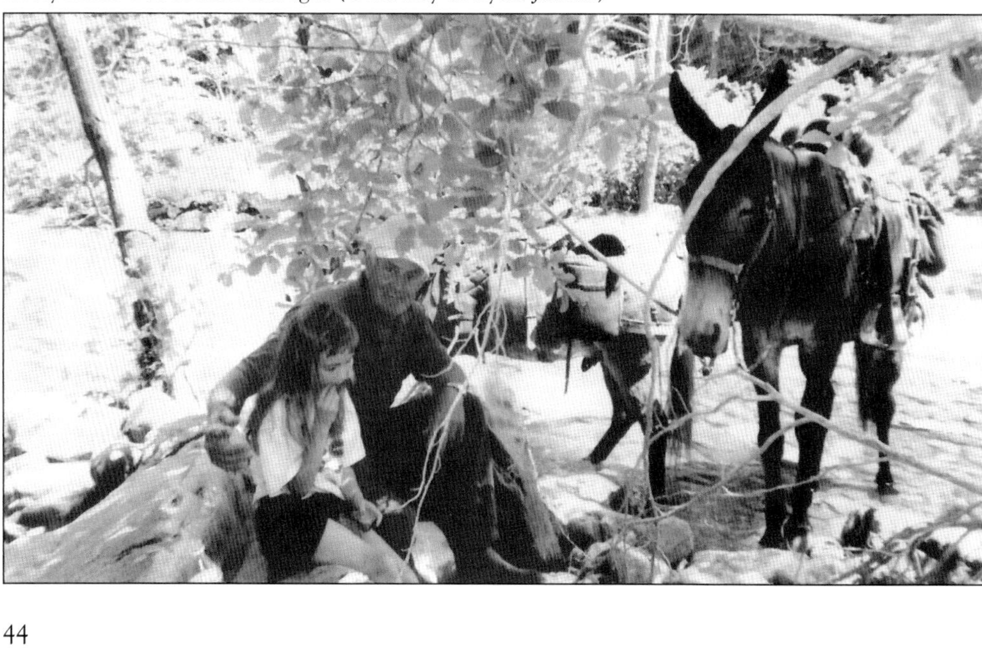

Three

Working Hard to Earn a Living from a Rocky Land

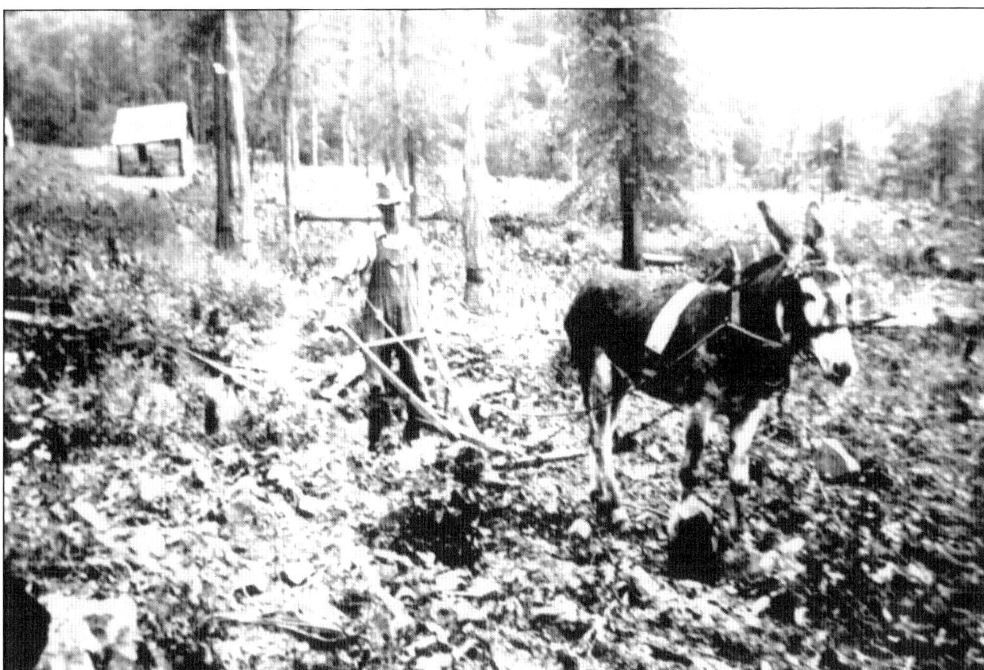

Vance Randolph, collector of Ozark folk tales, documented the following in 1951: "When a feller owns a forty in Newton County he farms the top and all four sides." Farming in the most mountainous and rocky county in the state was never easy, especially in the age before motorized equipment. With the help of mules, however, a farmer, like this one in the 1930s, was able to grow cotton and other crops on his mountaintop. Yields would be small, perhaps a bale or two of cotton or a few bushels of corn; however, it would provide much-needed cash money to buy essentials the farmer could not produce for his family. The farmer seen here was named Joe Rich, pictured with his mule, John the Baptist. (Photograph by Ernest and Opal Nicholson; courtesy of Shiloh Museum of Ozark History, Katie McCoy Collection.)

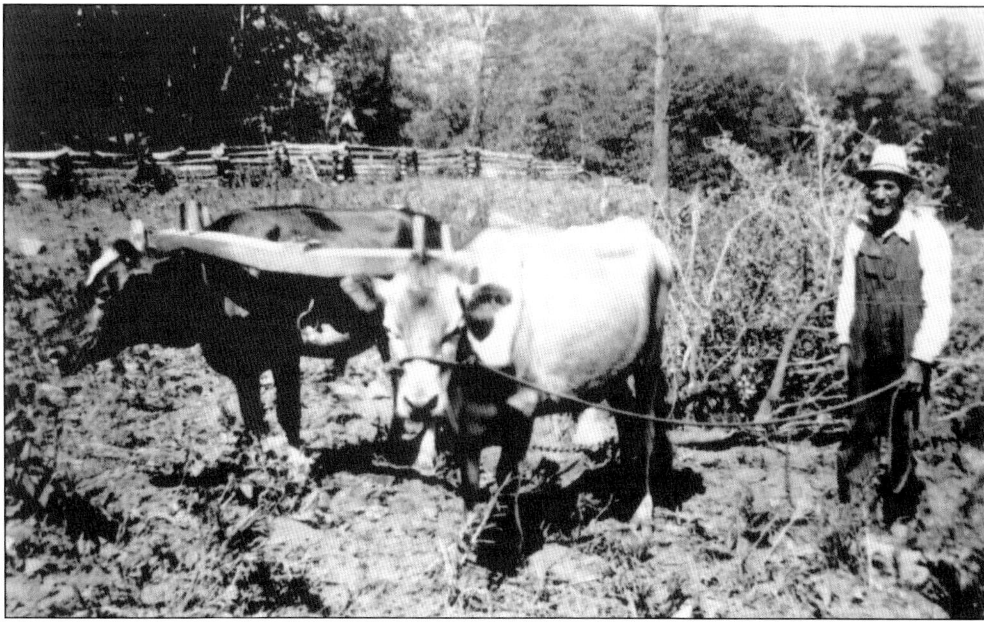

Some farmers resorted to multiple uses of their cattle to earn a living, in this case yoking the animals to a plow. In the background, the unidentified farmer has built a split rail fence on the edge of his field. (Photograph by Ernest and Opal Nicholson; courtesy of Shiloh Museum of Ozark History, Katie McCoy Collection.)

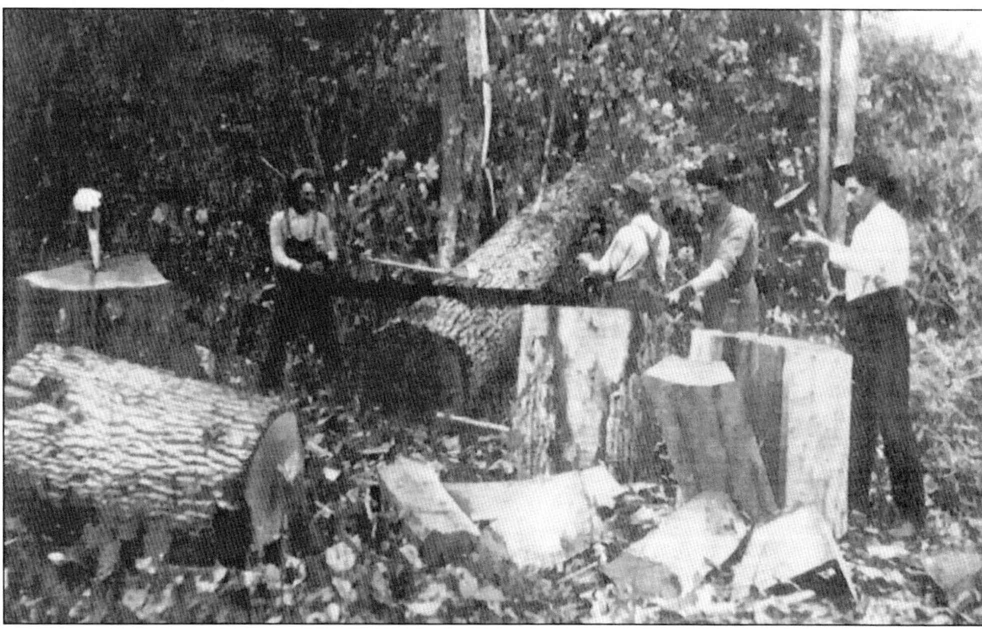

Timber has been a means of making a living from the land since the early pioneers. Until around 1900, timber harvesting was intended more for building homes and fences. Then, the lumber barons arrived and began to clear the stands of majestic centuries-old trees. Local men worked smaller projects for sometimes $1 or $2 a day. Seen here around 1900, lumbermen were cutting stave bolts from a large oak tree sectioned with a crosscut saw. The staves would have to be split and then shipped by wagon for making barrels. (NCL.)

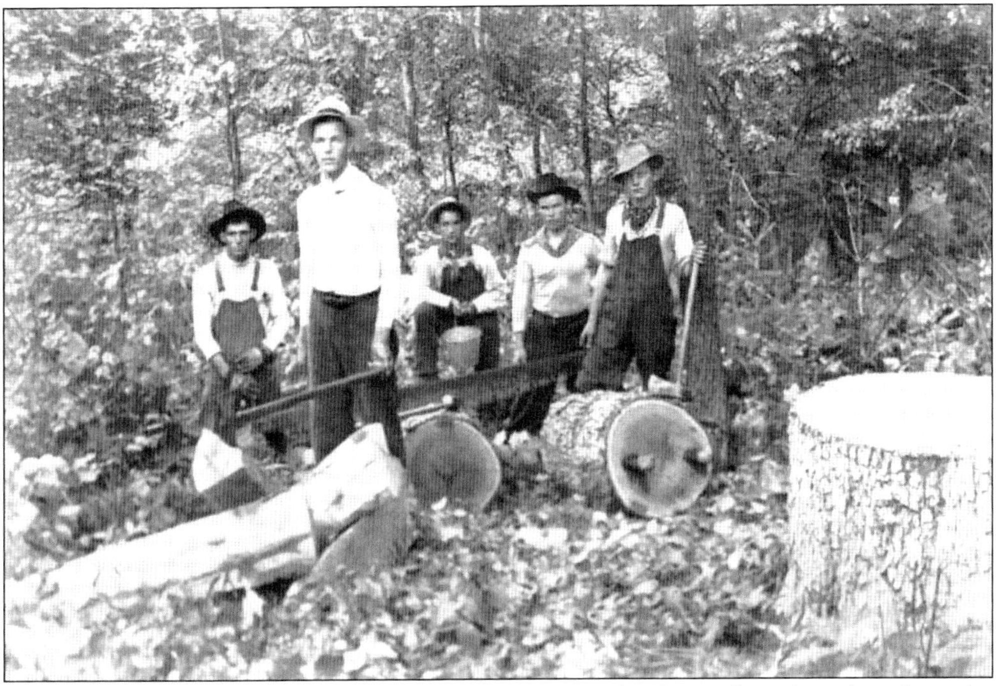

Standing in the foreground, 25-year-old Albert Raney posed in better dress than the others who had been cutting the 32-to-36-inch logs, which would later become barrel staves. Cutting staves was hard, dangerous work, and injuries were common. Albert Raney would later become the postmaster and a store merchant for many years in the community of Marble Falls north of Jasper. He was also a founding member of the Newton County Historical Society. (NCL.)

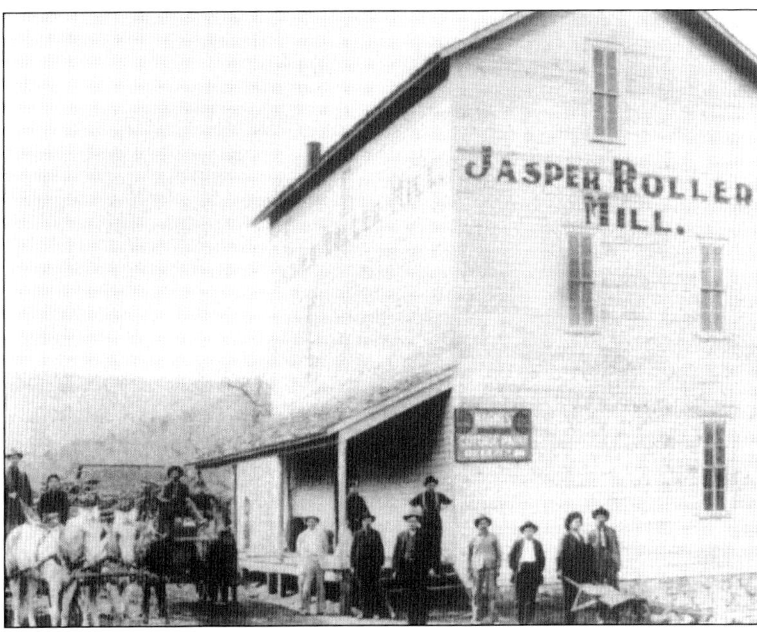

While some corn and other grain went to the distillery to make whiskey, more went to mills like the Jasper Roller Mill located on the edge of Jasper around 1908. Water-powered gristmills were found at Boxley, Marble Falls, Cave Creek, Vendor, as well as other locations around Newton County. (NCL.)

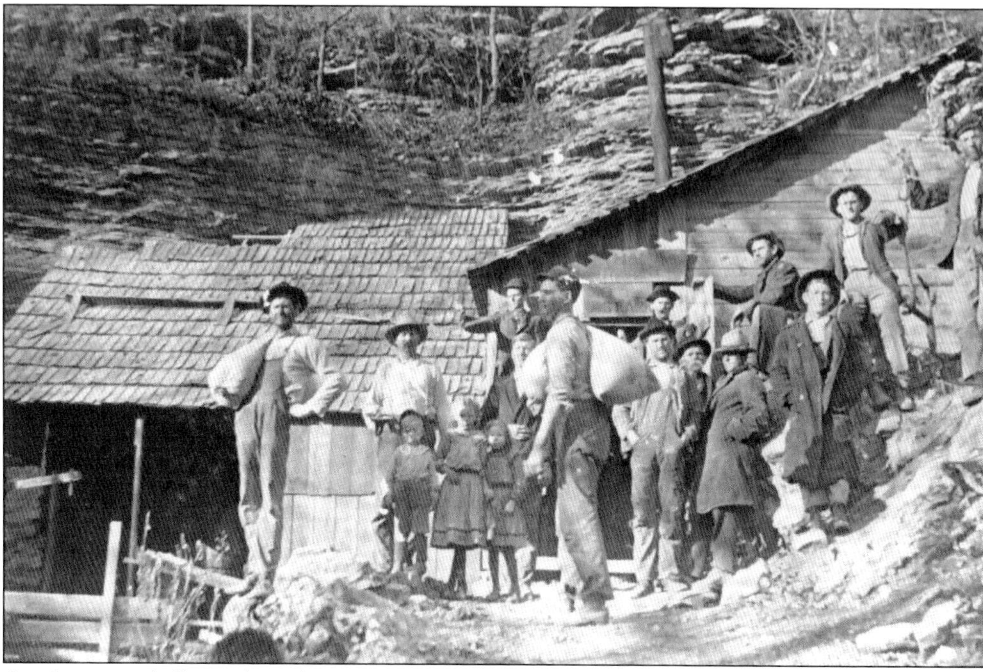

A reference to hill people making whiskey would immediately suggest an illegal still. However, in the early 1900s, Newton County was home to two very legal, federally approved distilleries. The c. 1900 photograph above was of the gristmill and whiskey distillery at Bat House Cave in eastern Newton County. Some of the people included, from the far left, Charley Bethany, Darrell, Kate and Corie Bethany, Calvin Quals, Eli Martin, Tom Ramey, Dick Knox, Riley Lee, and Bill Hill. The photograph below was taken in the interior of the cave, where a spring fed the distillery. The man on the far left is Levi Pinkney Bethany, sitting next to Charles Bethany. The legal allotment for the "still" was 12 gallons per day. Affixed to each gallon was a government stamp costing $2.10; half of this cost represented a federal tax. Prohibition closed the still in 1917. (NCHS.)

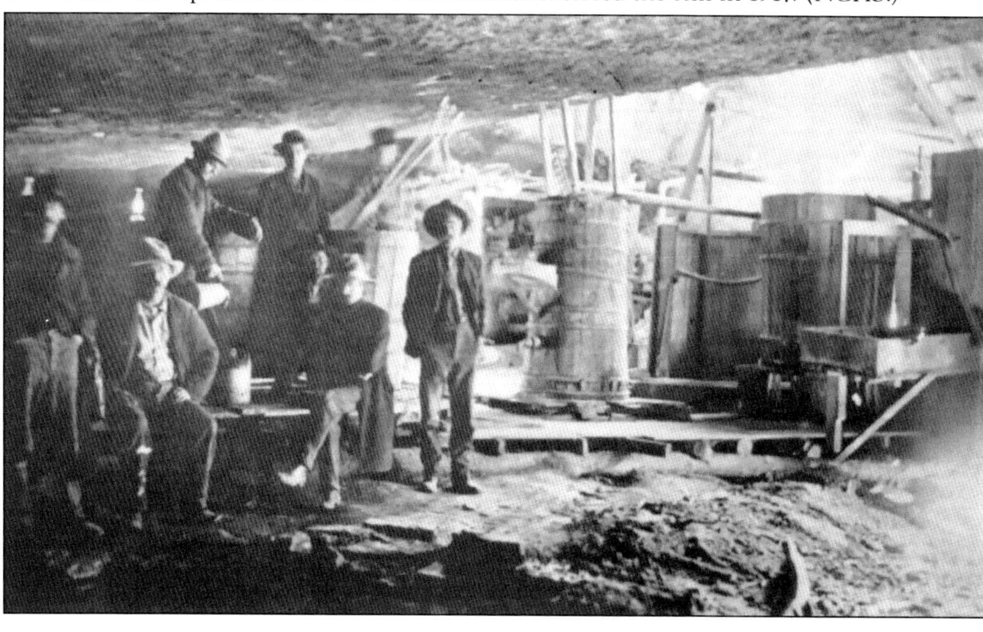

“Hog killing time,” beginning in the early days of Newton County, was signified by the arrival of the first cold days of winter. Farmers often grew some corn to supplement the acorns and food scraps they fed their hogs, the better to fatten them for the slaughter. Seen here in the 1940s, a slaughtered hog has already been dipped in boiling water; the farmer is scraping the hide as part of the preparation. (NCL.)

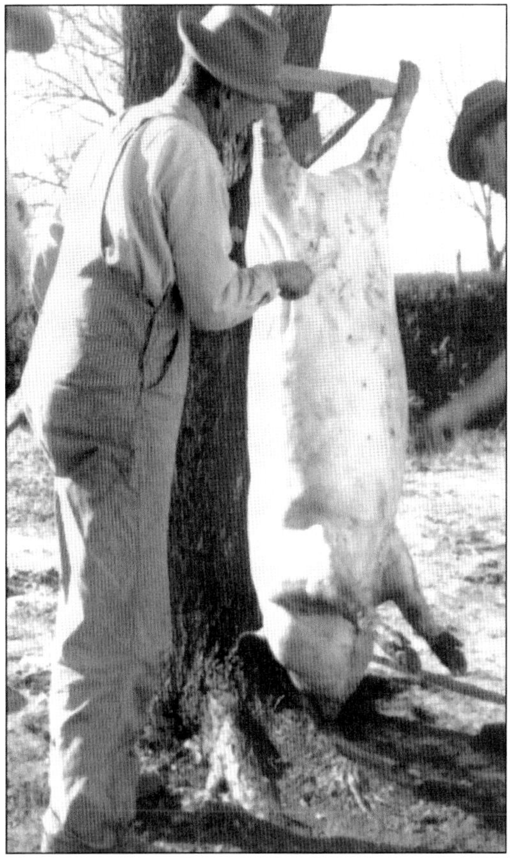

The ham and bacon produced from the annual hog killing were often stored in the smokehouse that was usually located behind the farmer’s cabin home. Seen here around 1910 was Henry Rush’s smokehouse in Sycamore Hollow on Cave Creek in eastern Newton County. The dog would have been helpful in keeping bears and other would-be meat thieves away from the smokehouse. The building is also adorned with raccoon hides and other pelts. (NCHS.)

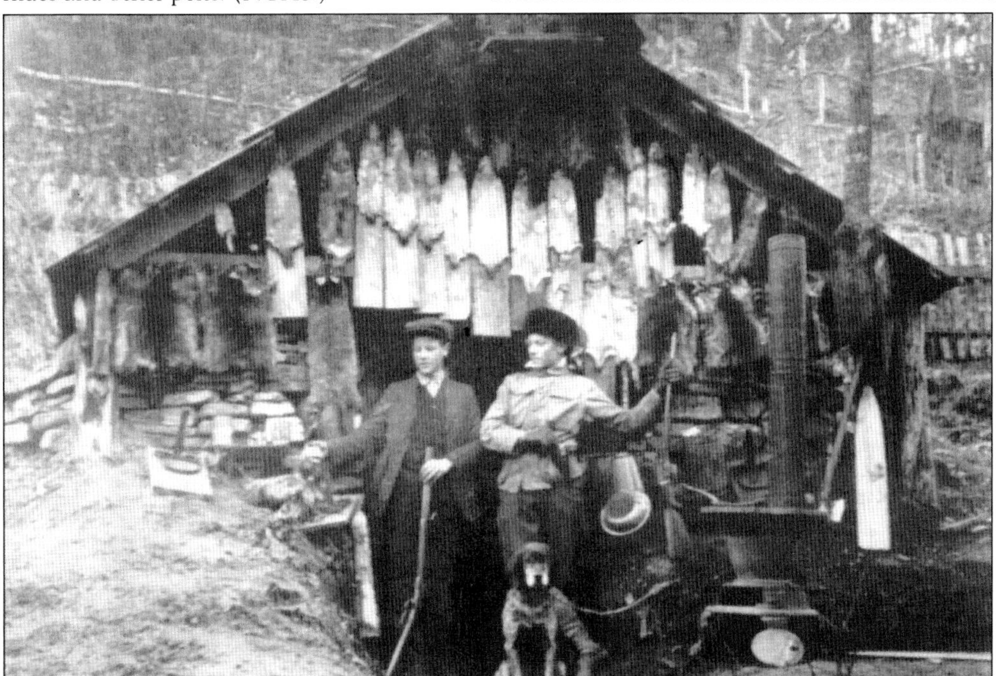

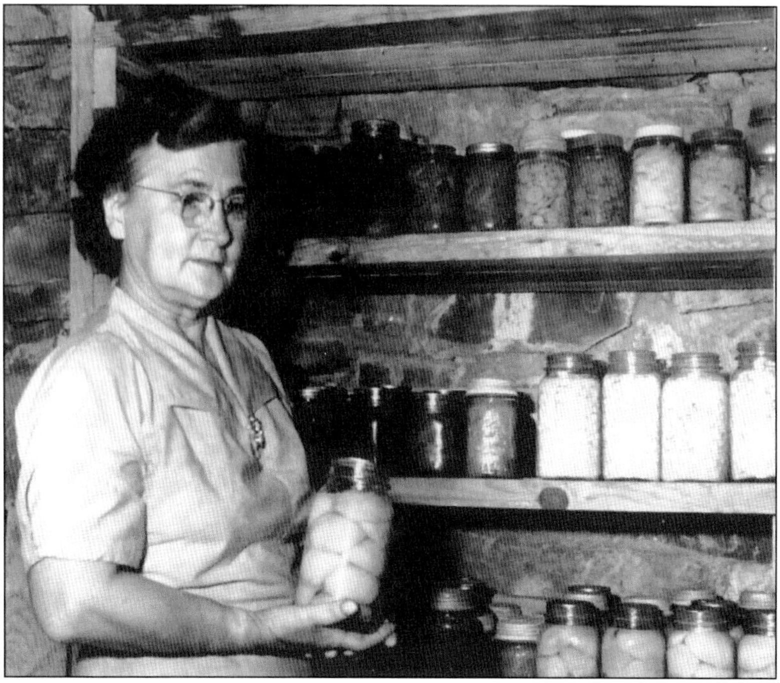

Ham from the smokehouse was not all that helped Newton County families remain self-sufficient and dine well over the decades. Seen here in the 1940s is Mrs. Gussie Ball in her root cellar near the Bass community, about 20 miles southeast of Jasper. She was proud of having put up 500 quarts of fruits and vegetables from the family's garden. (NCL.)

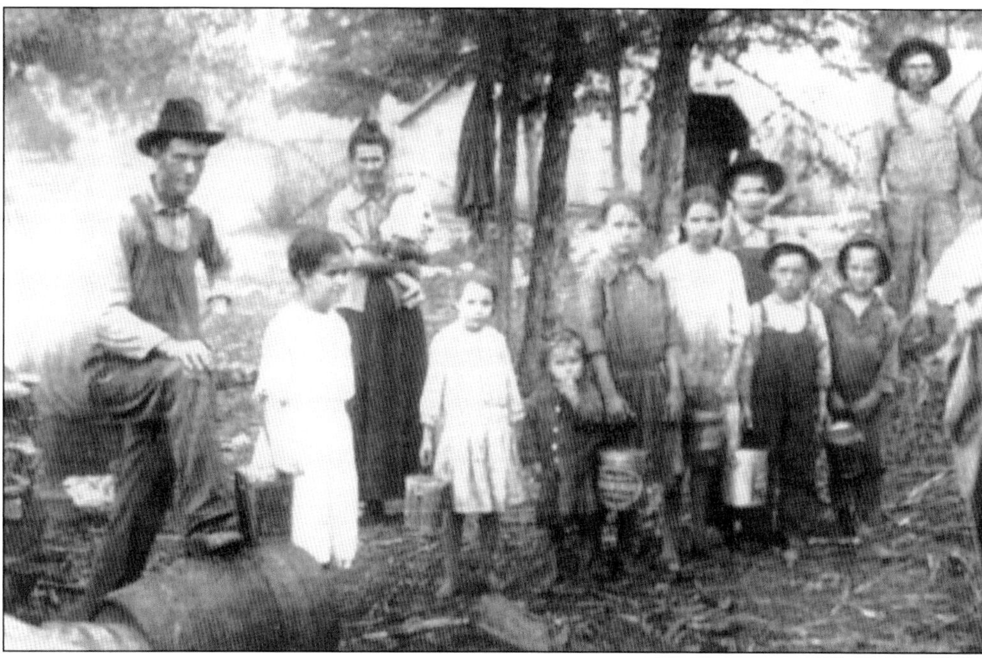

Another fall ritual for some families in Newton County was producing sorghum molasses. The sweet syrup pressed from sorghum grain has been made in the United States since the 1850s. It represents a skill brought to Newton County by the early pioneers, who favored the treat on their breakfast biscuits and corn cakes. The 1910 operation here had pressed into service a number of children helping to fill syrup buckets. From left to right are Billy Robinson, Mamie Dixon, Missie Caroline Dixon holding baby John Dixon, Walcie Dixon, three unidentified, Dason Waters, two unidentified, and James Waters. (NCHS.)

C.W. Clayborn and his father, C.C. Clayborn, were photographed on a wagon on their farm near Nail around 1930. Horses, mules, and wagons were Newton County mainstays well into the 1950s, before tractors started to become more common in the area. In the case of the Clayborns, they were transporting some very large rocks out of their field. (Courtesy of John Clayborn of Conway, Arkansas.)

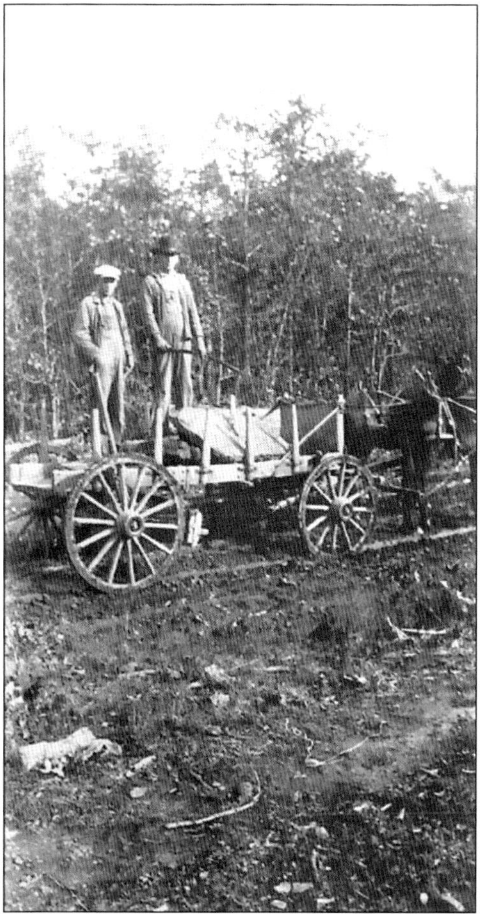

Newton County was known for its lead deposits even before the Civil War, which made it a target especially for the Confederacy that was much in need of ammunition. Saltpeter, or "niter," which some say came from bat droppings found inside local caves, was used in making gunpowder. A major lead-mining boom was underway by 1916, when this postcard of mine workers at Ponca was made. This site is listed as the Eleventh Hour Mining Company.

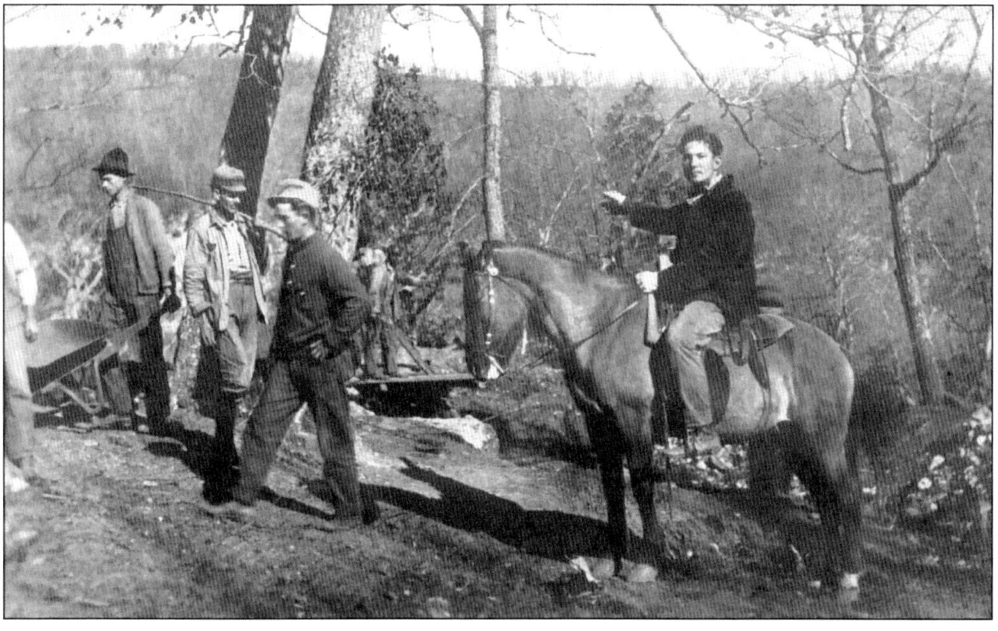

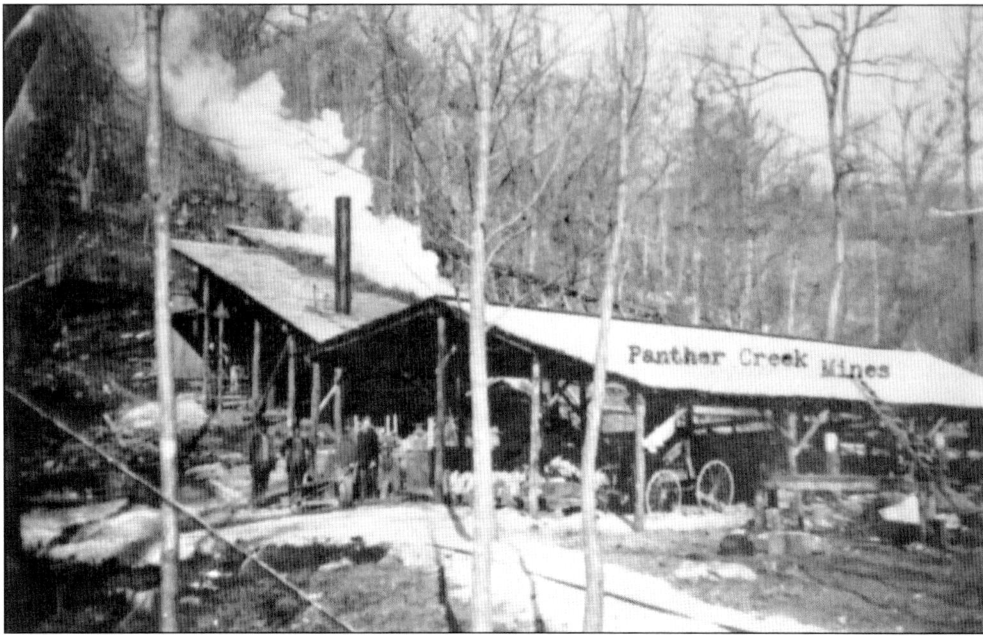

The Panther Creek mines near Diamond Cave became a major site for taking and processing lead, as well as some zinc. The creek supposedly got its name in the 1800s when settler Sam Hudson, on his way home from gathering honey and armed only with a knife, killed a panther (actually a mountain lion) that had attacked him. The lead ore was discovered by accident by a man digging for ginseng roots. (NCL.)

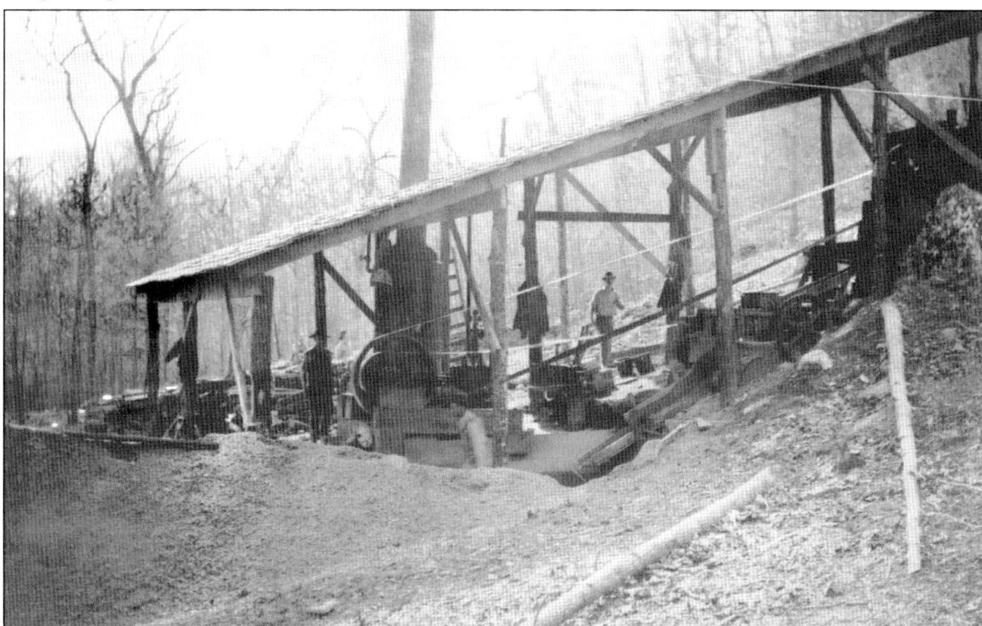

In 1916, Walter Lackey, who earned $40 a month as a schoolteacher, went to work at the Panther Creek mines when school was not in session. He earned $1.50 for a 10-hour day of backbreaking work. The steam engine covered by the shed drove the machinery that separated the waste rock from the lead, helping to process it for shipment by wagon out of the rugged valley. (NCL.)

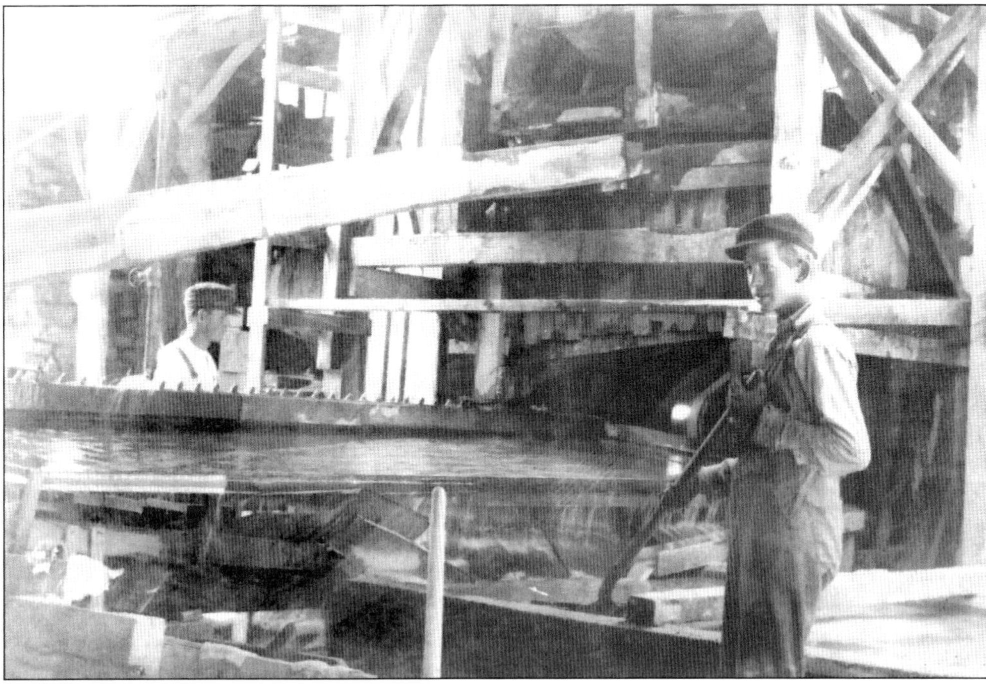

The mines of Newton County were dangerous. The surrounding soil and rock were unstable, which necessitated shoring up with beams often cut on site from the surrounding forests, as at the Panther Creek Mine. (NCL.)

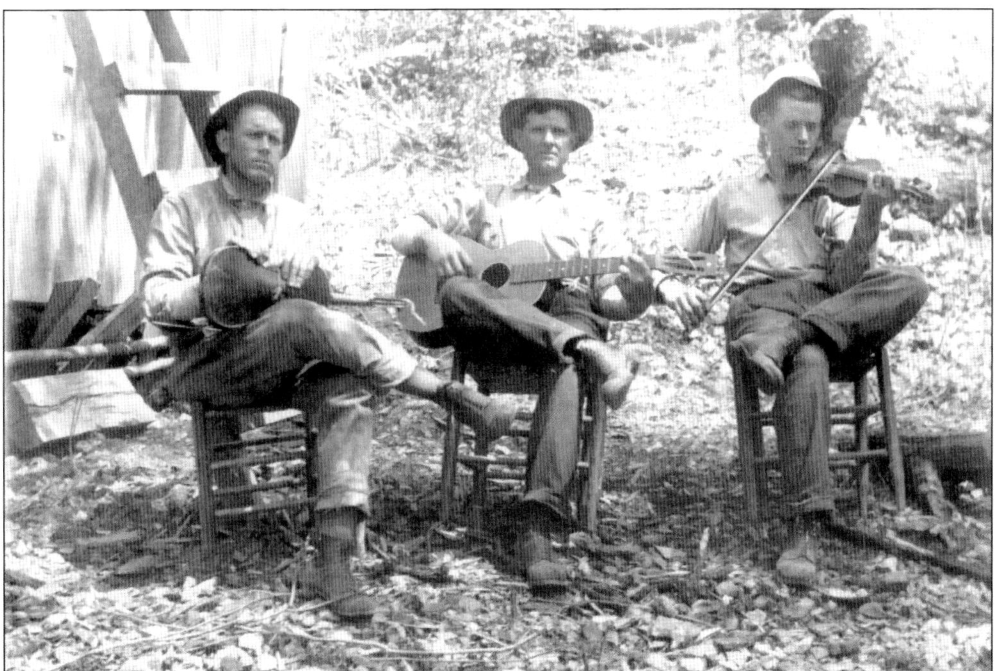

There was not a lot of energy left after a hard 10-hour day working in the lead mines, but (from left to right) Jim Vaughn, Noah Goss, and John Cline had the desire to play some tunes on their fiddles and a guitar in 1916. (NCL.)

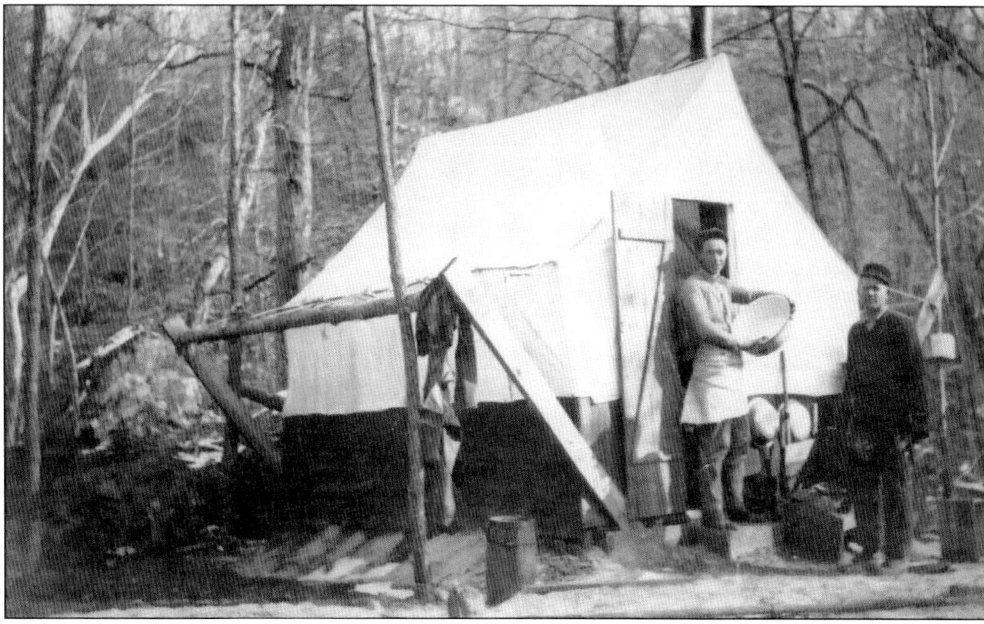

With earnings of $1.50 for a 10-hour day, miners did not have a lot of extra money to pay room and board in local communities. Hence a number of workers lived in tents around the mine. In this tent was housed the cooking facilities for the miners in Panther Creek in 1916. Jim Vaughn (left) and Noah Goss posed for the postcard photograph. (NCL.)

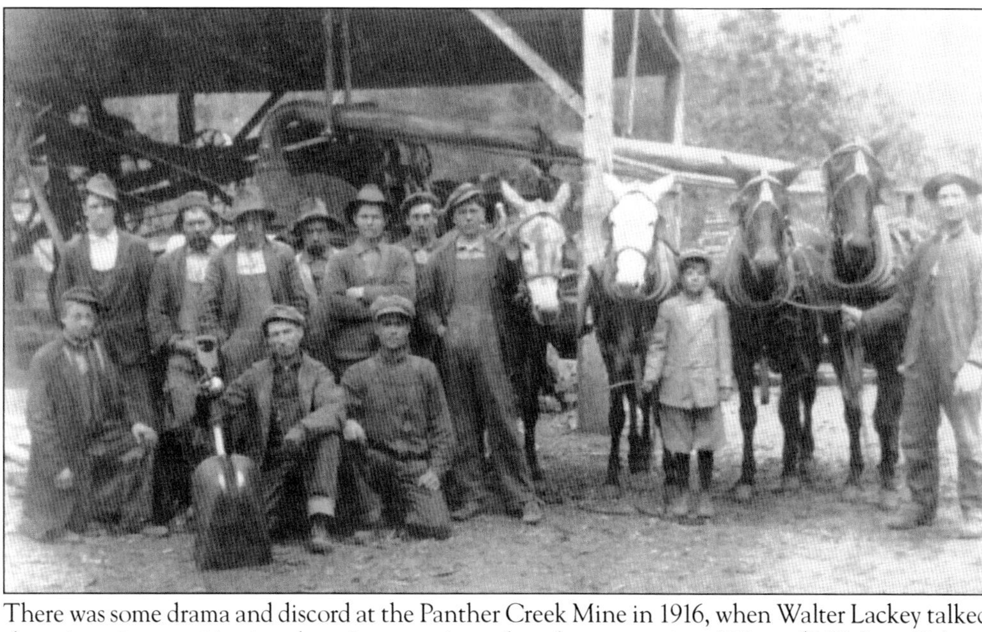

There was some drama and discord at the Panther Creek Mine in 1916, when Walter Lackey talked the miners into petitioning the mine superintendent for a pay raise of 25¢ to $1.75 for a 10-hour day, or cut the hours and get $1.50 for an eight-hour day. The mine boss nailed their petition to a post and said, "If you men don't like your work and pay you can quit." Most did quit, and the mine soon closed. The Panther Creek Mine would be bought and sold a number of times over some 50 years, with tons of ore being extracted. Today, very little trace of the mining activity remains. The forest has reclaimed the land. (NCL.)

Four

HARDSHIP AND PERSEVERANCE IN THE 1930s

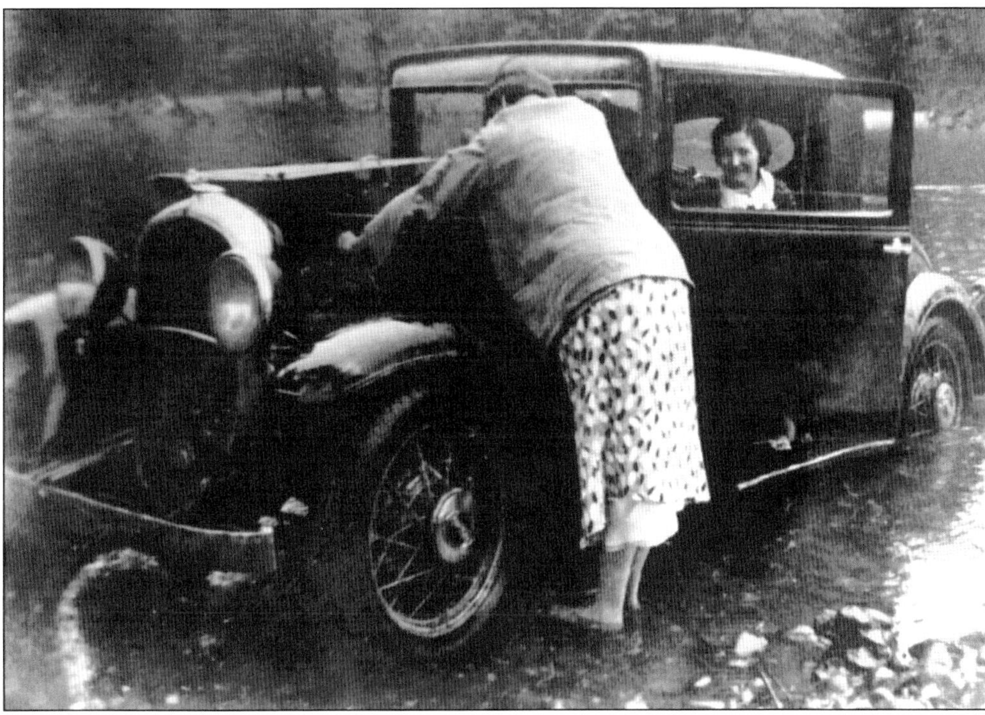

In the mid-1930s, Ernest and Opal Nicholson served as Newton County administrators of the Works Progress Administration (WPA). In this position, they supervised caseworkers who traveled the county seeking to assist the most needy, often the elderly or disabled, who could not generate an income. The photographs making up this chapter were taken and chronicled by the Nicholsons; they offer a unique window on daily life in a challenging period. The photograph above captured two of the caseworkers, with Opal Nicholson likely behind the wheel, when their automobile stalled while crossing a stream. Note that the quotations and photographs throughout this chapter are from Ernest and Opal Nicholson. (Photograph by Ernest and Opal Nicholson; courtesy of Shiloh Museum of Ozark History, Katie McCoy Collection.)

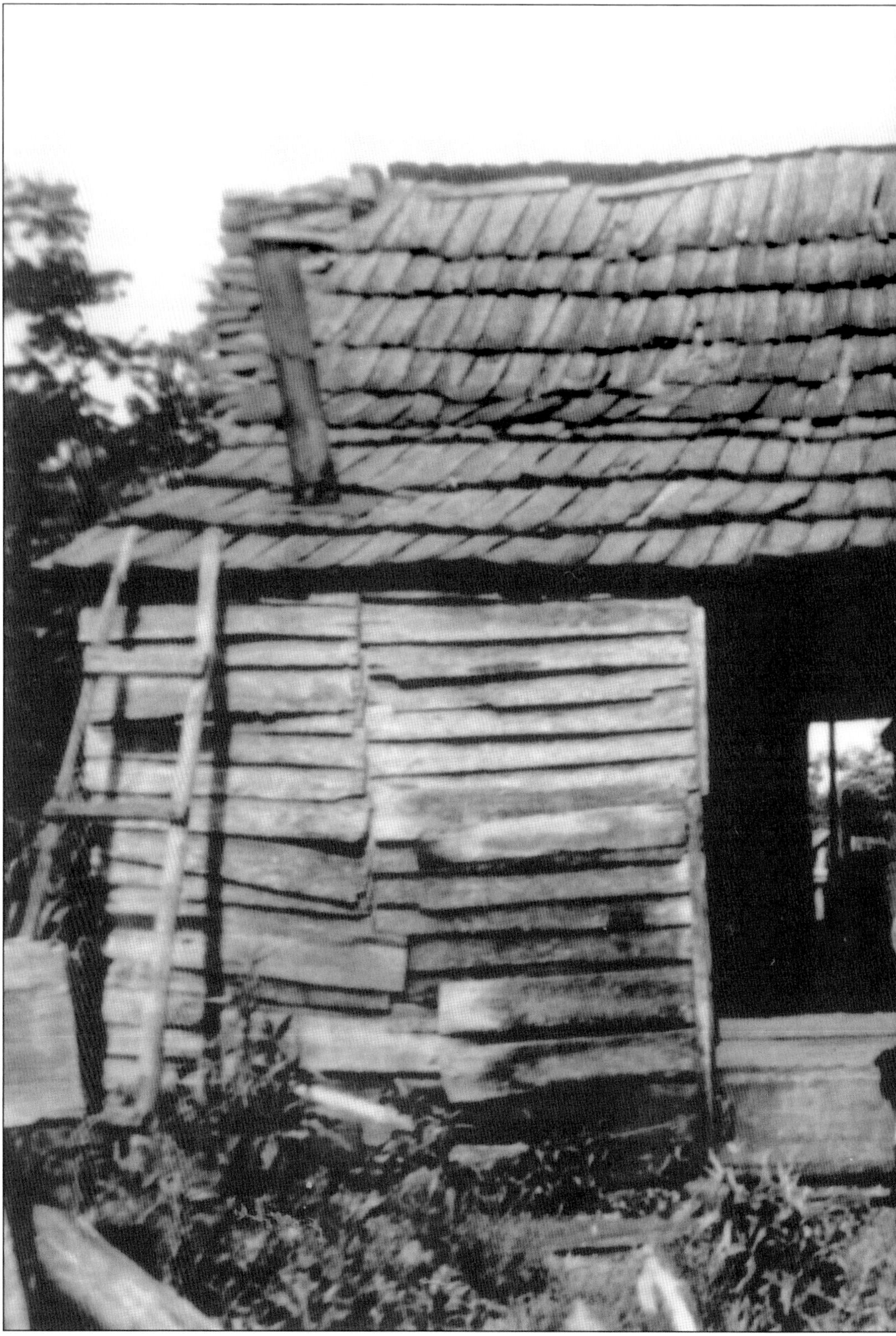

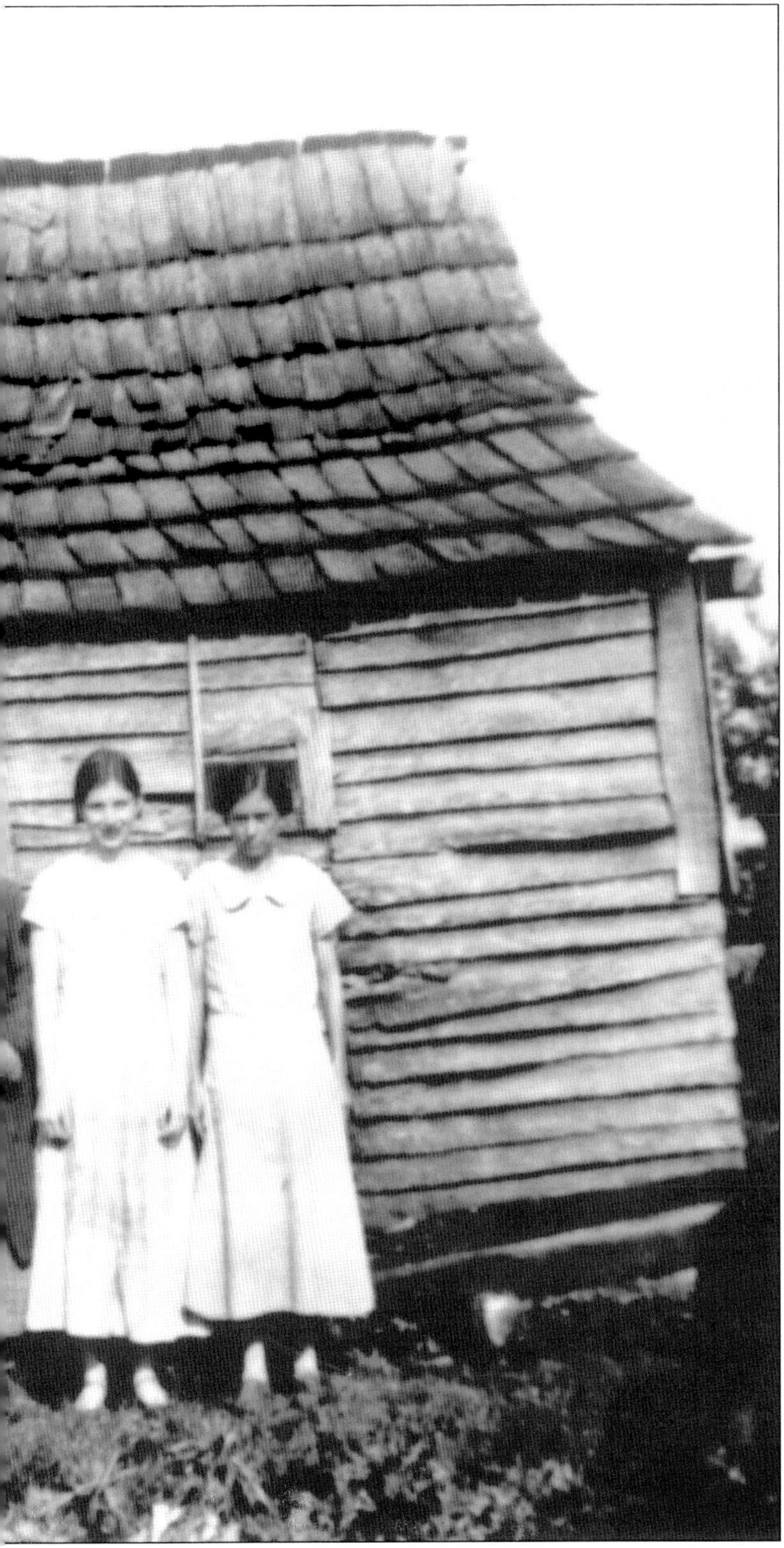

The Nicholsons' photographs often carried detailed notations about who was depicted and their circumstances. "This is the cabin of Aunt Vina Jones. She is very ill with dropsy and will probably not live long. Her sister has come to try to help her by administering tea made of Wahoo roots. The other two women are daughter and granddaughter of Mrs. Jones. Even while this picture was being made the caseworker could hear Mrs. Jones calling for her deceased husband to come take her to her new home." (Photograph by Ernest and Opal Nicholson; courtesy of Shiloh Museum of Ozark History, Katie McCoy Collection.)

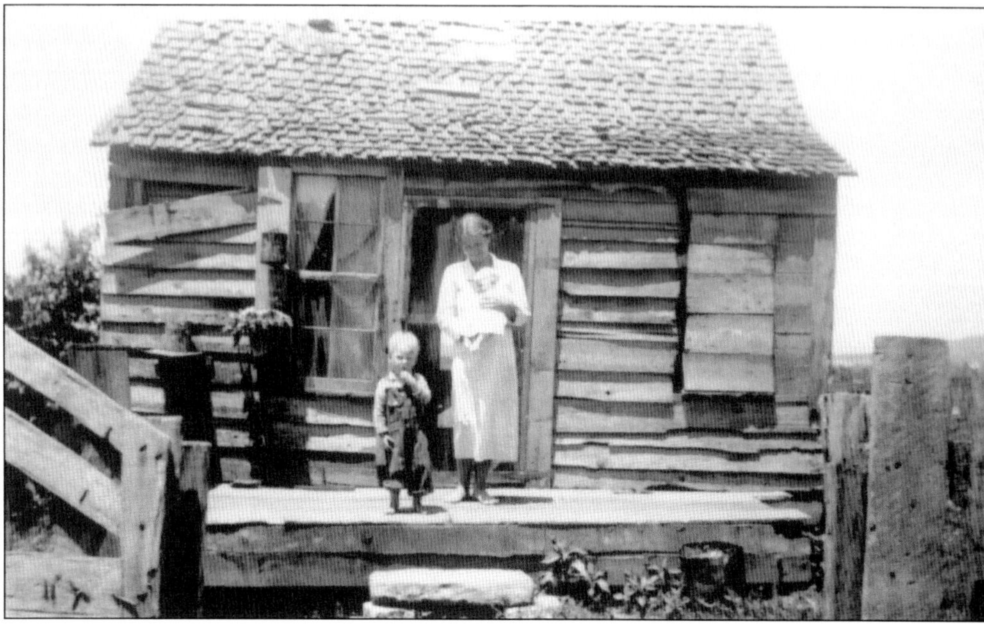

Some of the homes the caseworkers called upon were cobbled together out of whatever scrap materials the resident could obtain. This small cabin was constructed of rough slabs of lumber and a shake-shingle roof. The rural relief program's caseworkers provided beef or canned goods, reading material, and sometimes even funds for windows and screens. (Photograph by Ernest and Opal Nicholson; courtesy of Shiloh Museum of Ozark History, Katie McCoy Collection.)

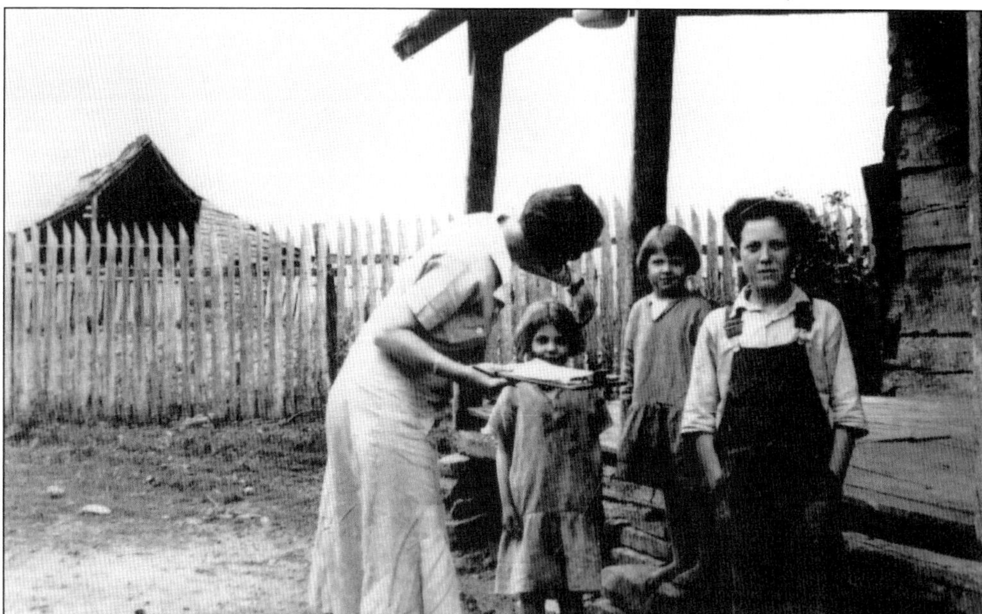

"The caseworker is telling this pretty girl how nice she would look with her face washed and her hair combed. Our caseworkers have accomplished some desirable results by simply mentioning the nice things which the clients had done and suggesting other improvements." (Photograph by Ernest and Opal Nicholson; courtesy of Shiloh Museum of Ozark History, Katie McCoy Collection.)

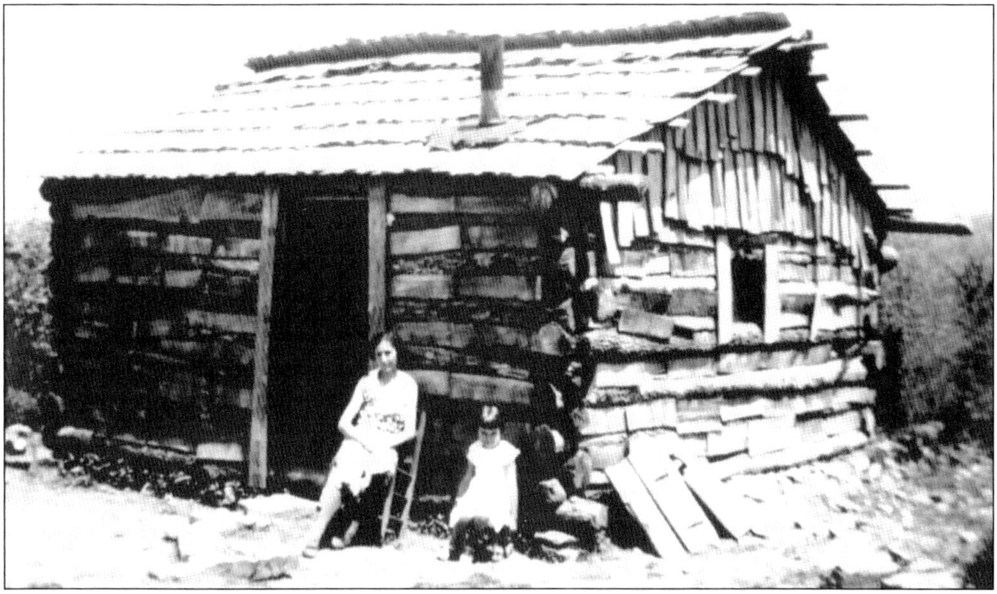

"This house was built by two women. They made the boards, cut the trees, hewed the logs and did all the work. One of the women, Mrs. Loyd Cooksey and her daughter are shown in the picture." The ladies are labeled as the "Carpenterettes." According to public records, Loyd Cooksey, then age 25, married 27-year-old Argie Marion of Swain in 1931. It is unclear what happened to Loyd Cooksey that would lead his wife to build her own home. (Photograph by Ernest and Opal Nicholson; courtesy of Shiloh Museum of Ozark History, Katie McCoy Collection.)

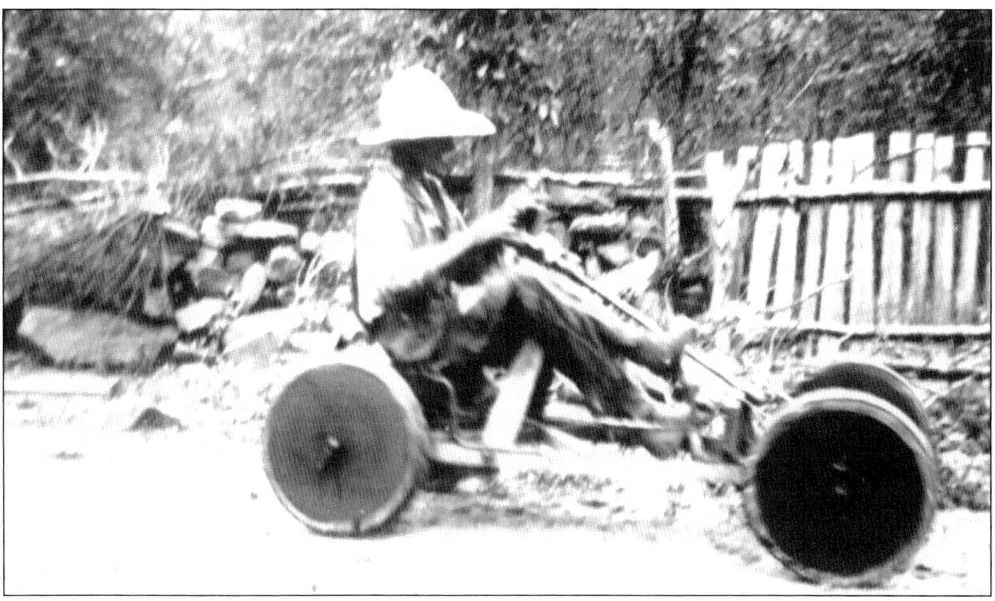

The caseworkers were quite taken with a young boy who had built his own car. "Hemmed in by barriers of rocks and trees, but he has the same desire to travel that has brought this age of speed. He has expressed it in this little homemade coaster. It is 'knee action' and has front wheel drive . . . It is a pity that desire and ability and energy like this is lost and often misdirected. This is our greatest undeveloped resource." (Photograph by Ernest and Opal Nicholson; courtesy of Shiloh Museum of Ozark History, Katie McCoy Collection.)

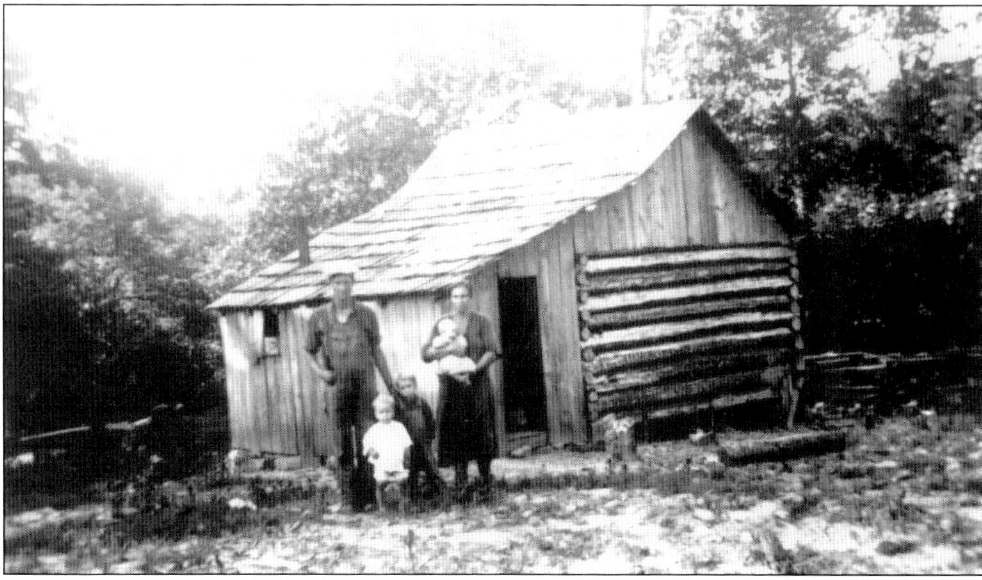

"Hardworking young family . . . from the picture one is inclined to think this an old cabin but it is only a few months old, having been built in March. The logs for the house were taken from the spot where this house is now located. Since he has moved here, Mr. Riddle has cleared about four acres." (Photograph by Ernest and Opal Nicholson; courtesy of Shiloh Museum of Ozark History, Katie McCoy Collection.)

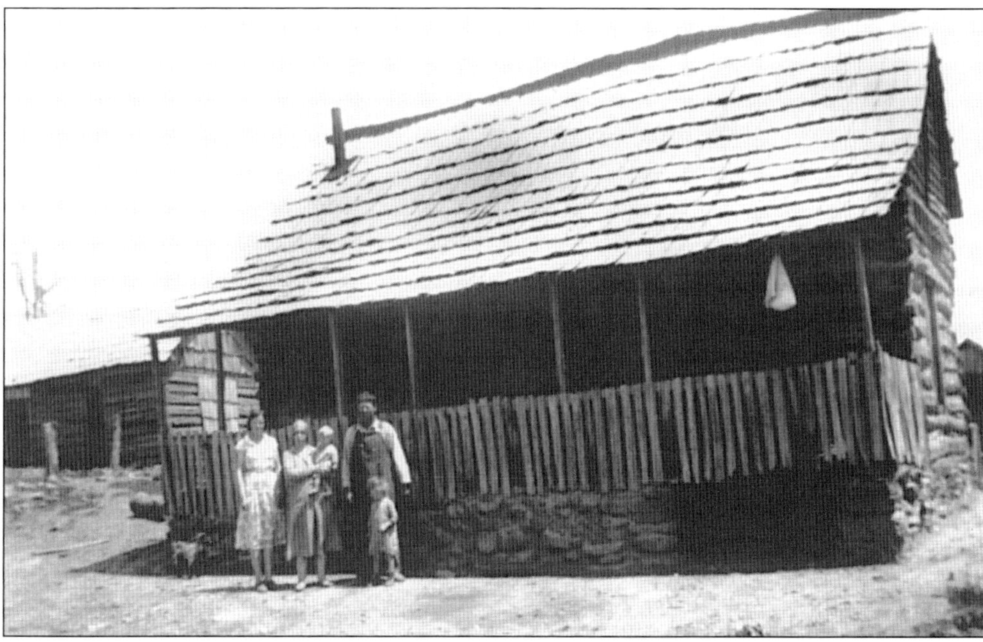

"Newcomers . . . this client came here from Illinois two years ago. He was sold on the Ozarks by a real estate agent and paid $2,000 for a place of uncertain value. He did not know how to farm here and soon spent all his money and energy with no return. He has turned his attention to milk goats and is now milking 35 head. We are encouraging this new undertaking and buying a goat from him now and then for other clients who have babies and no milk." (Photograph by Ernest and Opal Nicholson; courtesy of Shiloh Museum of Ozark History, Katie McCoy Collection.)

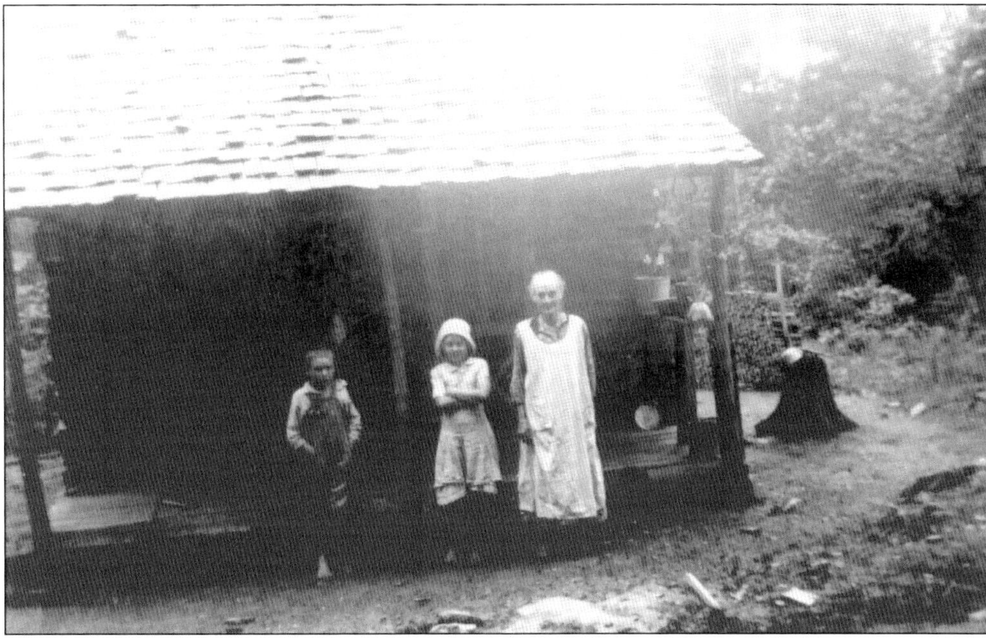

"Staying with grandma . . . after the death of their mother, these children of Robert Plumlee, disabled world war veteran, came to the home of their grandmother. Mrs. Plumblee says they are good workers. They have a splendid garden and a small crop. When groceries must be brought from the nearest store three miles away, the children are glad to walk and carry them home." (Photograph by Ernest and Opal Nicholson; courtesy of Shiloh Museum of Ozark History, Katie McCoy Collection.)

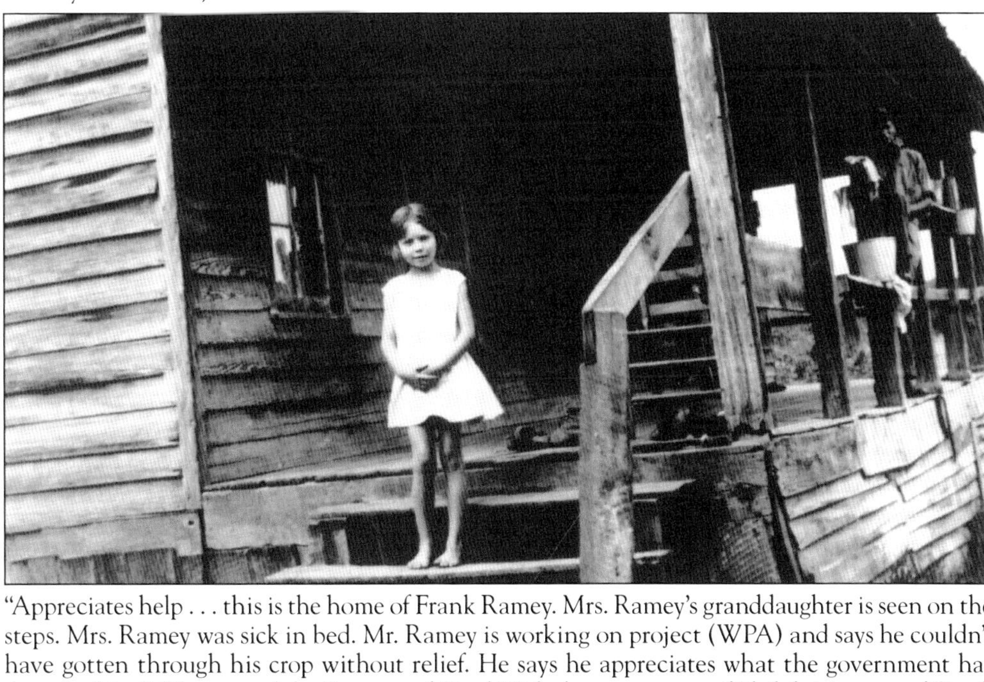

"Appreciates help . . . this is the home of Frank Ramey. Mrs. Ramey's granddaughter is seen on the steps. Mrs. Ramey was sick in bed. Mr. Ramey is working on project (WPA) and says he couldn't have gotten through his crop without relief. He says he appreciates what the government has done for him." (Photograph by Ernest and Opal Nicholson; courtesy of Shiloh Museum of Ozark History, Katie McCoy Collection.)

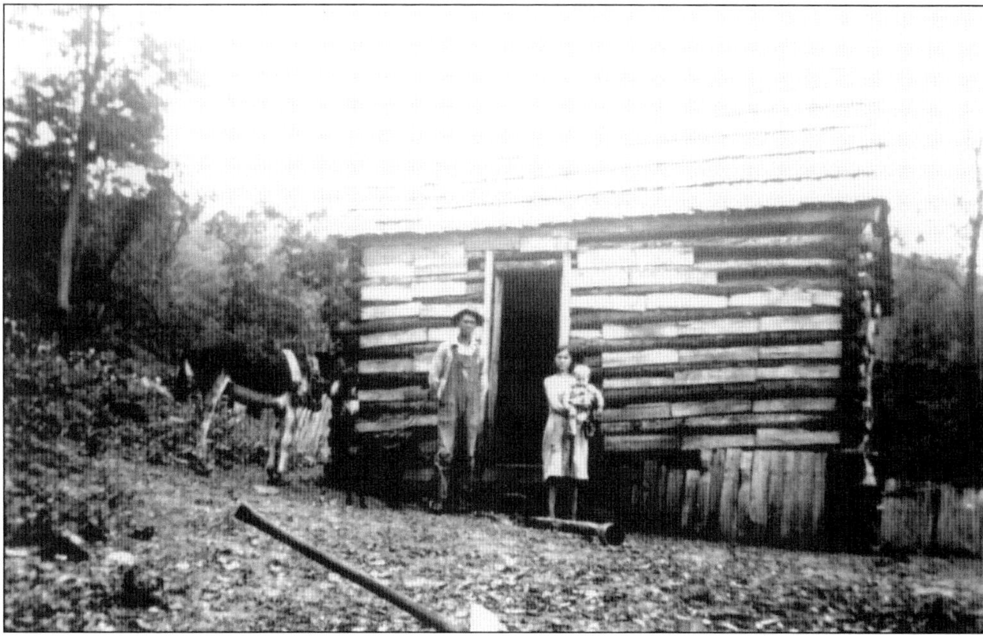

"Pioneering in 1935 . . . with trusty axe shown in the foreground Mr. Rich is chopping his way to independence. He cut logs, made boards and floor for the cabin, made palings and cut poles for fences and gates for his bench homestead. He cleared the land using the best timber for bolts which he sold for subsistence." (Photograph by Ernest and Opal Nicholson; courtesy of Shiloh Museum of Ozark History, Katie McCoy Collection.)

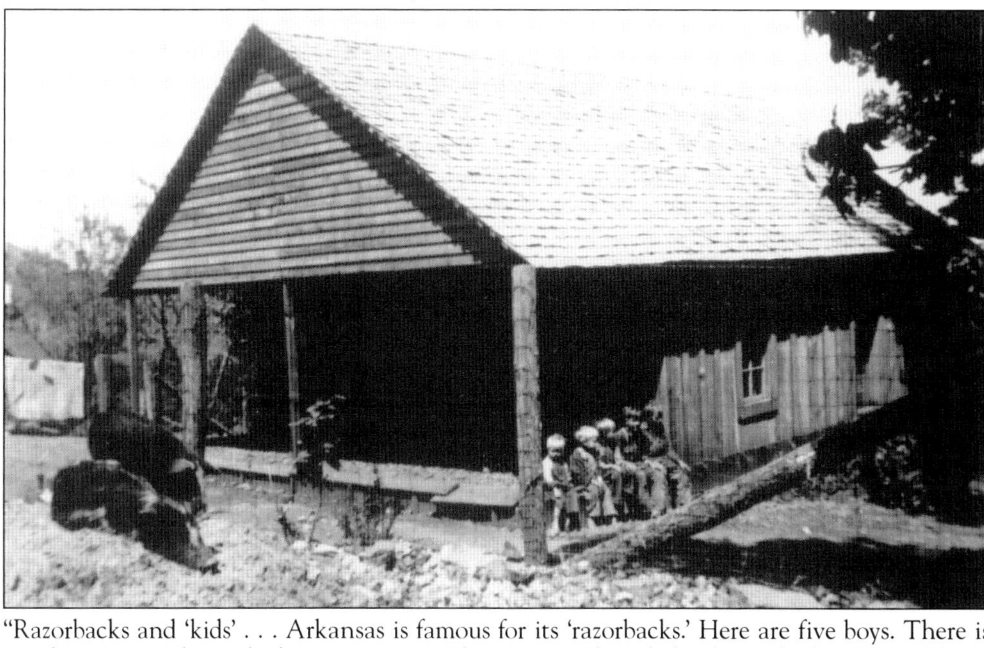

"Razorbacks and 'kids' . . . Arkansas is famous for its 'razorbacks.' Here are five boys. There is another one inside too little to come out. This man cut logs, helped saw the lumber and build the house. It cost him less than $40 in cash. He has also put a wire fence around his place. Along with helping to provide for his family, this represents a lot of work." (Photograph by Ernest and Opal Nicholson; courtesy of Shiloh Museum of Ozark History, Katie McCoy Collection.)

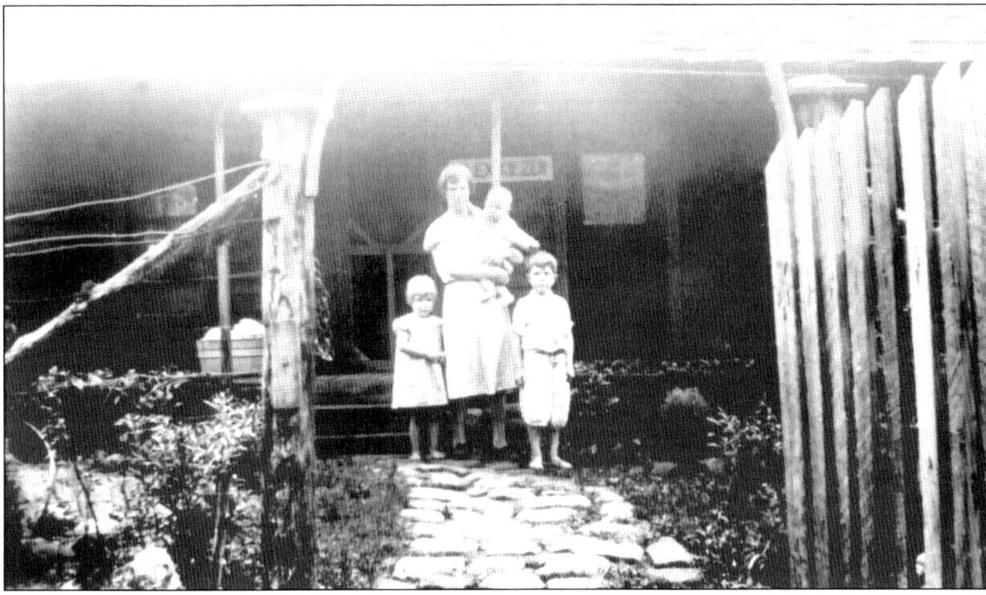

"This is a family of the former boxing coach. He has hopes of a business of his own, training his boys to be prizefighters. This man carried the rocks from his garden to build the rock walk and a wall around his garden. He also carried sediments from the creek to fertilize his garden." The hardworking family's name was recorded as Kiezer. (Photograph by Ernest and Opal Nicholson; courtesy of Shiloh Museum of Ozark History, Katie McCoy Collection.)

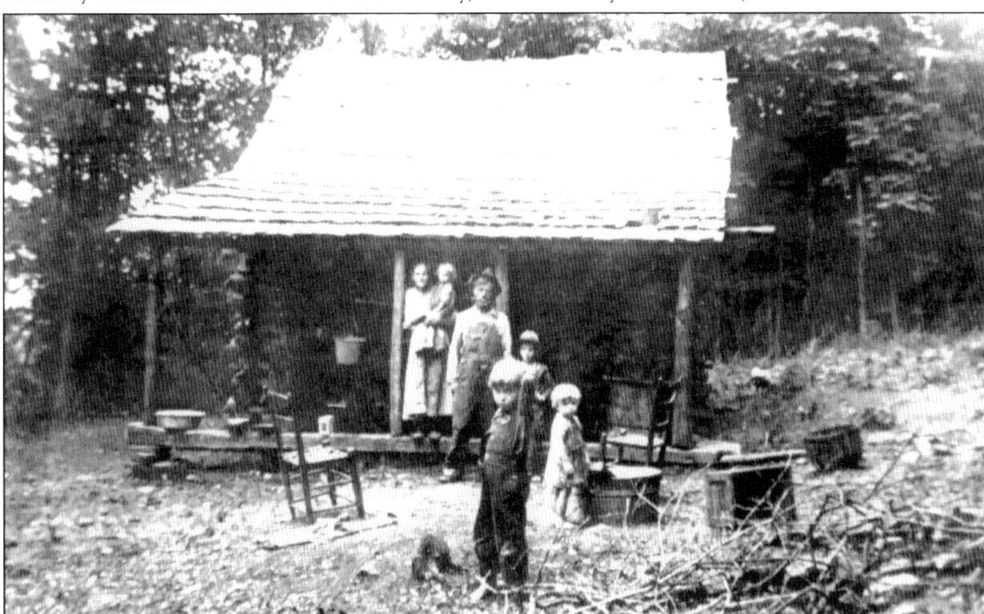

"Monroe Middleton (1879–1951), an ex-mail carrier, has made many trips from Jasper to Vendor by foot, carrying the heavy mail bags. This is a distance of about 15 miles. Now Mr. Middleton lives in a small house, newly built. The kitchen has no floor, nor walls. At the time this picture was made, he had 'running water' in his kitchen due to a heavy rain causing a mountain spring to overflow and run into the house." (Photograph by Ernest and Opal Nicholson; courtesy of Shiloh Museum of Ozark History, Katie McCoy Collection.)

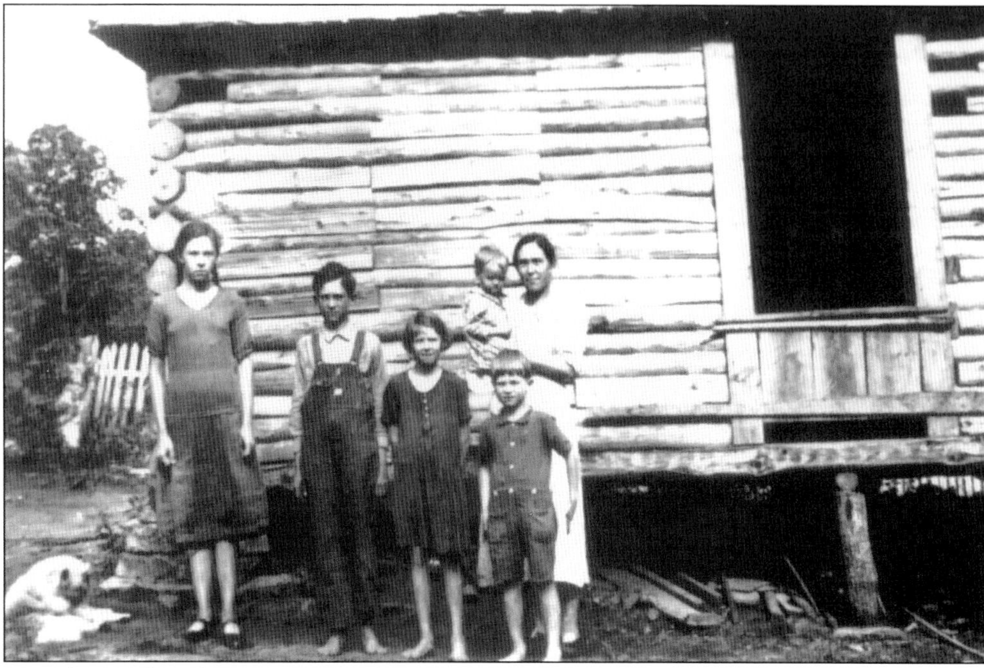

"New home of Frank Ramey. Since the picture was made, Mr. Ramey has put in windows and has the house well screened. The windows and screen wire was bought with the special disbursing order issued from the special fund for relief clients." Mr. Ramey had married Georgia Cooper in 1909. (Photograph by Ernest and Opal Nicholson; courtesy of Shiloh Museum of Ozark History, Katie McCoy Collection.)

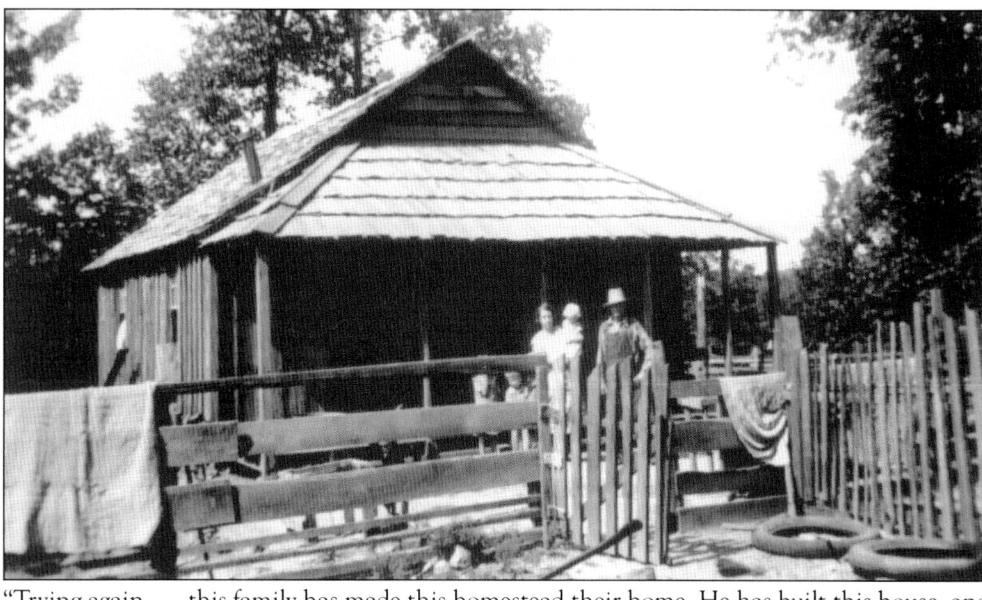

"Trying again . . . this family has made this homestead their home. He has built this house, and cleared about three acres. After losing his crop, which was on Big Creek during the floods, he has made another near his house. His crop is small but well kept. He cannot depend on farming alone to make a living." (Photograph by Ernest and Opal Nicholson; courtesy of Shiloh Museum of Ozark History, Katie McCoy Collection.)

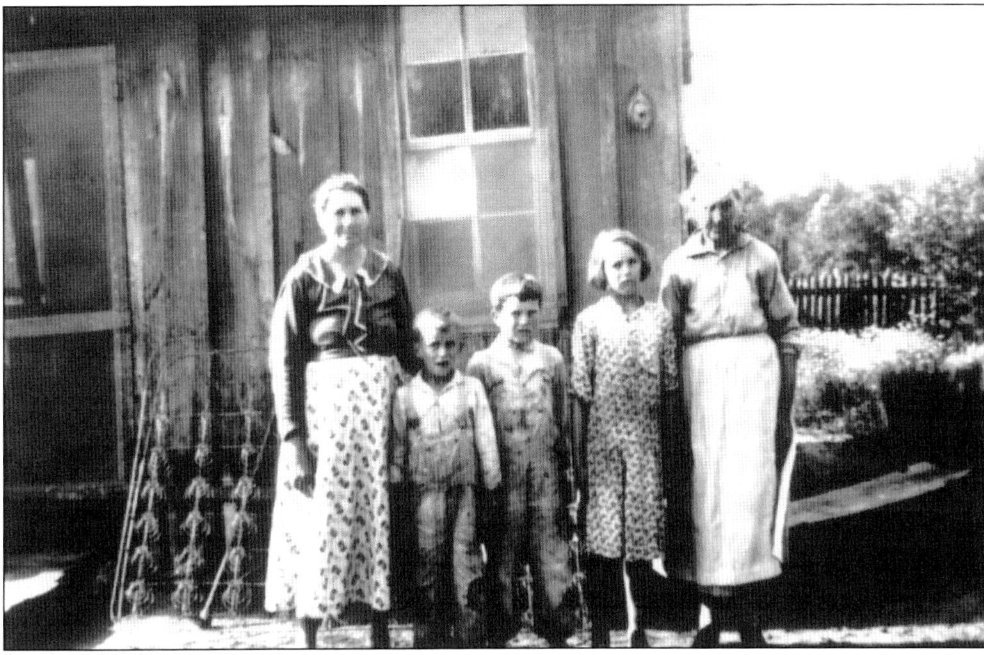

"Pioneer women . . . with nothing but a single hoe, these courageous women have made a crop. Mrs. Treadway and her mother live alone with the three small children. Two other children were killed not long ago in a school bus wreck." (Photograph by Ernest and Opal Nicholson; courtesy of Shiloh Museum of Ozark History, Katie McCoy Collection.)

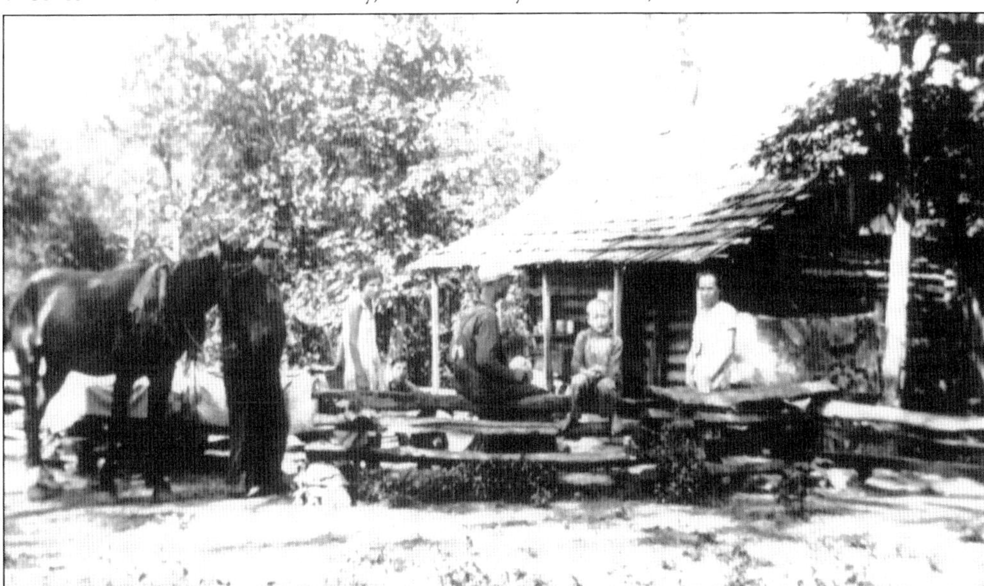

"You-all come and see us . . . this is the house of John Smith (not captain). At the time the caseworker arrived, some of Mr. Smith's relatives who had spent the night here were preparing to hitch the old mare to the buggy and start home. The house has been cleaned and the beds, which were "made down" on the floor, are out on the line for necessary airing. All is ready for the departure." (Photograph by Ernest and Opal Nicholson; courtesy of Shiloh Museum of Ozark History, Katie McCoy Collection.)

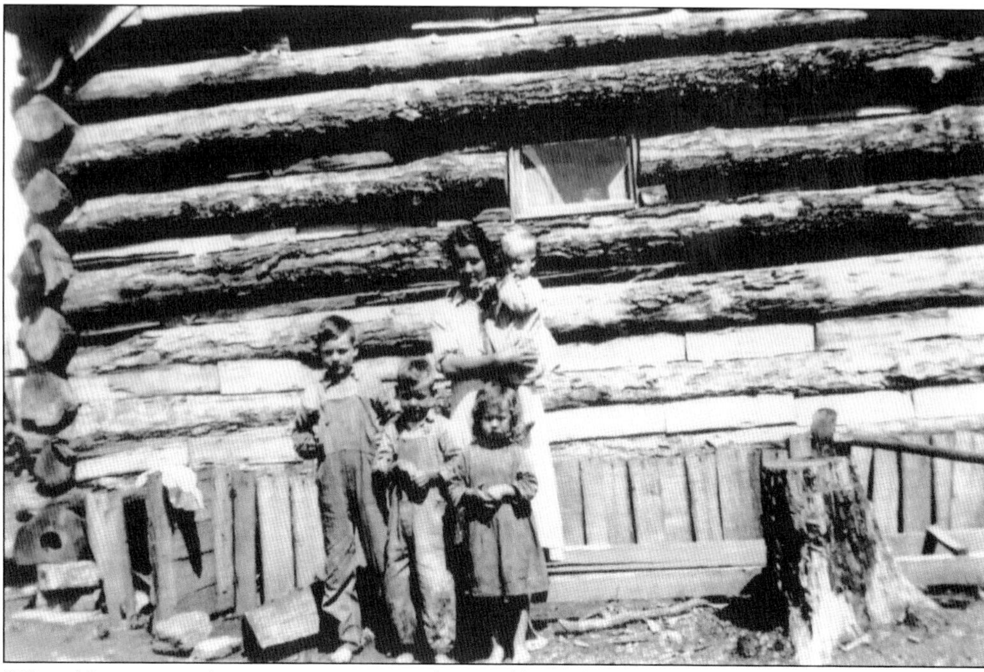

"The oldest one in the picture acts as mother and housekeeper, while her father and mother are working in the field and making stave bolts. The father is the local 'Holy Roller preacher.' He is a good, industrious man and above the average in mentality, but limited in education, honestly following what he believes. He was forced to apply for relief by a long illness but since then they have made quite an improvement in the home[stead], built the house, started a barn, cleared and fenced 15 acres and planted a crop." (Photograph by Ernest and Opal Nicholson; courtesy of Shiloh Museum of Ozark History, Katie McCoy Collection.)

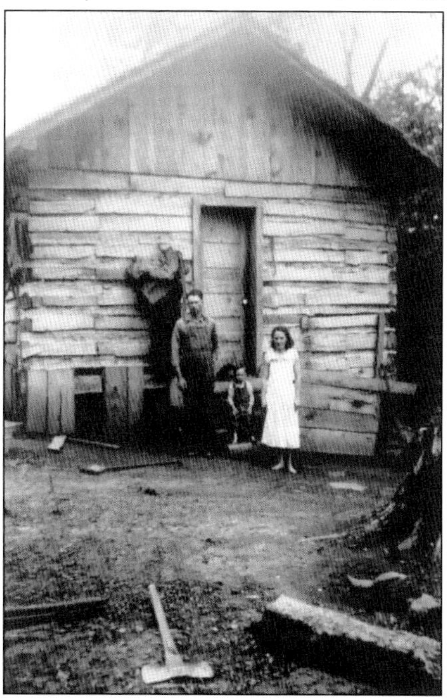

"Determined to succeed . . . Mr. Clyde Hudson has built a new room to his house. Put in windows and made screen shutters. Cleared some land and planted a young orchard. This young couple is very happy in their improved home. Sammy, their five-year-old son says he is going to start school this fall. He will have to walk two and one half miles." Clyde Hudson (1908–2001) married Jessie Brasel (1910–2003) in 1929; she gave birth to two sons, Samuel and Richard. (Photograph by Ernest and Opal Nicholson; courtesy of Shiloh Museum of Ozark History, Katie McCoy Collection.)

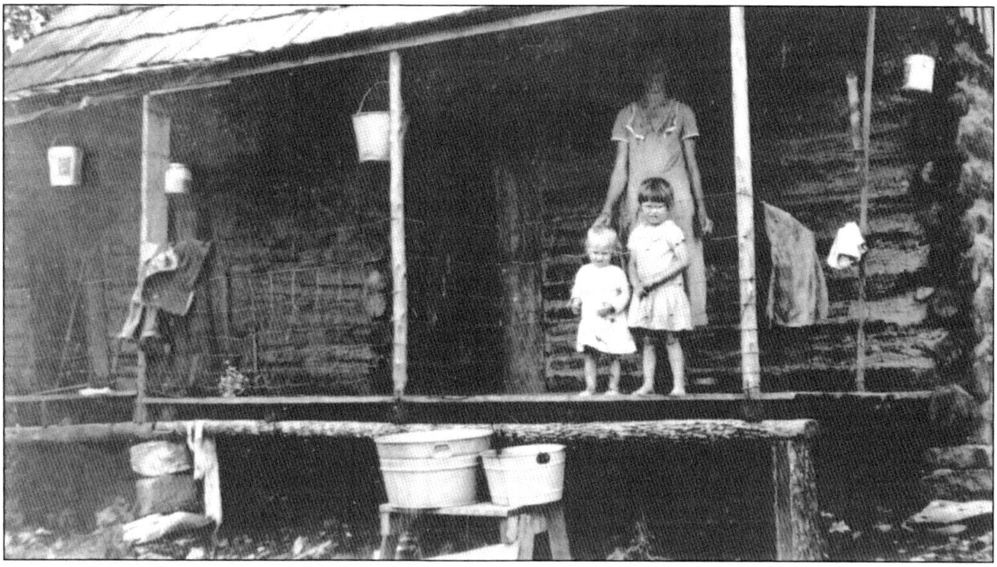

"This is the wife and children of Dallas Jones. When Mr. Jones moved into this house it was only a one-room log house with a lean-to for the kitchen. He cut logs and built one log room [on]to the house. Mrs. Jones has papered all rooms with newspapers. The inside of the house is very neat." Dallas Lee Jones, age 19, and Ruby, age 20, had been married for about a year as of the 1930 census, living in the New Hope Township between Bass and Western Grove. (Photograph by Ernest and Opal Nicholson; courtesy of Shiloh Museum of Ozark History, Katie McCoy Collection.)

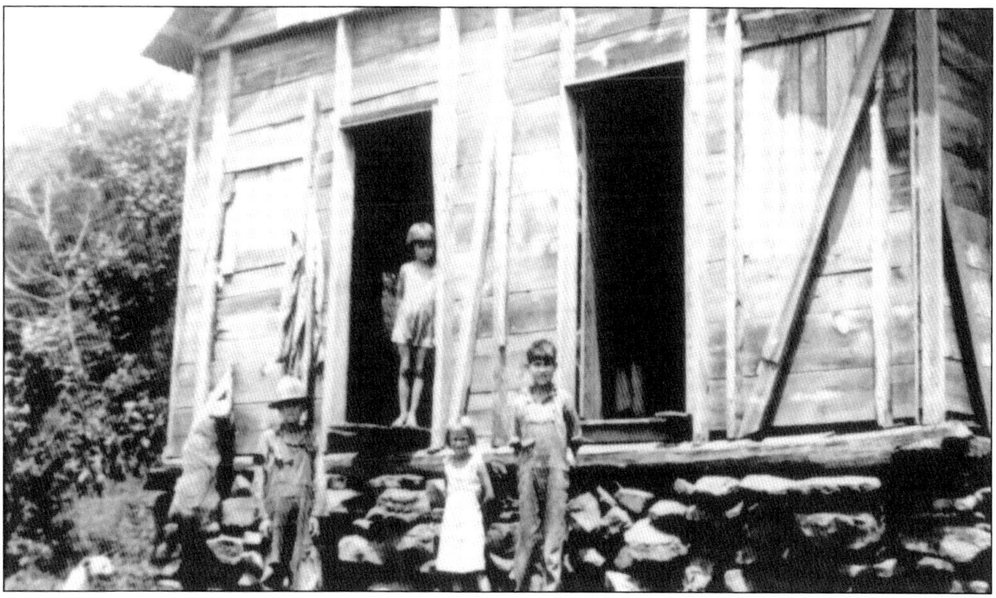

"There are eight living in this small house located on a high mountain overlooking the Red Rock valley. The only way of getting to the house is to walk about a mile. The only amusement the children have is playing with their white dog, which you see at the corner of the building. These children who know no other life seem happy here, but will of course become individualists and will hardly know how to adjust themselves to society when they get out into the world. The caseworker is hoping to help with reading material." (Photograph by Ernest and Opal Nicholson; courtesy of Shiloh Museum of Ozark History, Katie McCoy Collection.)

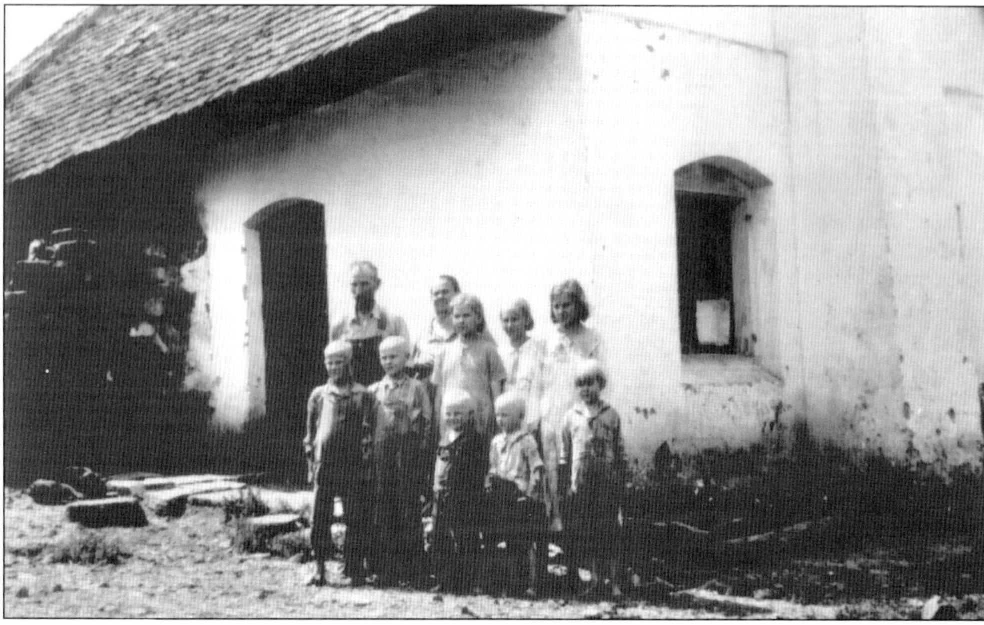

"Twenty in the family . . . this is only half of the Wasco family. There are sixteen children living and two dead. The first sixteen children were born a year apart. The last two were twins. Mr. and Mrs. Wasco are very happy in their little home. They are very thrifty and have a nice vineyard and a variety of small fruit. They were compelled to apply for relief because of the drought last year." (Photograph by Ernest and Opal Nicholson; courtesy of Shiloh Museum of Ozark History, Katie McCoy Collection.)

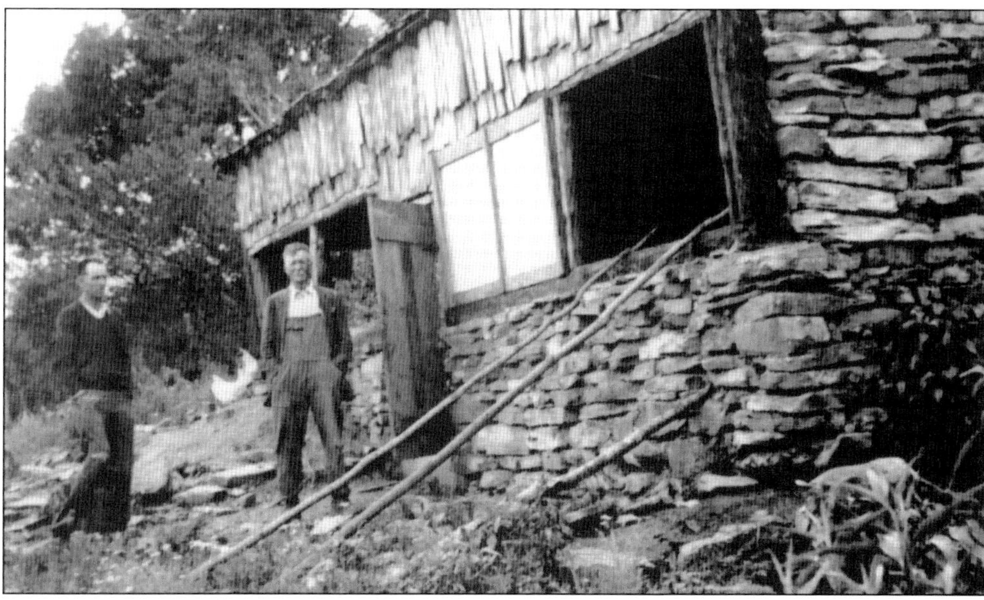

"Mr. J.R. Brantley and son, Ervin . . . the Brantleys came to Arkansas from the North, bought this little farm, paid part down and undertook to make a living on it. They are trying to prepare to raise chickens and hope to become independent in this way. This is a picture of a chicken house they have just built. The materials were acquired with almost no cost." (Photograph by Ernest and Opal Nicholson; courtesy of Shiloh Museum of Ozark History, Katie McCoy Collection.)

Five

Hamlets and Crossroads

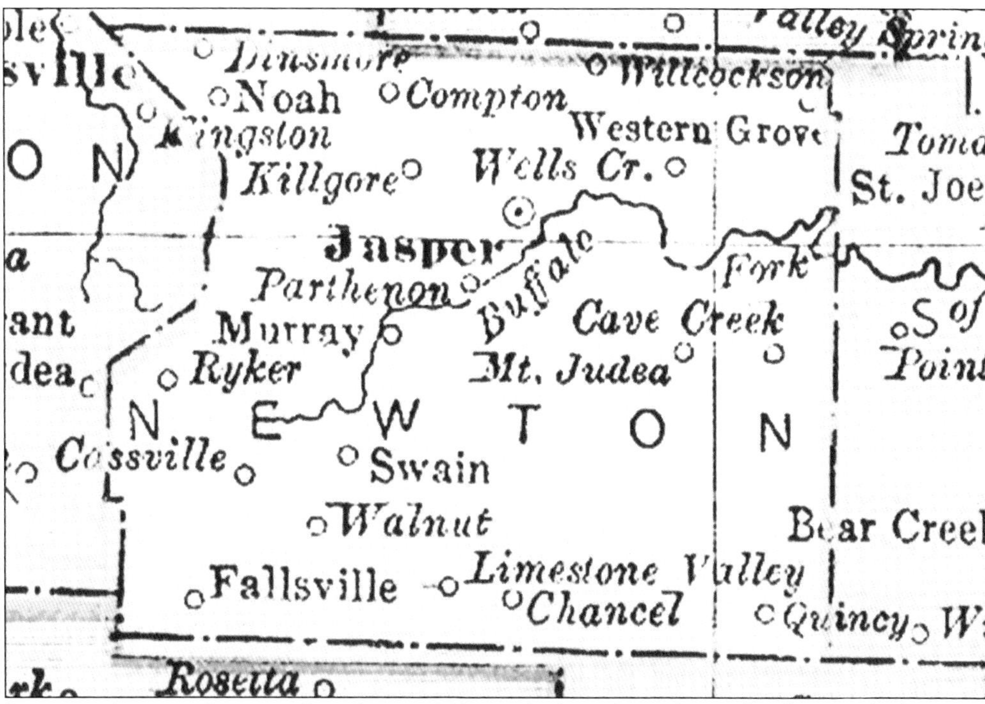

Jasper, with a population today of some 460 people, has always been the "big city" of Newton County, but this 1900 map shows that a number of other communities were spread across the mountains and valleys of the rugged county. More than 50 years before paved roads arrived in the area, settlements, like Low Gap, Fallsville, Nail, Deer, Parthenon, Ponca, and Mount Judea, were linked by rough, sometimes impassable wagon roads. Some towns would later be renamed, as with Wilcockson becoming Marble Falls. Some, like the towns of Ryker and Noah, would disappear from modern-day maps. All the tiny communities were home to hardworking people, schools, churches, and even, for most, a post office.

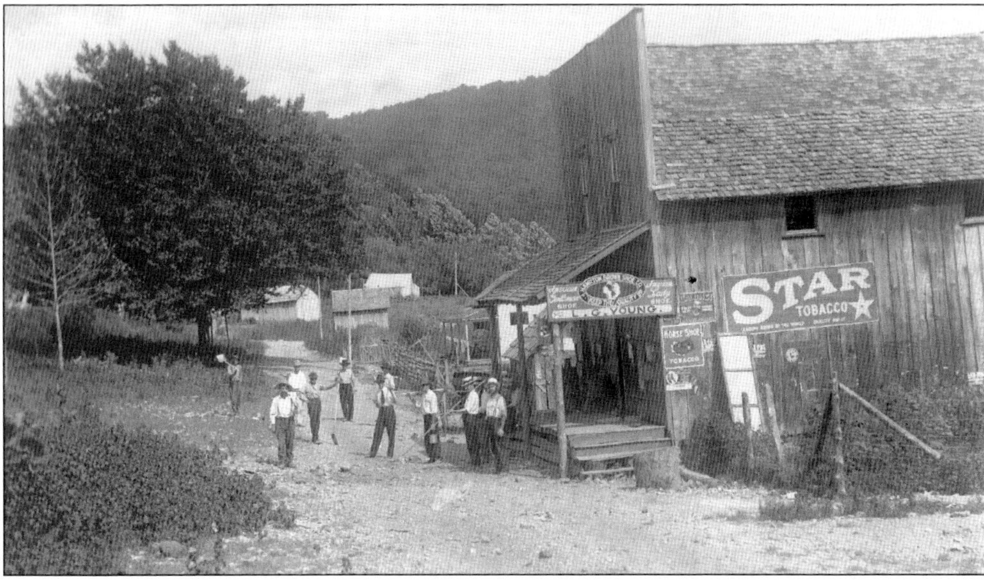

Ponca, seen here in 1916, was a booming mining community with ample jobs digging for zinc and lead in the surrounding hills. A crew of men appeared to be working on the little village's main street in front of L.G. Young's store. The town took its name from the Ponca, Oklahoma, mining company, which subdivided the land and plotted the valley into city lots, an enterprise that faded with decline of the mining.

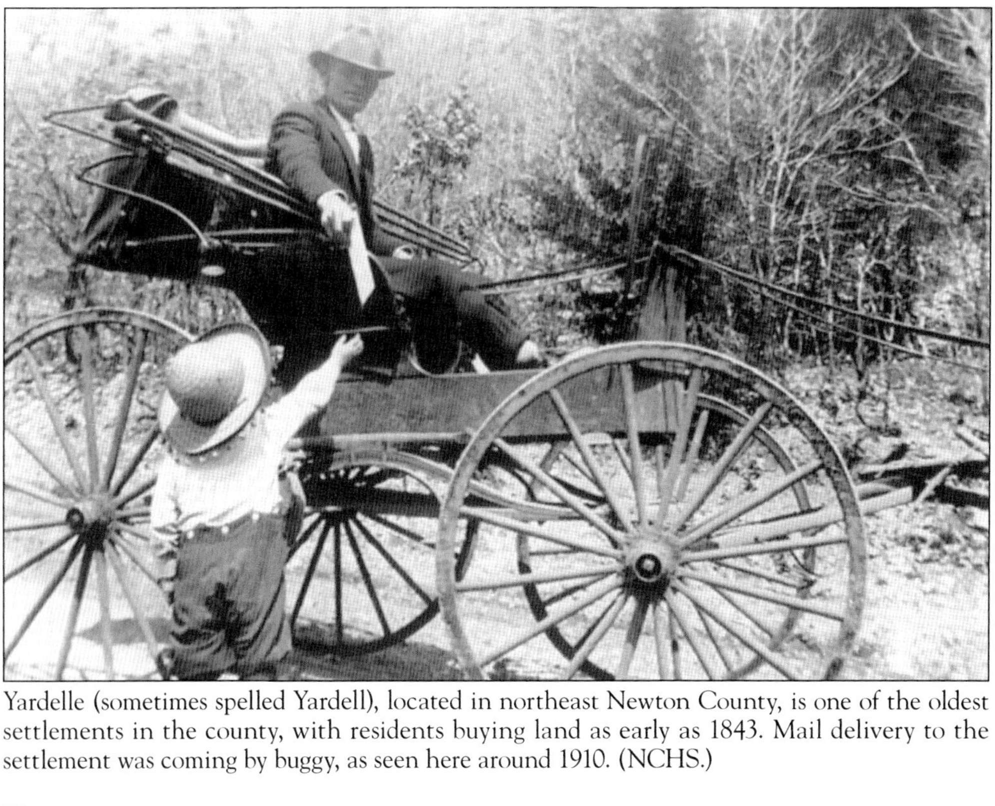

Yardelle (sometimes spelled Yardell), located in northeast Newton County, is one of the oldest settlements in the county, with residents buying land as early as 1843. Mail delivery to the settlement was coming by buggy, as seen here around 1910. (NCHS.)

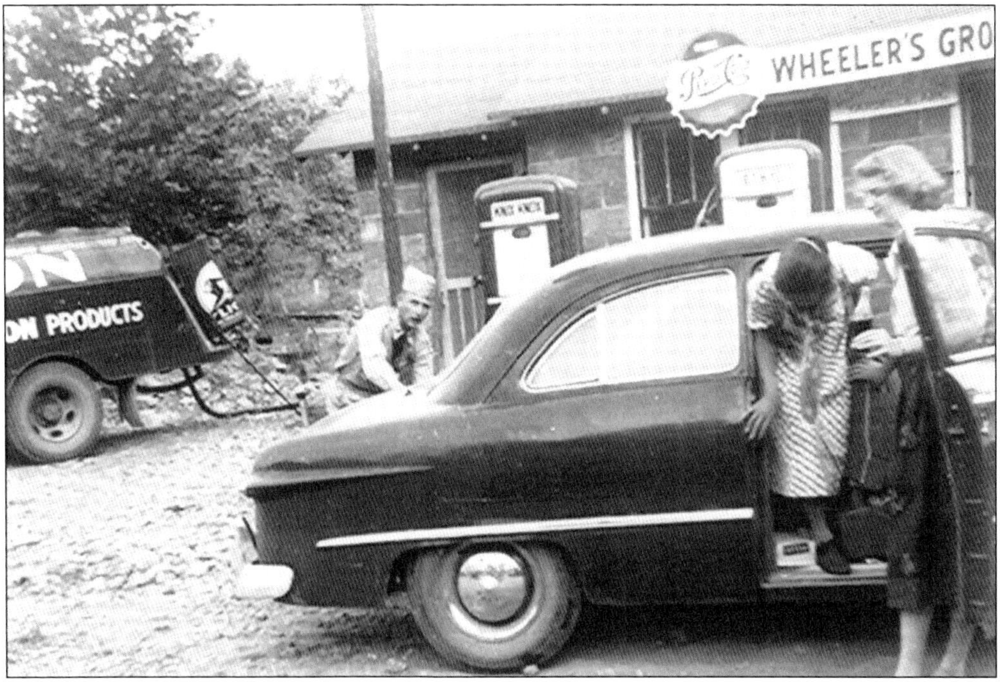

By the 1940s, Highway 123, though unpaved, was maintained well enough to allow travel from southeastern Newton County to the northern part of the county. Wheeler's Grocery and post office was one of the few places to gas up in the area. The store building, though altered, still stands. (NCHS.)

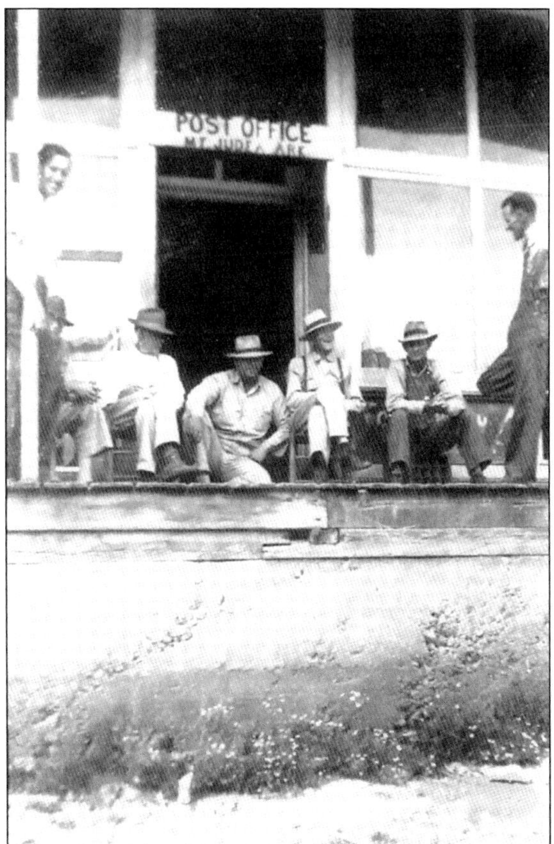

The porch of the general store, which housed the post office, was often the center of community conversation in the eastern Newton County community of Mount Judea. The sprawling, white wooden building that housed the store remains today in the community. (NCHS.)

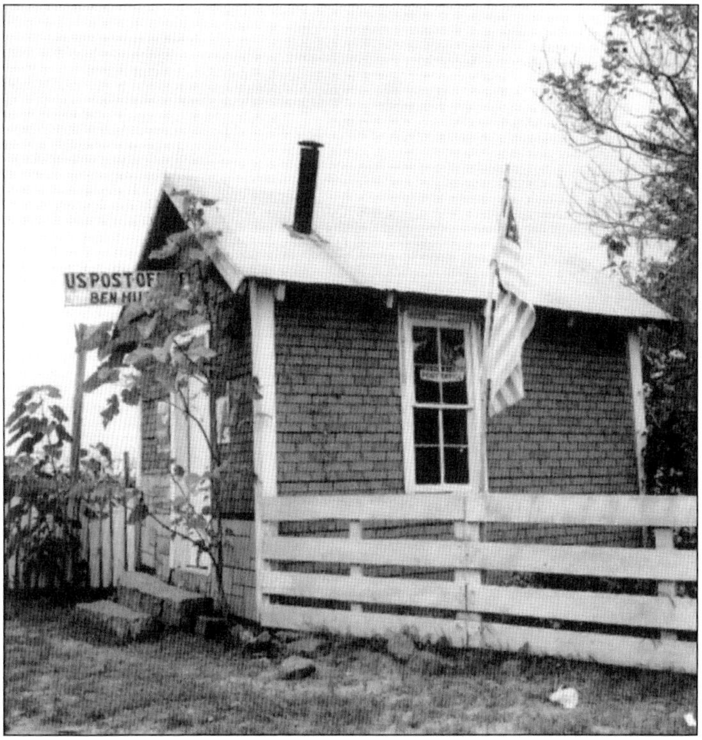

Ben Hur is a remote village hugging the Pope County line in southeast Newton County, having been named after the book written by Union general Lew Wallace after his Civil War service. The town's tiny one-room post office is seen here around 1940 but was closed by the US Postal Service in 1975. The still-remote community is reached today via paved State Highway 16; it is seen by many Arkansans en route to the Richland Creek campground and wilderness area. (Courtesy of Arkansas History Commission.)

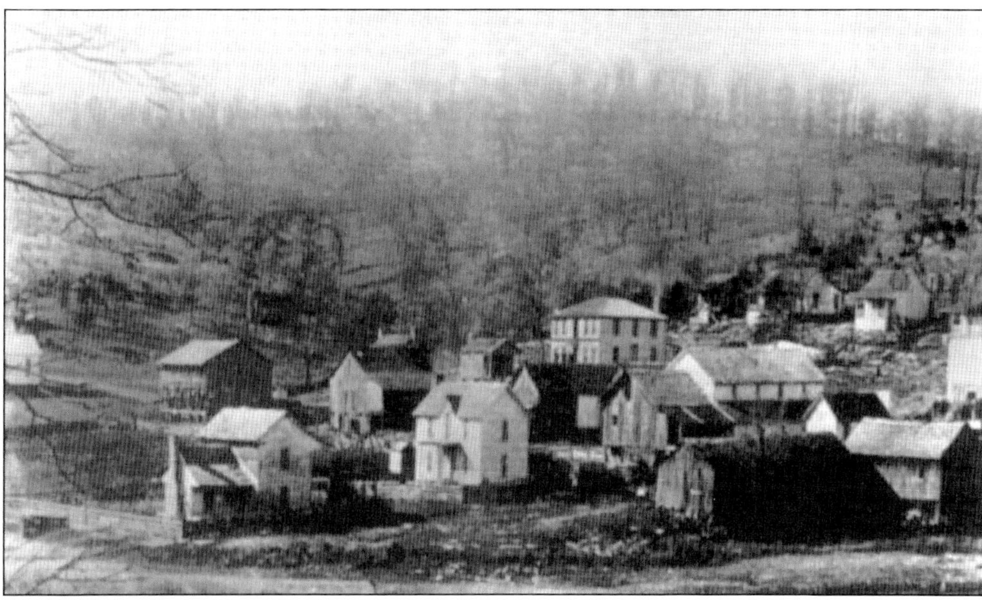

Marble Falls, located north of Jasper, was first named Wilcockson and later Marble City, in recognition of the limestone, which looked like marble, that was mined in the area. It boomed beginning in the 1880s, taking on the reputation of a health resort due to the numerous mineral springs that seeped up through the rocky valley. The town would later fade away to be revived in the 1960s and renamed Dogpatch, after a theme park of that name that was built on the land. Today, the theme park is gone, and the name Marble Falls has been restored to the quiet collection of rural homes. (NCL.)

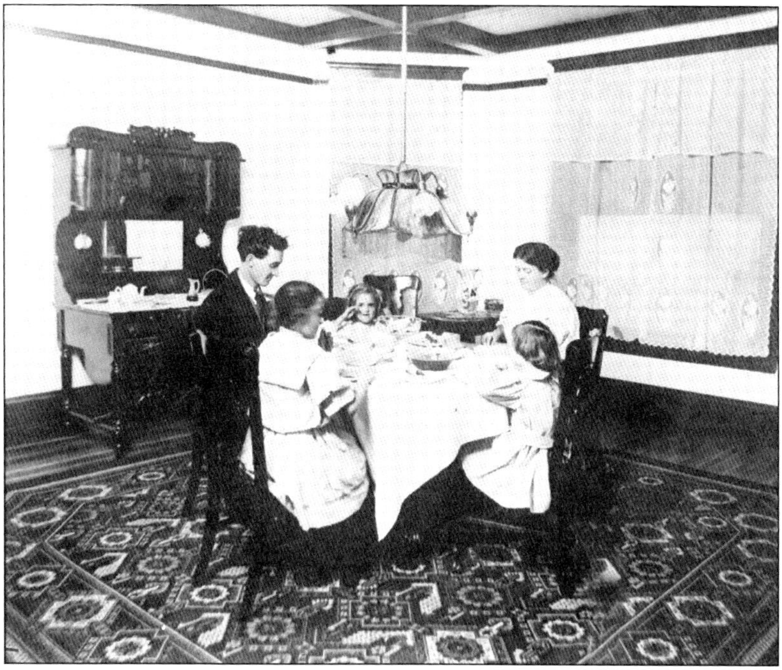

Marble Falls prospered for several decades early in the 20th century. Evidence of that prosperity can be found in this c. 1910 photograph, which captured the interior of a well-to-do family's dining room in Marble Falls. The postcard's message read, "We wish that you could eat with us. This is of our dining room."

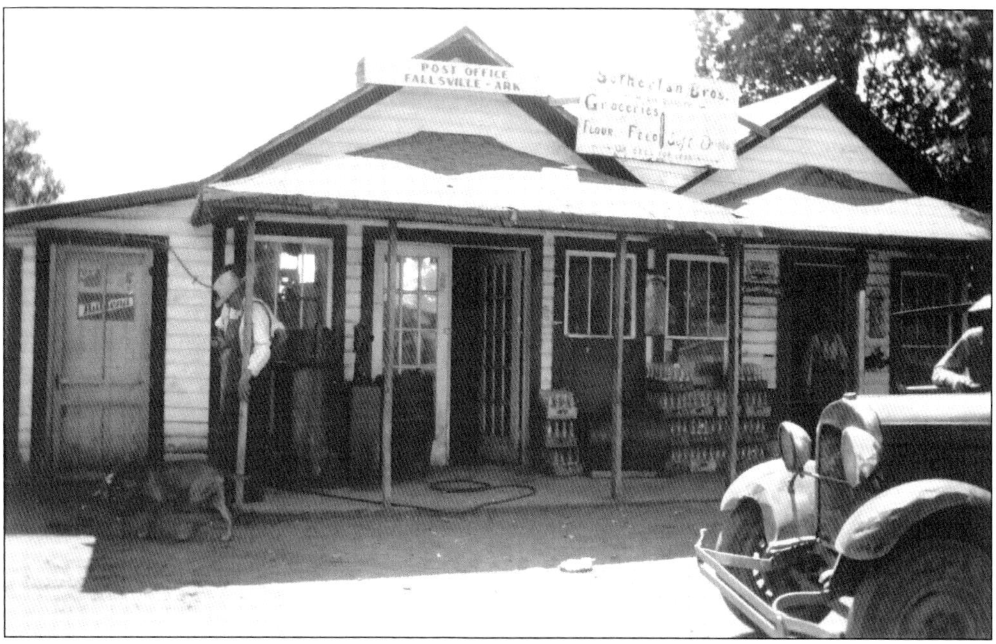

A tourist passing through the southwest corner of Newton County stopped to photograph the Fallsville Post Office and General Store in 1946. The Sutherlan Brothers, in addition to handling the mail, advertised groceries, flour, feed, and soft drinks. The US Post Office Department closed the community's post office in 1955.

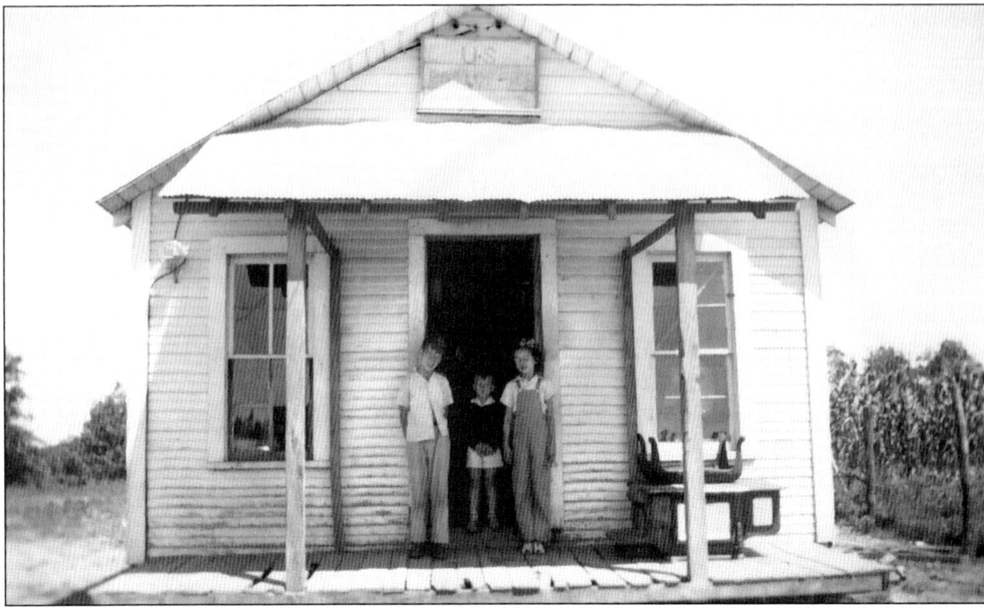

The community of Deer, located in south-central Newton County, had in the 1940s the county's largest school enrollment. The same tourist that visited Fallsville in 1946 also stopped to photograph the Deer Post Office, where three children posed on the rough board porch. Unlike other small communities, Deer, which first saw a post office in 1898, today boasts a modern, brick postal facility that serves the remote but still very viable community.

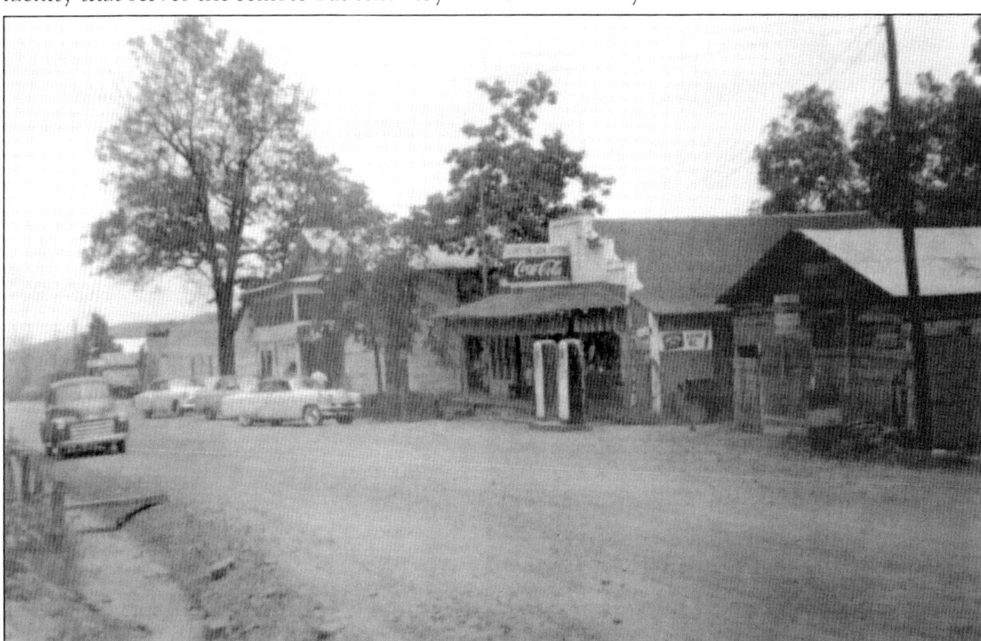

Lurton, located in the southern part of the county, was a thriving manufacturing center for hardwood tool handles in 1925 and for furniture later. The town's still-unpaved main street was photographed in the early 1950s, showing the general store and gas station with the two-story hotel just beyond. (NCHS.)

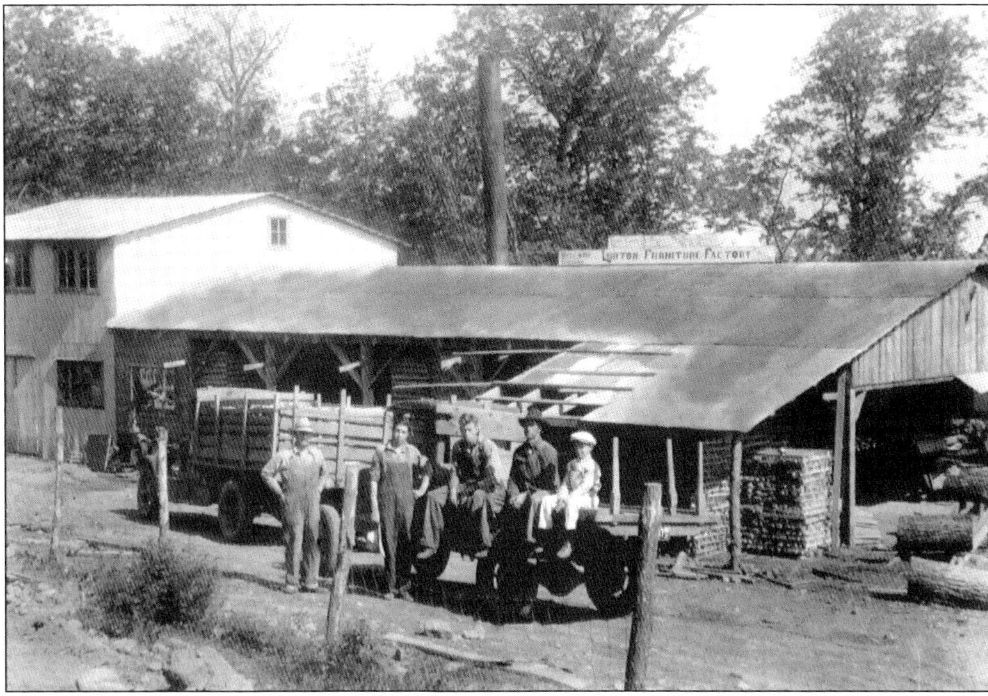

The Sutton handle factory of Lurton was the major employer in southern Newton County for many years, selling the US government $120,000 of hickory and ash tool handles during World War II. Workers posed here around 1940 at the factory, which crafted furniture as well as tool handles from the area's hardwood timber. Pictured from left to right are I.C. Sutton, Irving Sutton, Delbert Nichols, Bobby Boyd, and Alburtus "Burt" Sutton. Burt and Irving are sons of I.C. (NCL.)

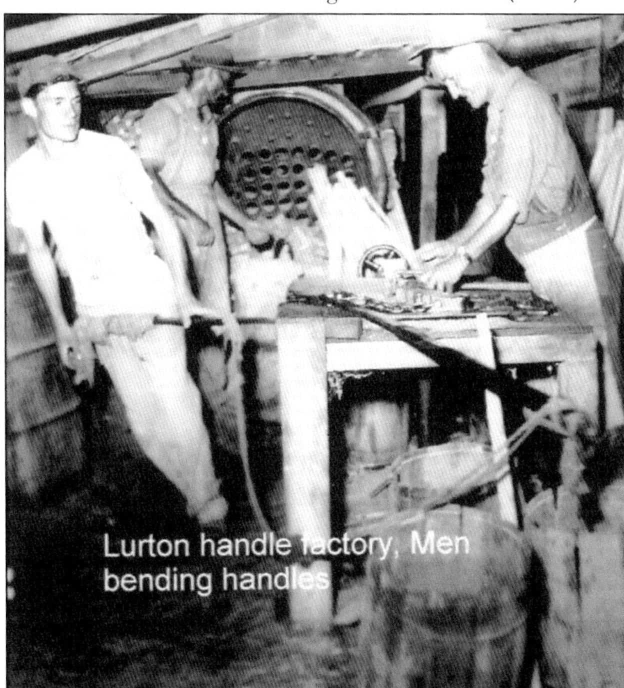

Some of the craftsmen that worked at the Lurton handle factory were photographed in the 1940s as they worked on the specialized equipment that bent the steamed, pliable wooden handles into the shape needed by the customer. The work of these skilled men would have been shipped to many locales to be affixed to a variety of tools. (Courtesy of John Clayborn of Conway, Arkansas.)

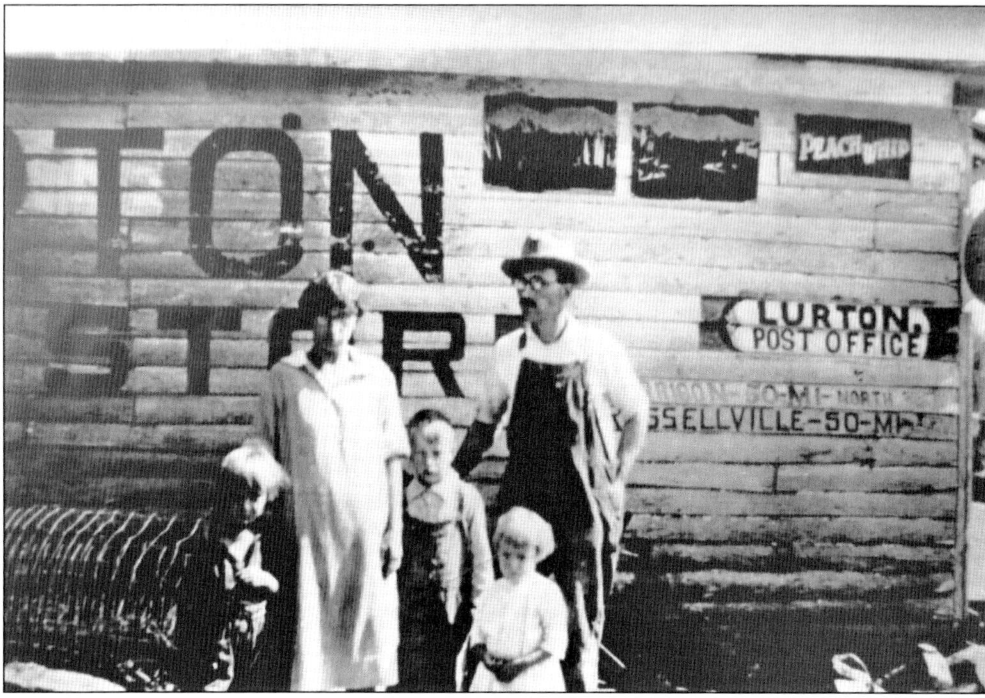

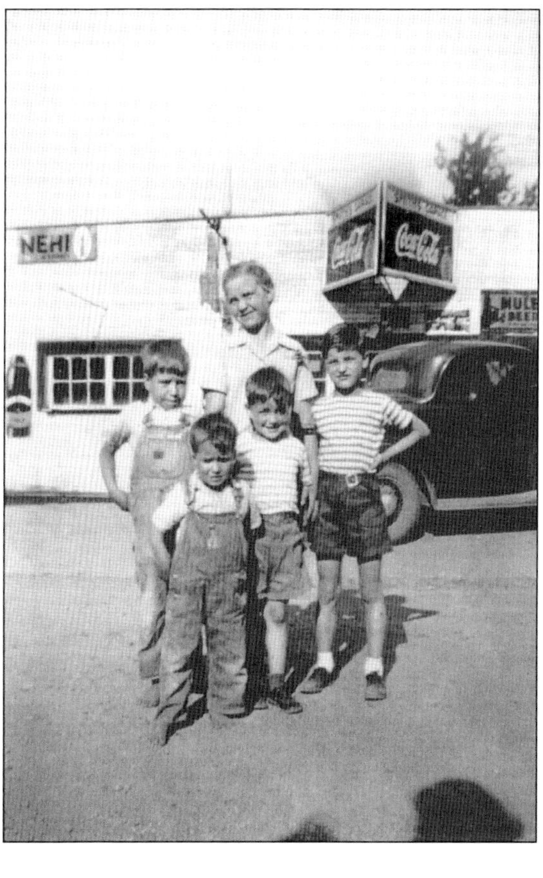

Posed by the side of Lurton General Store in the 1940s is the owner, Jason Sutton, with his family. From left to right are Mary, Libbie, Jim, Alice Mae, and Jason Sutton. The signs on the building identify its location as 50 miles north of Russellville. (NCHS.)

In 1941, Smith's garage in Lurton was the backdrop for a photograph of, from left to right (foreground) Don Sutton; (second row) William Sutton, Sonny Sutton, and Bobby Sutton; (background) and Halleen Sutton. Halleen, Sonny, and Bobby Sutton are the children of Irvin and Ruby. (NCHS.)

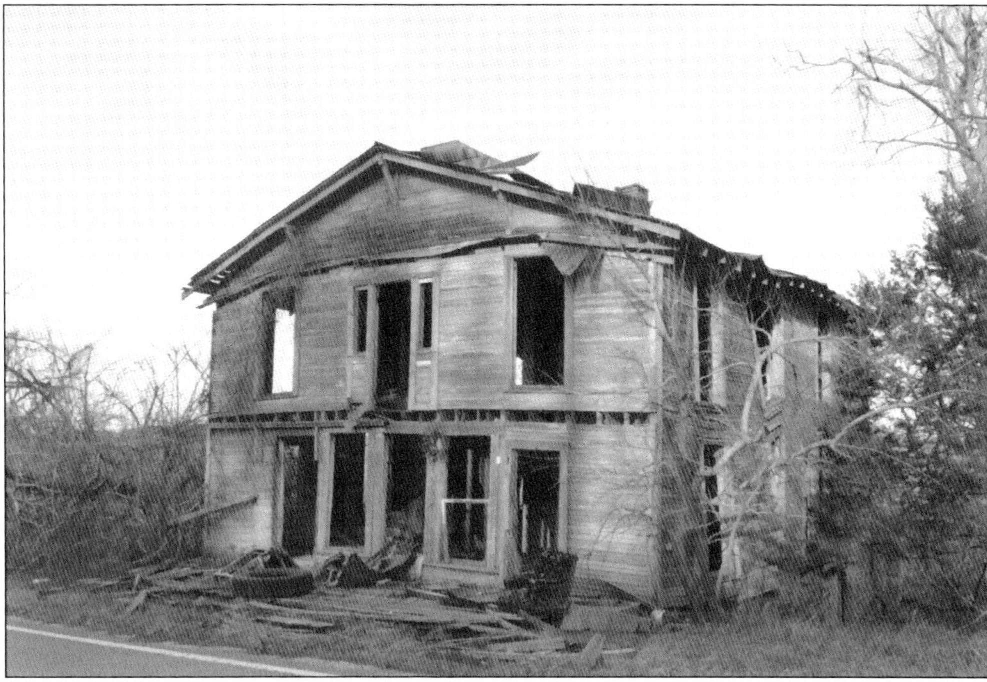

Today, the once small but thriving business district of Lurton is gone, and the area is a small collection of scattered homes and farms. The one remaining relic, the old hotel, seen at the end of the street on page 75, is slowly slipping away, a victim of rain and wind. (Photograph by Ray Hanley.)

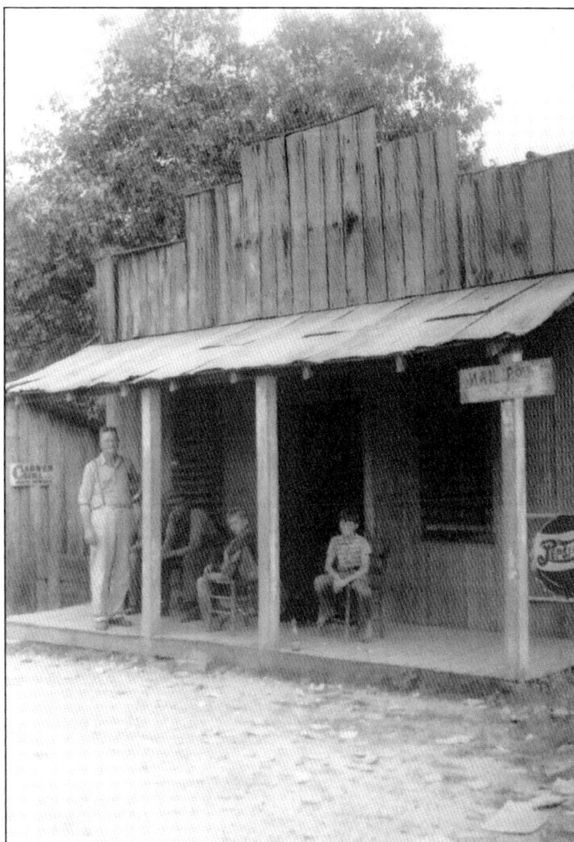

The post office at Nail, Arkansas, was photographed around 1950 in the building it shared with a general store. The name of the town is most likely due to a mix-up when the registration papers reached Washington, DC, misreading "Neal" as "Nail." (Courtesy of the University of Arkansas Special Collections.)

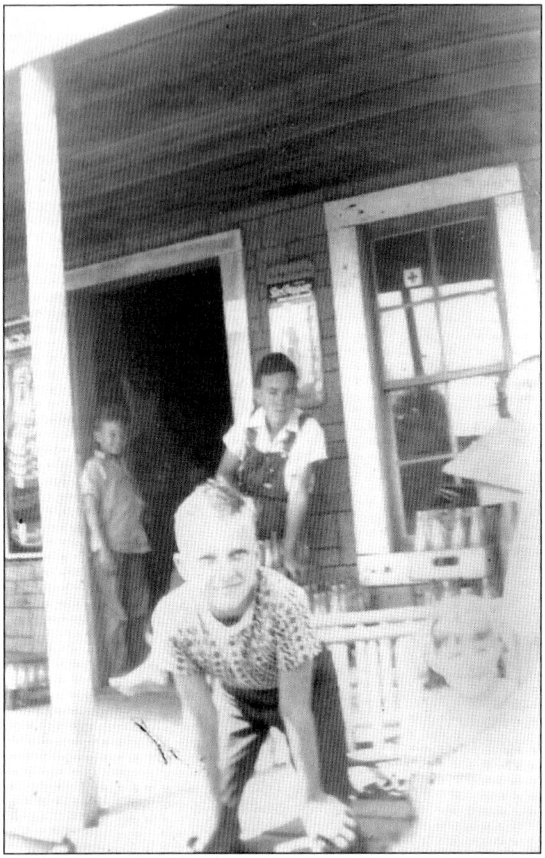

Clayborn's store at Nail, seen here in 1947, was a popular gathering spot. In the doorway in this photograph stands Jim Clayborn, with his brother Harold Clayborn in overalls; mugging for the camera up front is their cousin Gene Gash. (Courtesy of John Clayborn of Conway.)

Some of the tiny general stores of Newton County still stand, a few in surprisingly good condition. Seen here in 2012 is the old store in the community of Compton. (Photograph by Ray Hanley.)

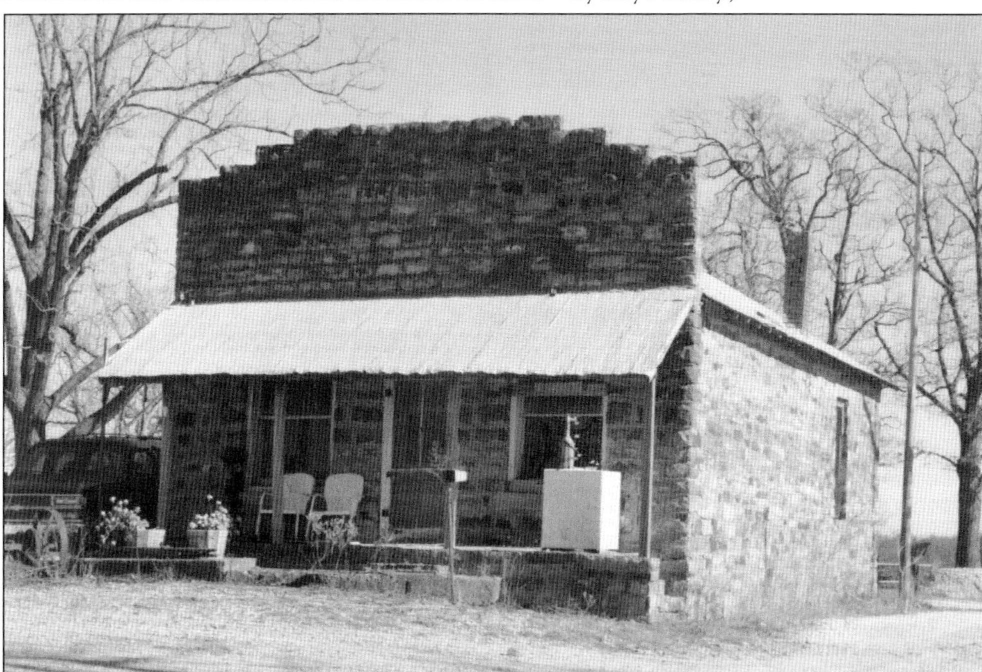

Six

Teaching and Preaching in Schools and Churches of Newton County

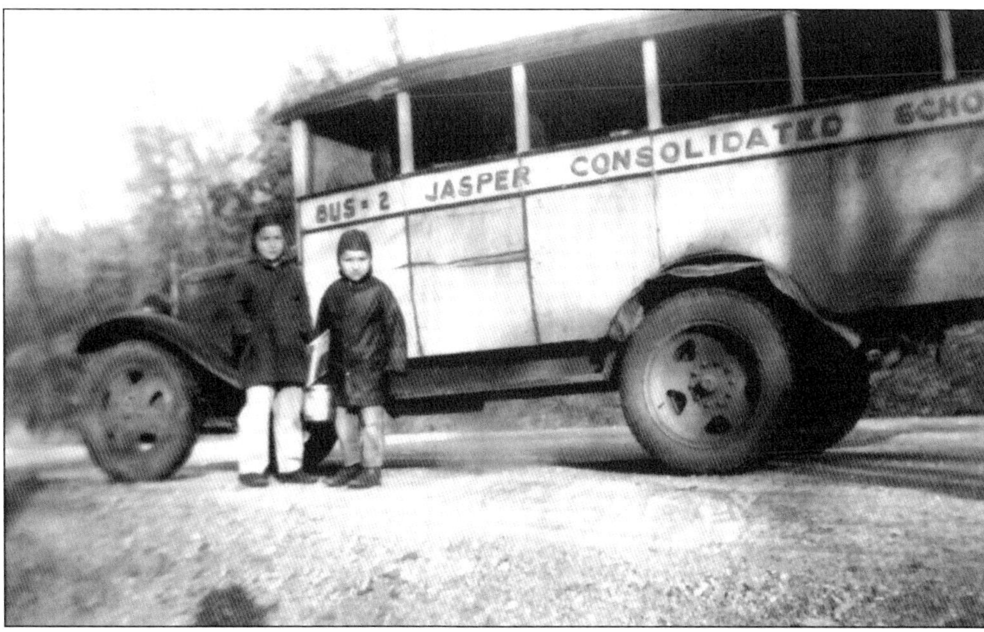

Schools and churches have always been central to the lives of the families of Newton County. In the 1934–1935 school year, Newton County had a reported 95 school districts, with 57 of these being one-room schoolhouses. F.G. Walton was the driver of Jasper's first school bus, seen here around 1940; it picked up children in the Erbie and Pruitt areas. A tragic episode occurred one day when the brakes on the bus failed and several children were caught beneath it. Barbara Sue Walton, age five, died after being rushed in her father's arms to a local doctor. (NCL.)

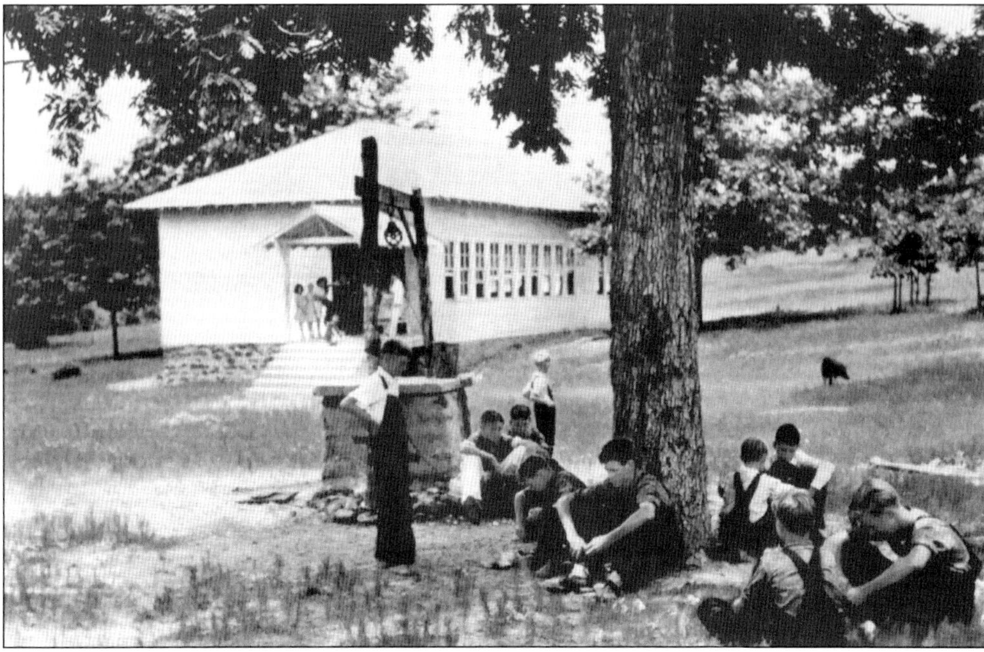

"Sometimes Sit and Think, Sometimes Just Sit," was the title of a scene at the Mount Sherman school west of Jasper on what is today State Highway 74. The salary of a Newton County teacher in 1897 ranged from $20 to $40 a month; by 1961 it had risen to be between $330 and $555 a month, depending on experience. Seen below, the Mount Sherman student body expressed its honor of country around 1920 in saluting the American flag in front of the whitewashed frame building. The school served students through the fifth grade, all studying within one room. (Both, NCL.)

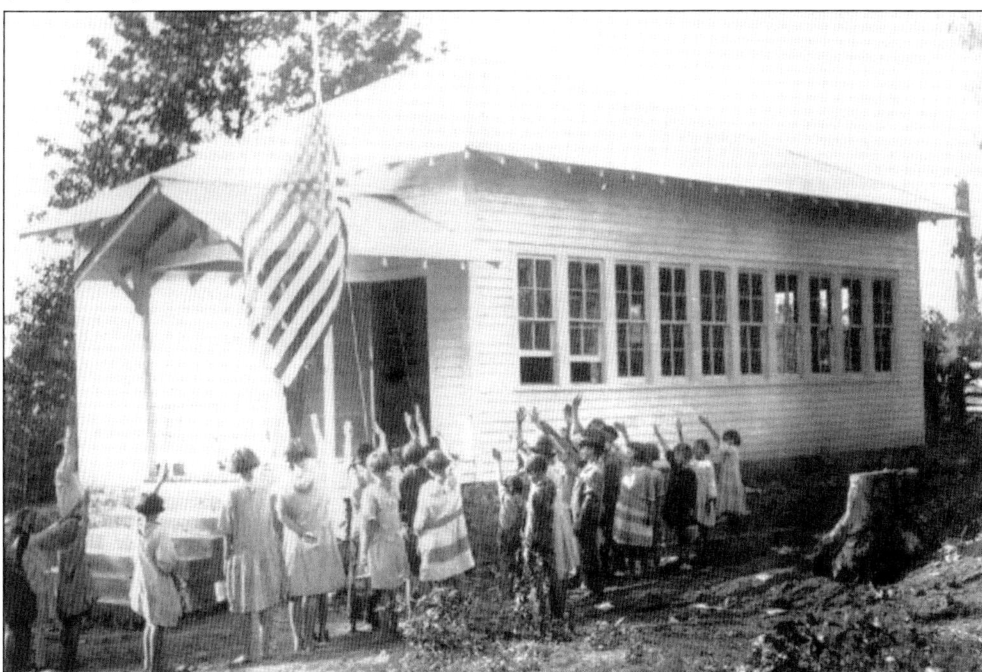

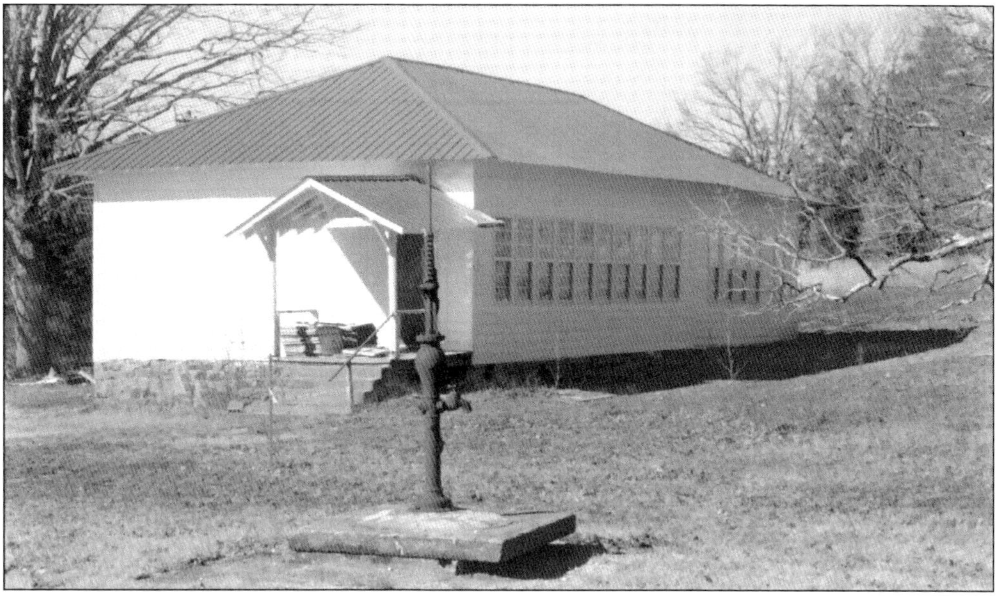

The restored school building sits today on the edge of the Mount Sherman community; a pump now sits where the well was in the schoolyard image on page 80. It is one of the very few one-room schoolhouses left standing in a state that was once dotted with such places of education. (Photograph by Ray Hanley.)

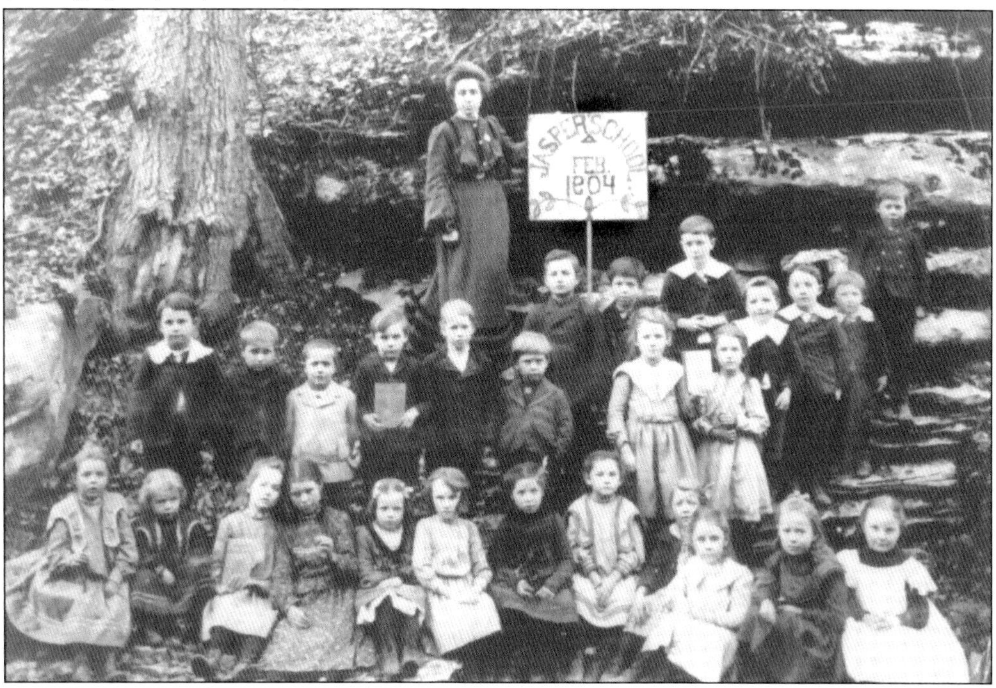

In 1904, a Jasper elementary teacher posed with her students on the side of a hill on a cold February day. The children came to school that day prepared for the photograph. Parents had carefully dressed each in what was likely their finest clothing, and every child's hair had been carefully combed. At the time, the average Arkansas teacher earned $166 for the 69-day school year. (NCL.)

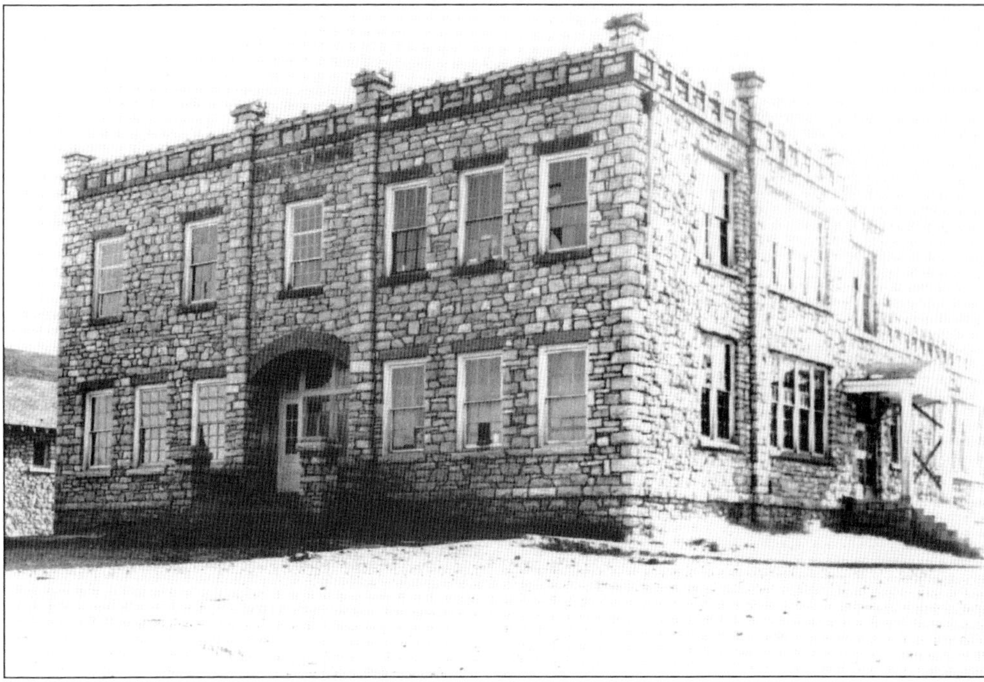

The native stone Jasper High School was built around the turn of the century, with an elementary school later added next-door. The stone schoolhouse entrance would prove a popular spot for class photographs over the years, for students of all grades. The average school year was 124 days for the larger schools in 1920 when the photograph below was taken. That year, the state counted more than 5,000 school districts. The school building was demolished in 1970, and the modern Jasper school buildings are located near the site. (NCL.)

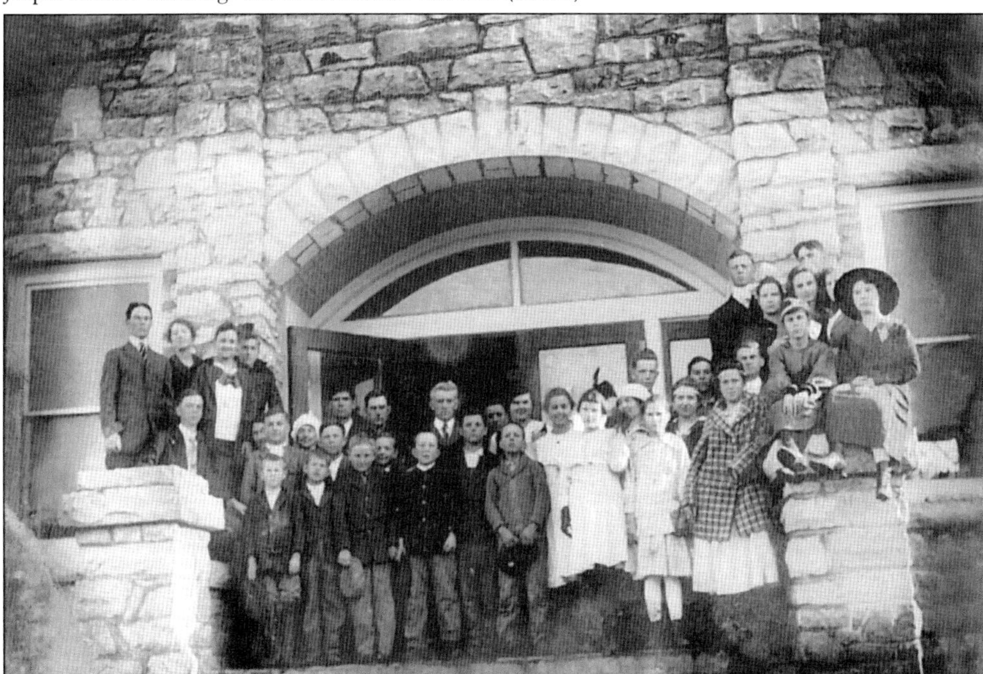

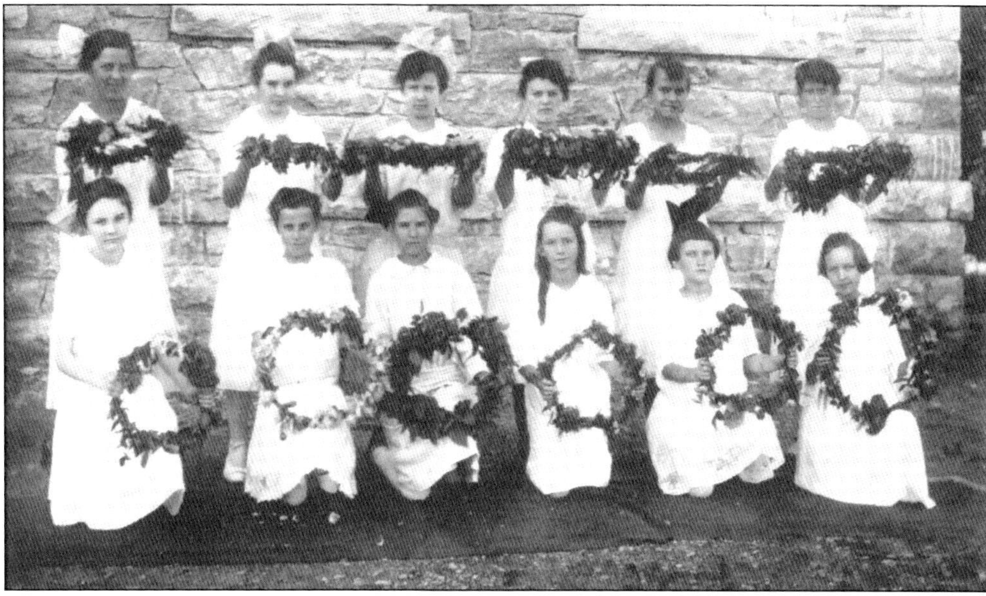

A dedicated Children's Day was first held in Jasper in 1868 and was reprised when these girls posed outside the Jasper High School dressed in white and carefully holding wreaths of flowers. Among the events was a ceremony where children marched to the local cemetery to place flowers on the graves of the areas veterans. From left to right are (first row) Mae McFerrin Case, Evelyn Booth, Ruth Earp Tuttle, Ava Perkey Smith, Dovie Moore Pruitt, and Lulu Brown; (second row) Oles Seals Allen, Eileen McFerrin, Margarite Murray, Nellie Henderson Loomis, Kathleen Spring, and Cora Leach Unwer. (NCL.)

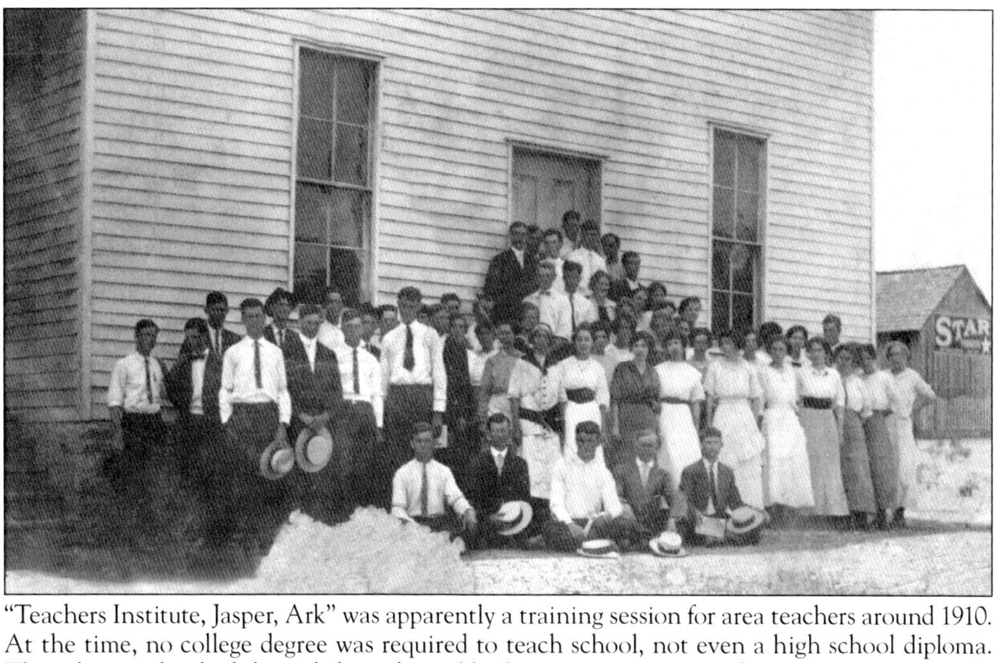

"Teachers Institute, Jasper, Ark" was apparently a training session for area teachers around 1910. At the time, no college degree was required to teach school, not even a high school diploma. Those having finished the eighth grade could take an examination and, upon passing, receive a teaching certificate. Teachers in rural areas had a trying job, earning perhaps $40 a month. Their conduct was expected to be exemplary; all eyes of the community were upon them. (NCL.)

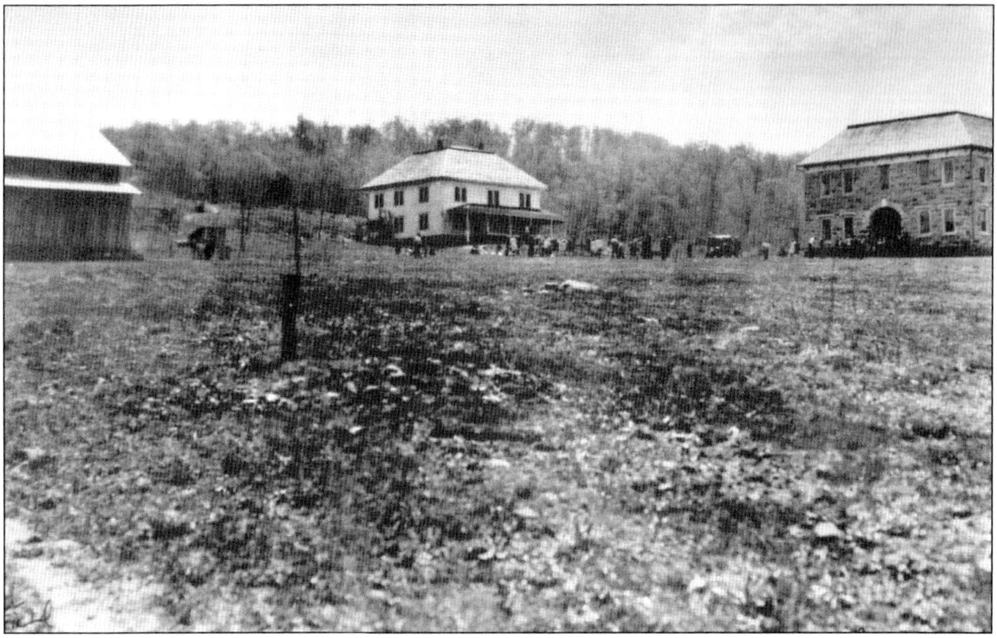

The Newton County Academy was built in 1920 on land donated by W.A. Casey. Its construction and operation was funded in part with the help of the Arkansas Baptist Convention, with the goal of providing extra help to disadvantaged students in the rural areas of Newton County. Located at Parthenon, the girls roomed in the dorm in the center, while the boys boarded with local families. The historic buildings are all gone today except the gymnasium, which has been restored. (NCHS.)

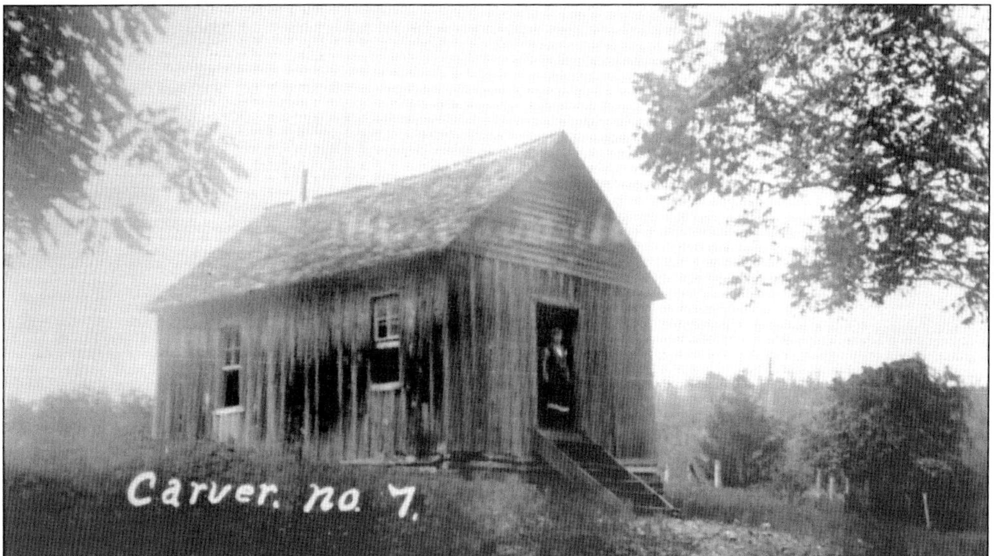

By the 1930s, many of the turn-of-the-century wooden one-room schoolhouses of Newton County were falling into disrepair, including the one shown here at Carver. In 1934, the Carver district, which trained students through the eighth grade, counted a total of 69 students; these children were surely taught in a larger building than the one seen here. (NCHS.)

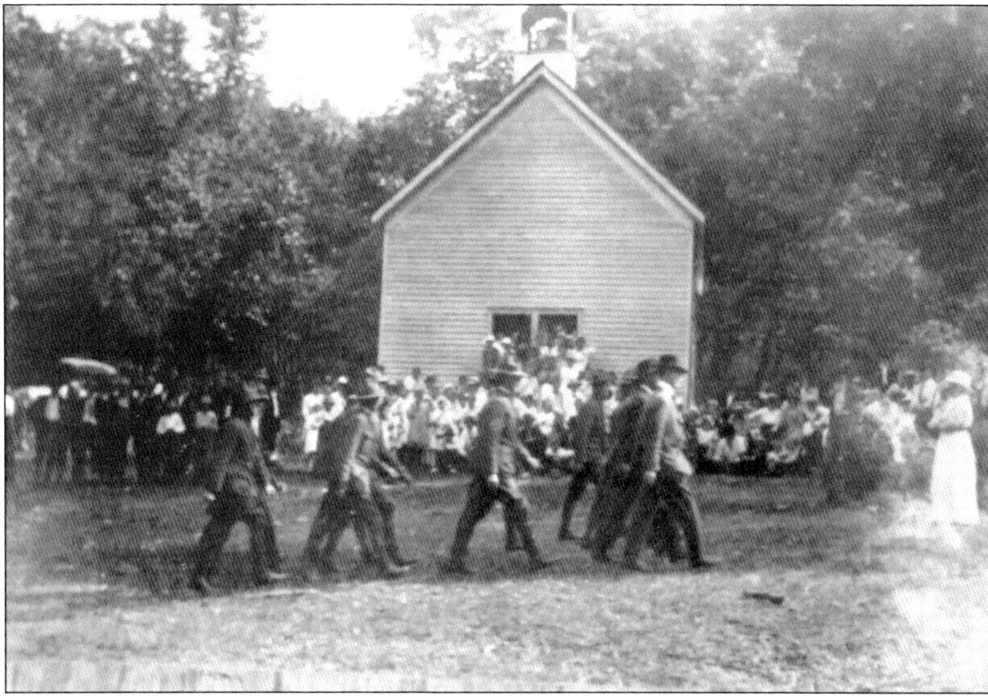

Schools sometimes served as the backdrop to community events. In this case, a Memorial Day parade passed through the yard of the Ben's Branch School around 1900. (NCHS.)

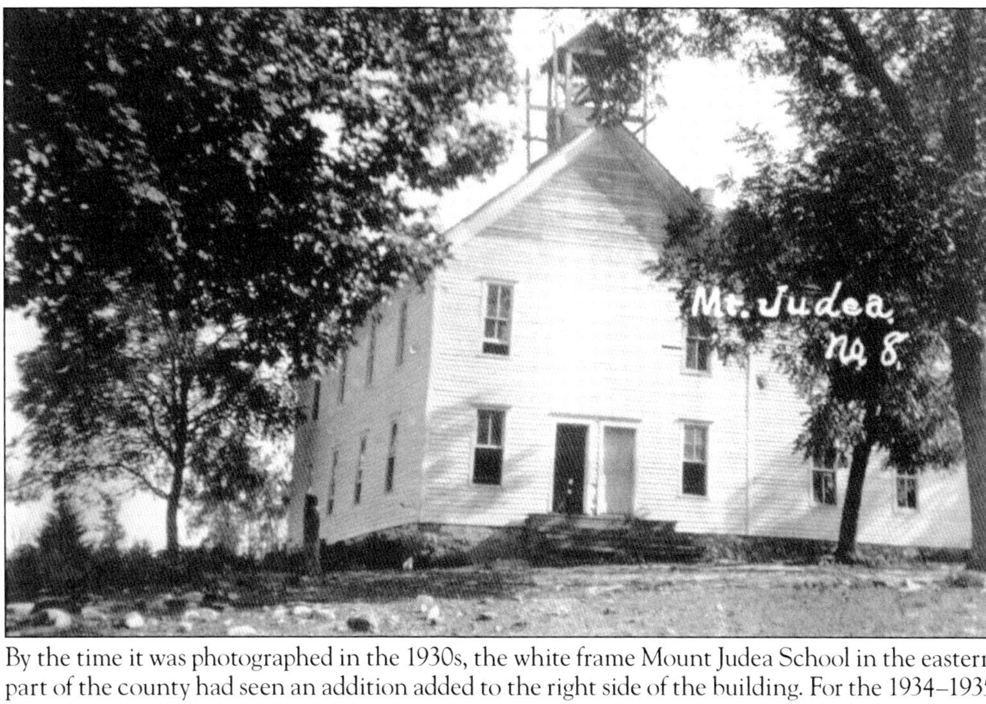

By the time it was photographed in the 1930s, the white frame Mount Judea School in the eastern part of the county had seen an addition added to the right side of the building. For the 1934–1935 year, the school offered classes to children through the eighth grade and counted 174 students. The average Arkansas teacher was earning $691 a year at the time, and the State of Arkansas contributed $35 per child per year to assist the districts. (NCHS.)

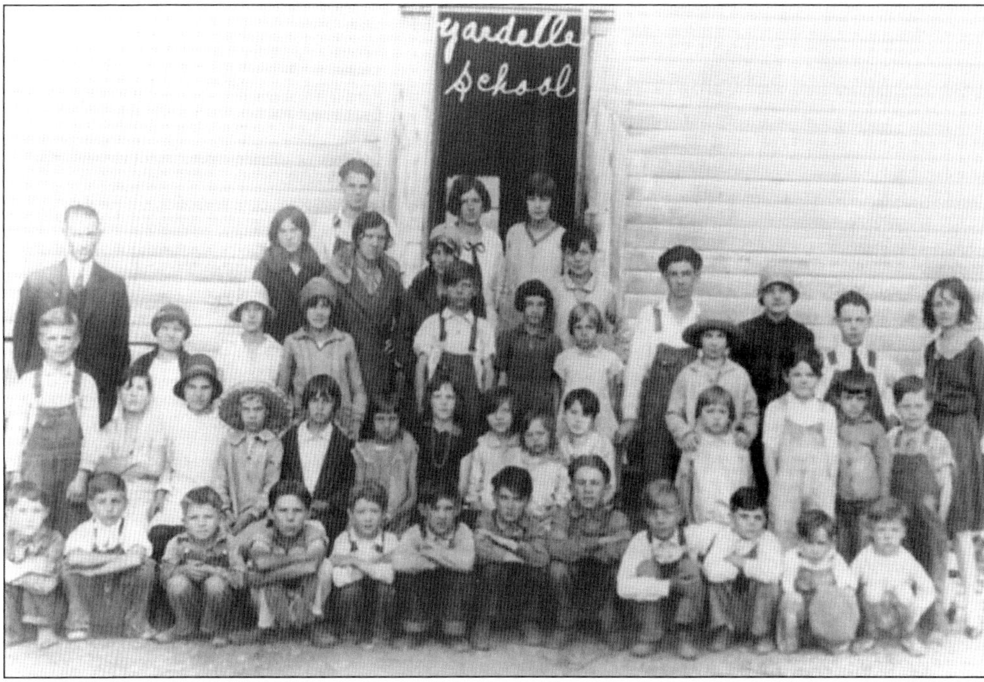

What was likely the entire student body of the Yardelle School posed with their teacher in front of their school around 1926. It would not have been unusual at the time for one teacher, such as the gentleman seen at the far left, to have had responsibility for all eight grades. (NCHS.)

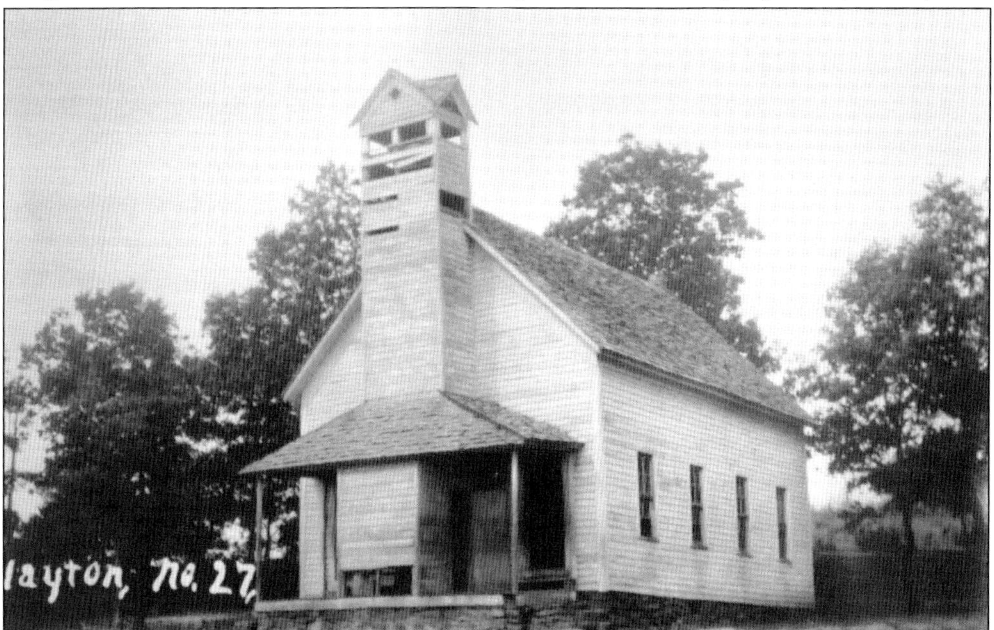

In the remote community of Wayton, the school building was in need of considerable repair by the time it was photographed here in the 1930s. Classes had apparently moved to another building at this time. The 1934–1935 enrollment through the eighth grade was reported to be 79 students. (NCHS.)

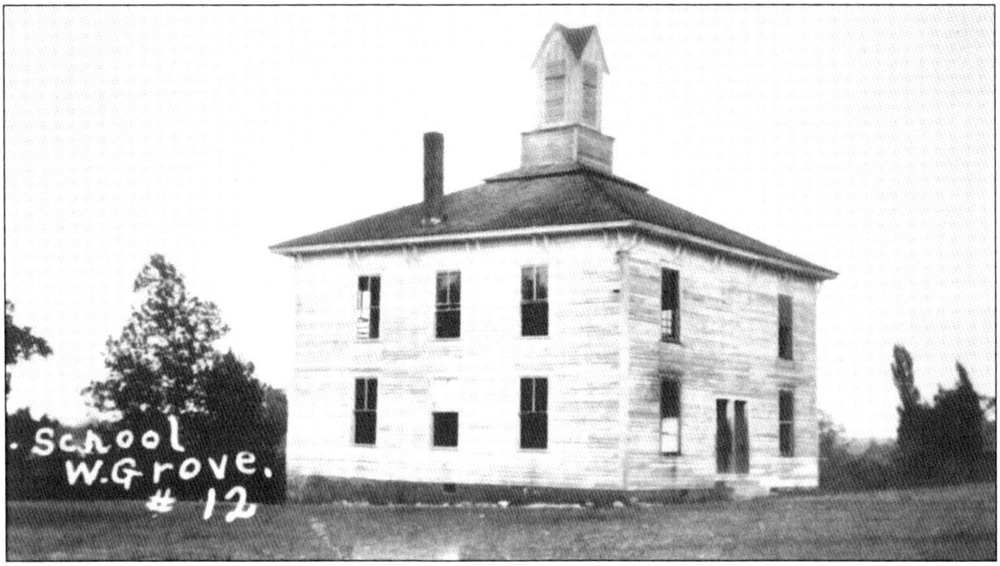

Western Grove, in the northeast corner of the county, saw its turn-of-the-century school also in need of repairs in the 1930s. At two stories, the building was larger than most in the county, reflective of the commerce in the area. Teachers employed in such a school would have been janitor as well as teacher and would have had to carry in firewood during the winter or drafted students for help. An elderly gentleman remarked to the Newton County Historical Society that "as a young boy in school, every time we went to the outhouse we had to carry a stick of firewood back with us." (NCHS.)

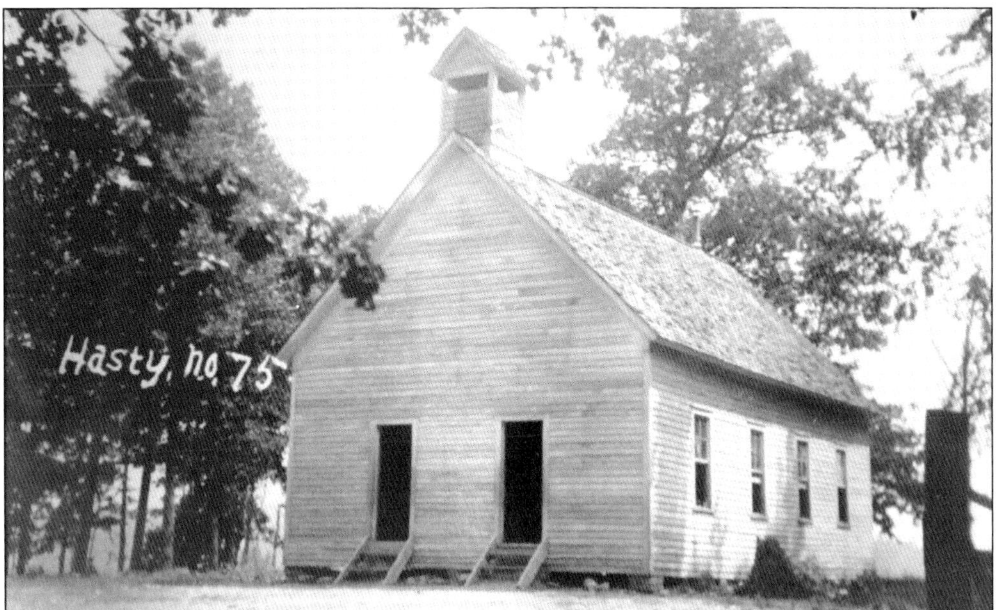

The paint was peeling, with some boards coming loose, when the Hasty one-room school was photographed in the 1930s. By then, the Hasty district had been consolidated into an adjoining district; the pace of such consolidations would pick up as the years moved along. Newton County, which had 95 districts in the 1930s, today has only three: Jasper, Deer, and Mount Judea (with two campuses). Western Grove is now part of the Ozark Mountain School District. (NCHS.)

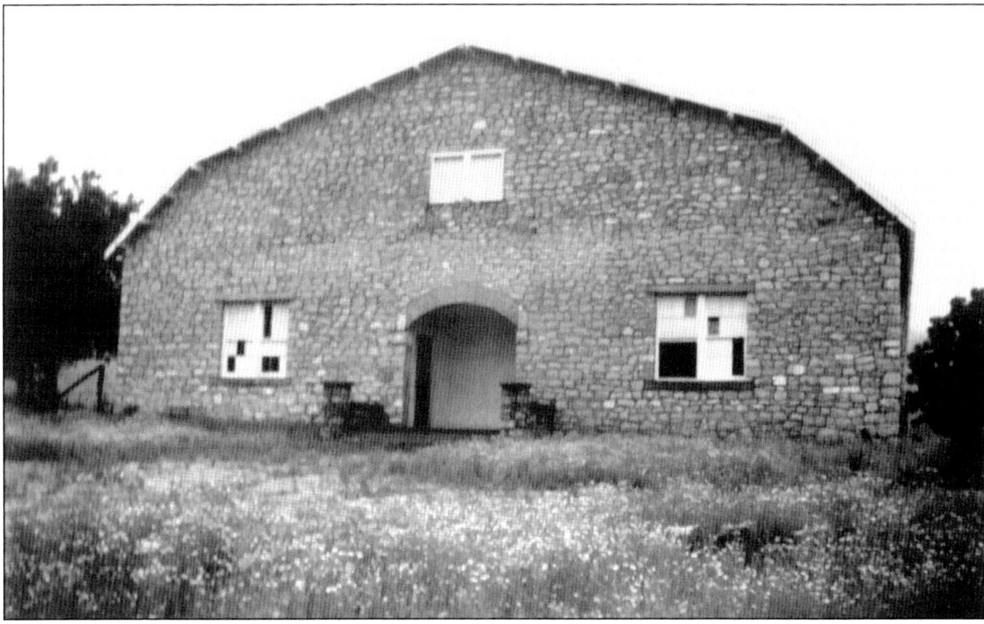

A gymnasium became a part of the campus at several Newton County school districts, as the popularity of basketball spread. This unique native stone gym was erected by the Works Progress Administration at the Parthenon school in 1936, with local materials donated "by subscription," presumably meaning from donations of local people. Though remodeled and given a different roof, the building still stands today. (NCL.)

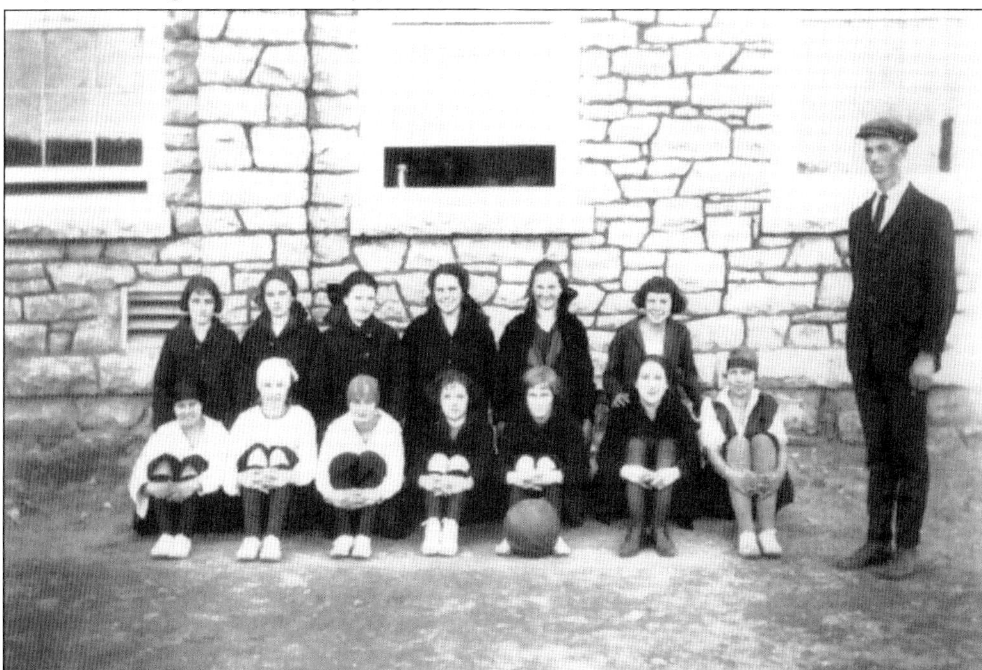

Over the decades, girls have been as competitive as boys in taking to the basketball courts of Newton County. Albert Raney was photographed here with the girls' team at Jasper around 1925. (NCL.)

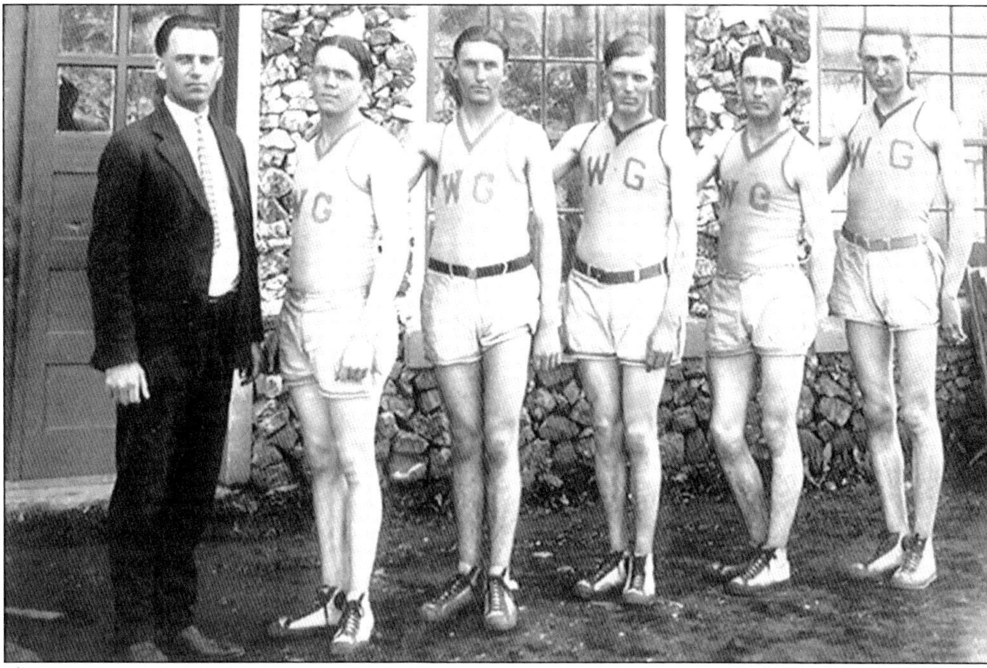

Schools in Newton County have always been too small to compete in football, but have embraced basketball for decades. The game was invented in Massachusetts in 1891; as early as 1912, Arkansas was awarding state championships in the sport. Photographed here around 1920 are members of the boys' team and their coach from the Western Grove School in the northeast corner of the county. Note the uniforms had belts. (NCL.)

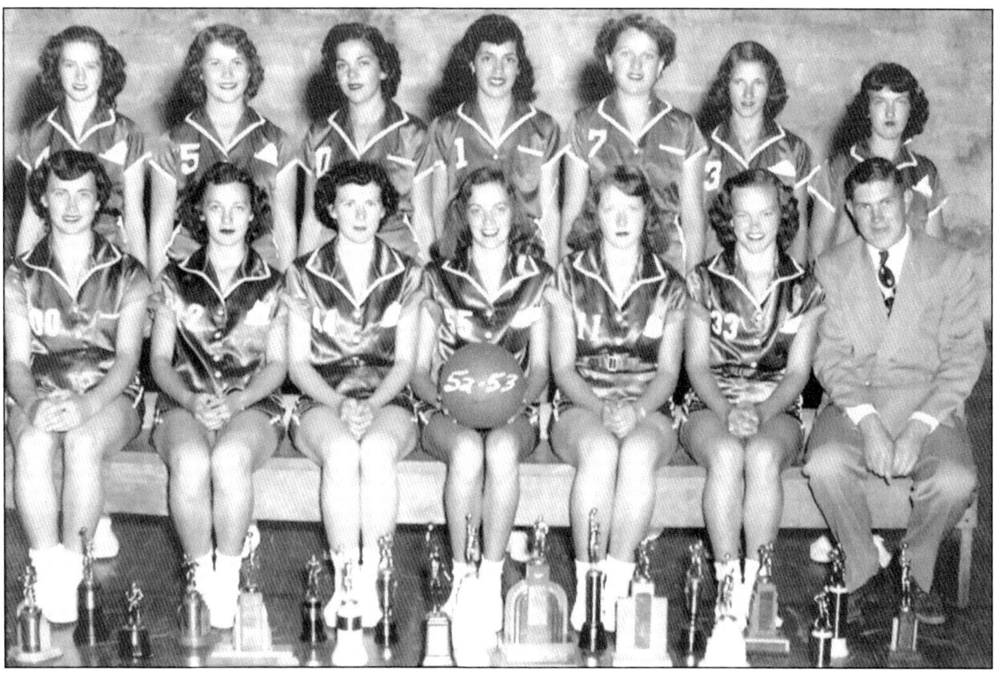

Mount Judea High School in western Newton County fielded a remarkably attractive and, by evidence of the trophies, very talented girls' basketball team for the 1952–1953 season.

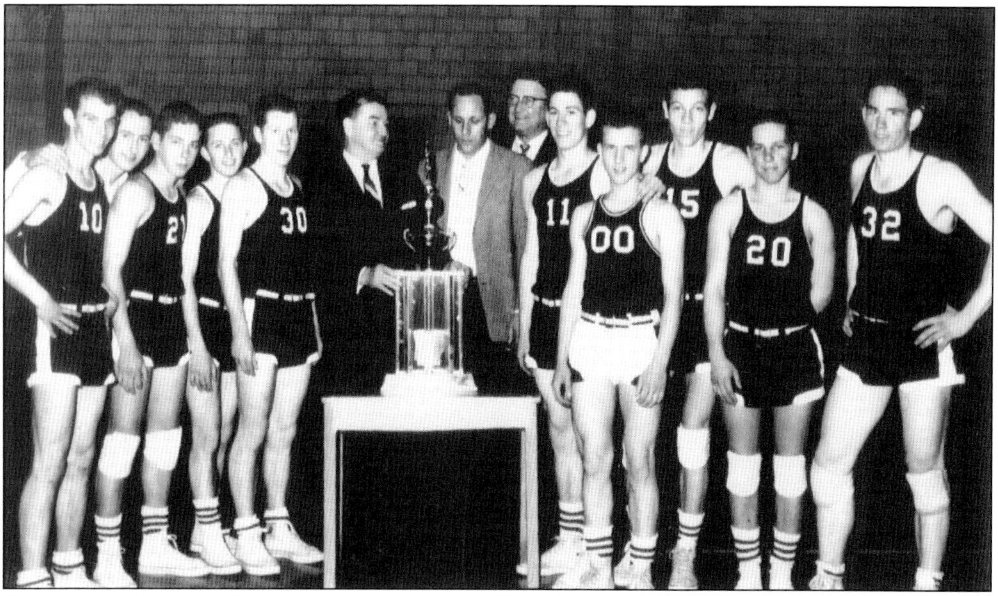
Players from Newton County not only competed but also sometimes won it all. Pictured here are the Jasper Pirates, who won the Arkansas State Championship in their division in 1960. Players pictured are, from left to right, Joe Brasel, Donnie Kilgore, Joe Thomas, Stanley Smith, Donnie Walton, Coach Gene Harness, unidentified, Karl Kelly, Donnie Hawkins, Rex Madewell, John Thomas, and Eddie Reynolds. (NCL.)

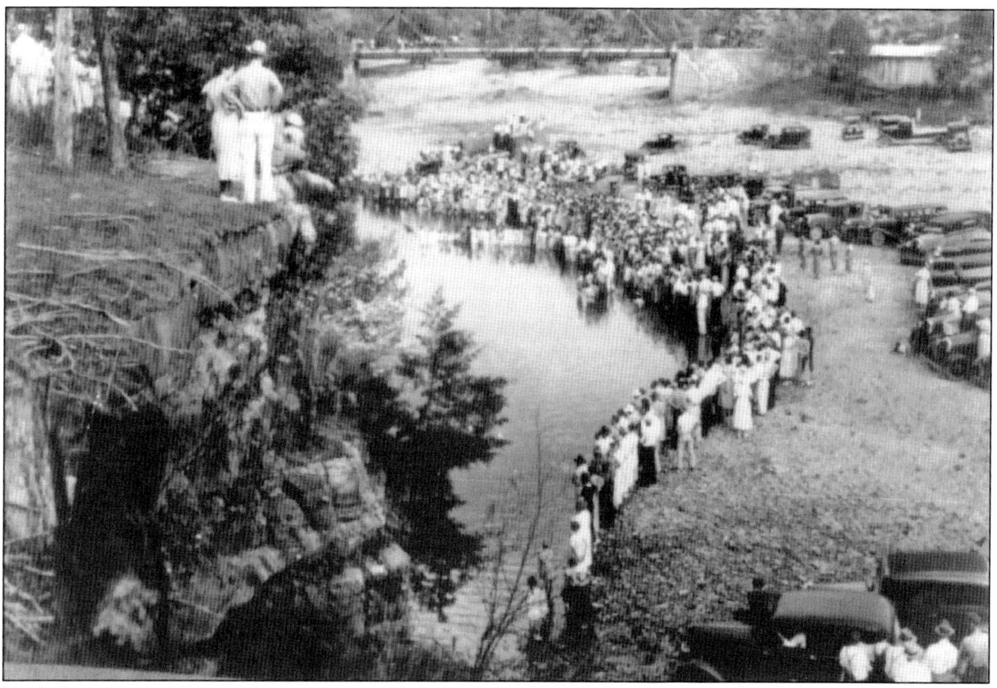
Faith has been a part of the fabric of life for Newton County's people since the first pioneers arrived with Bibles among their possessions. The Little Buffalo River, seen here just above the Highway 7 Bridge at Jasper in the 1930s, was a popular place for baptism ceremonies, sometimes drawing large crowds. (NCL.)

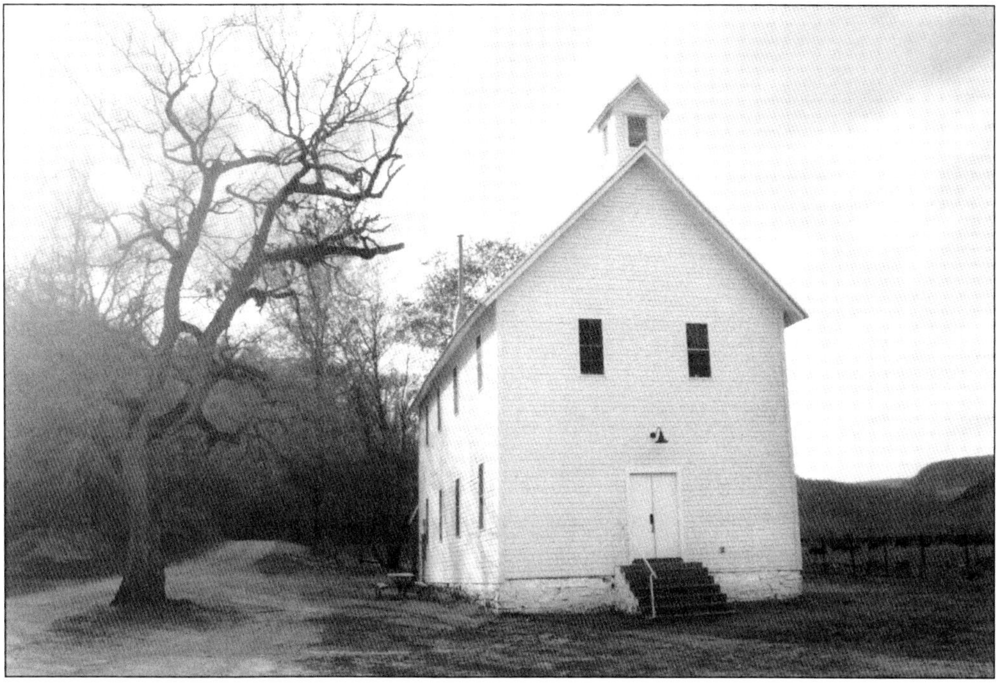

Perhaps the most photographed church in Arkansas, the Boxley Baptist Church in the historic Boxley Valley dates its founding back to 1838. The structure pictured here was built in 1899 and, for some 50 years, served as church, schoolhouse, and community center. A modern church was built next-door in 1956, but the historic white frame church continues to be maintained.

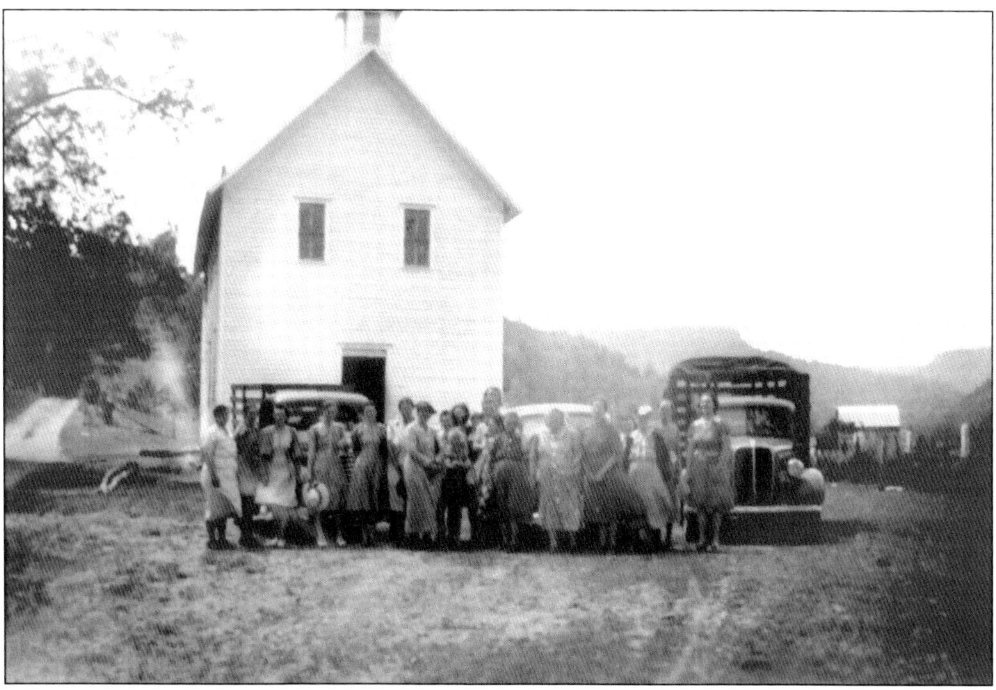

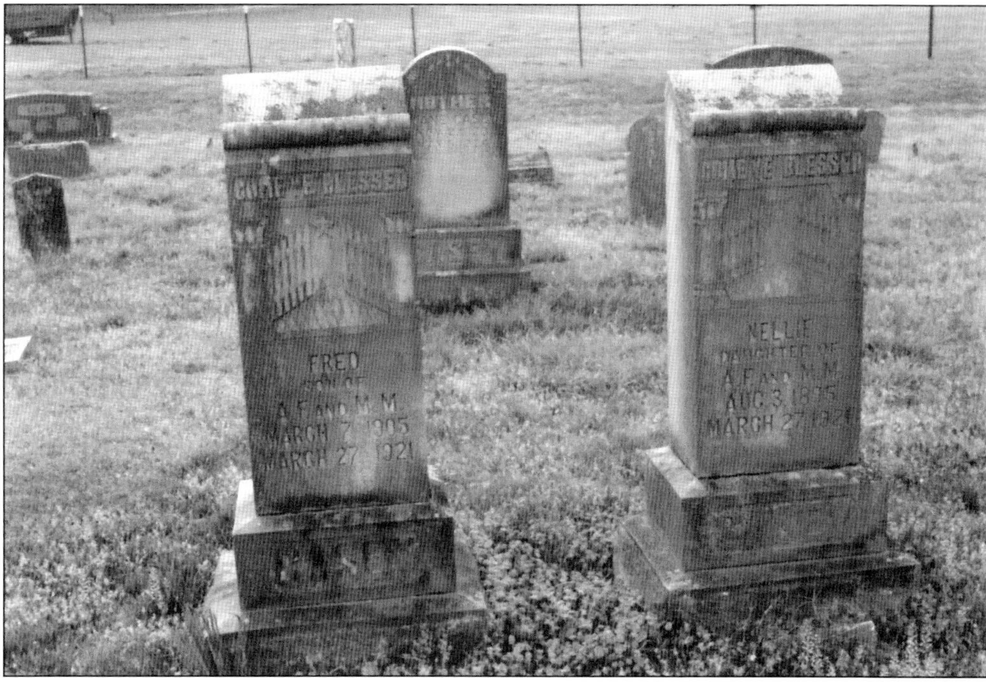

The cemetery next to the old Boxley Baptist Church, embraced by the surrounding mountains, is well worth a visit and quiet contemplation on the fragility of life. The small plot of land contains the graves of pioneers and Confederate soldiers; sometimes tragedy is set in the native stone markers. The gravestones of Fred Casey, age 16, and his sister Nellie, age 25, bear the same date of death, March 27, 1921. They were in Russellville some 60 miles to the south, borrowed an uncle's automobile for a ride, and were struck and killed at a train crossing.

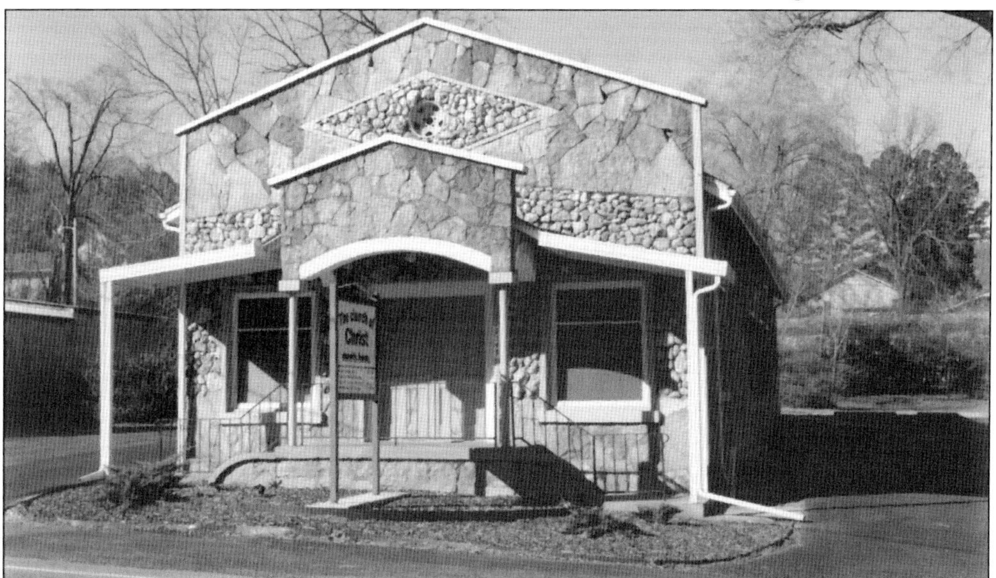

The Church of Christ building that stands on the south side of Jasper bears a bit of the whimsical touches of its builder, Gould Jones. An automobile wheel is placed inside the cobblestone diamond in the upper front section of the house of worship. (Photograph by Ray Hanley.)

Seven

BYGONE TOURIST ATTRACTIONS

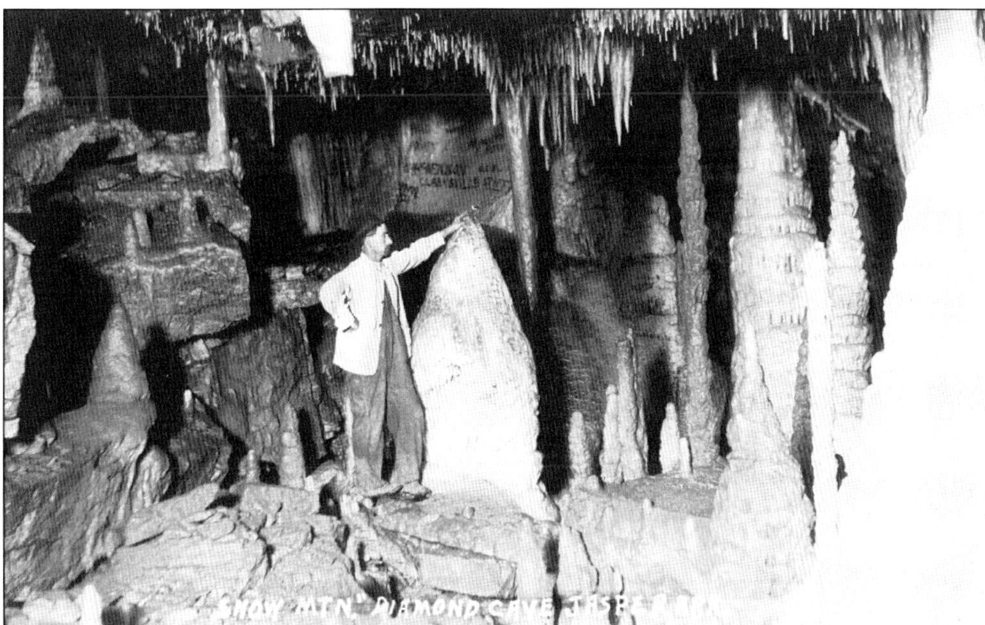

Diamond Cave was discovered, according to the most common legend, quite by accident in the winter of 1835, when the hunting dogs of Sam and Andrew Hudson chased a bear into a hole in the side of a mountain. A half mile inside the cave the brothers killed two bears, but only after losing one of their dogs. Located a few miles west of Jasper near Henson Creek, the cave would emerge over the next century and half as one of the best tourist draws in Newton County. This postcard, written by a tourist in 1927, said, "P.S. We are in the Diamond Cave."

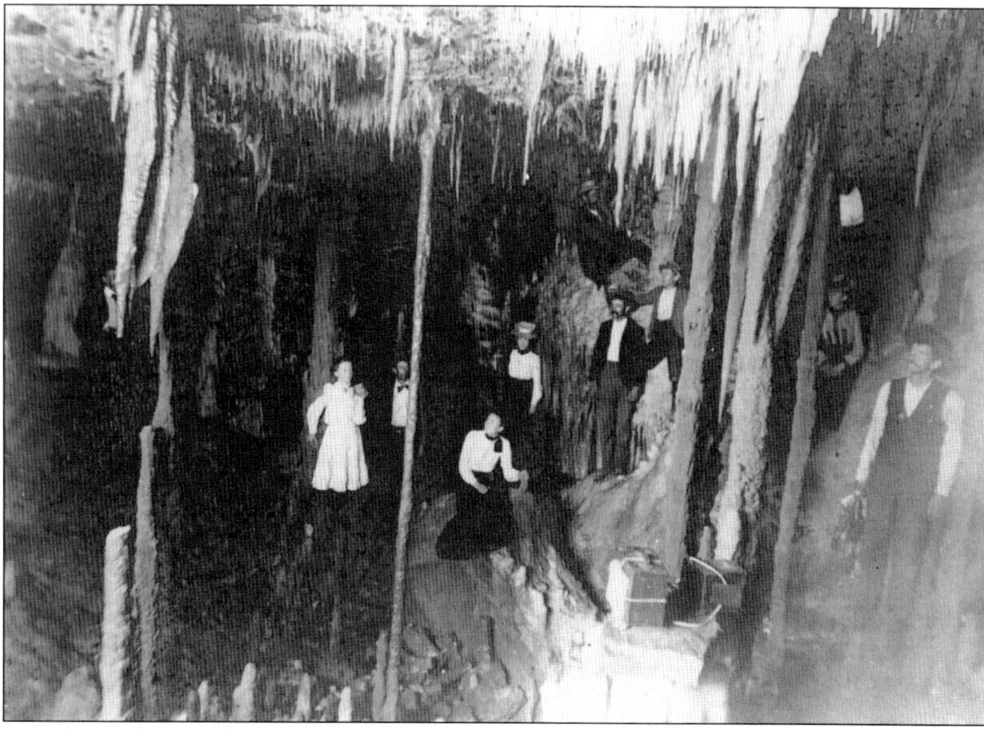

"Nearly a mile from daylight amid the charms of Diamond Cave," was the inscription on the bottom of this c. 1910 postcard image of a group posed among the stalactites, columns, and stalagmites. The name "Diamond Cave" likely came from the many minerals contained in the water that dripped from the ceiling, causing a display of colors.

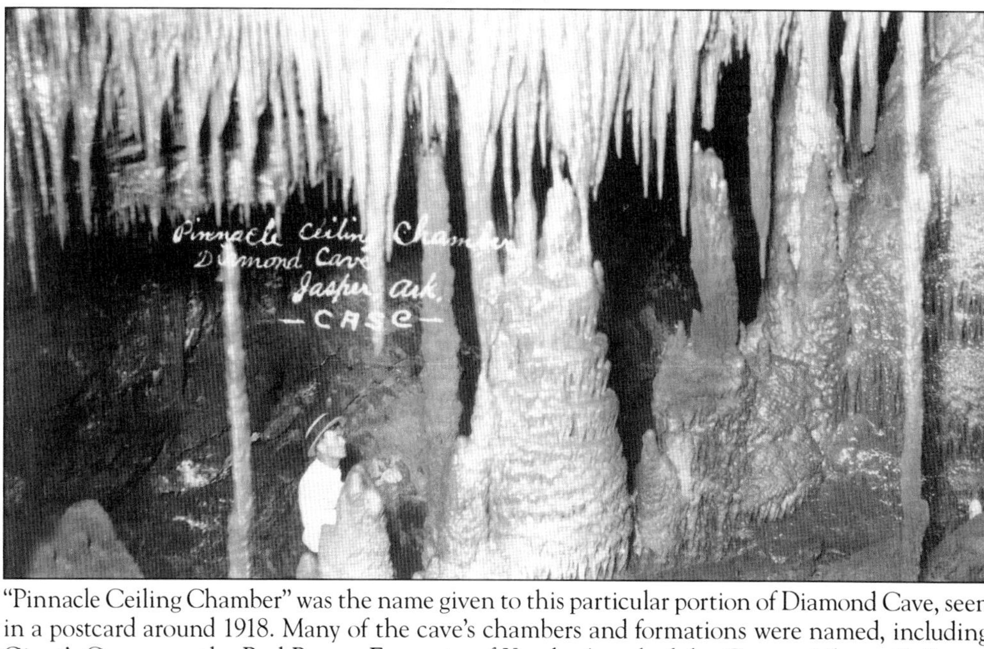

"Pinnacle Ceiling Chamber" was the name given to this particular portion of Diamond Cave, seen in a postcard around 1918. Many of the cave's chambers and formations were named, including Giant's Causeway, the Red Room, Fountain of Youth, Angel of the Grotto, Liberty Bell, and King Solomon's Temple.

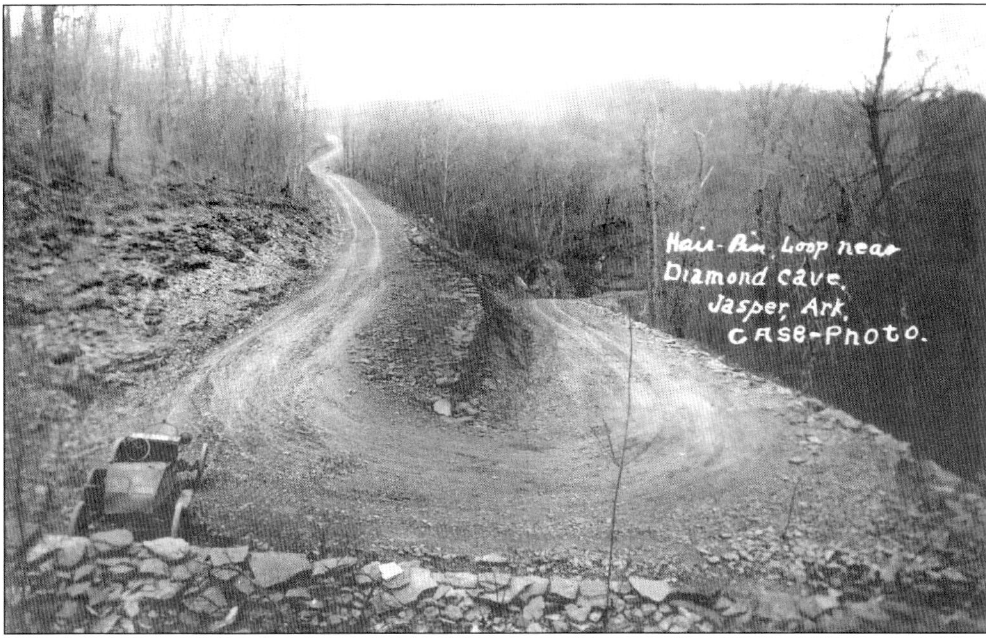

The road leading tourists to Diamond Cave, with its "Hair-Pin Loop," was in itself part of the billed attraction put onto postcards by around 1915.

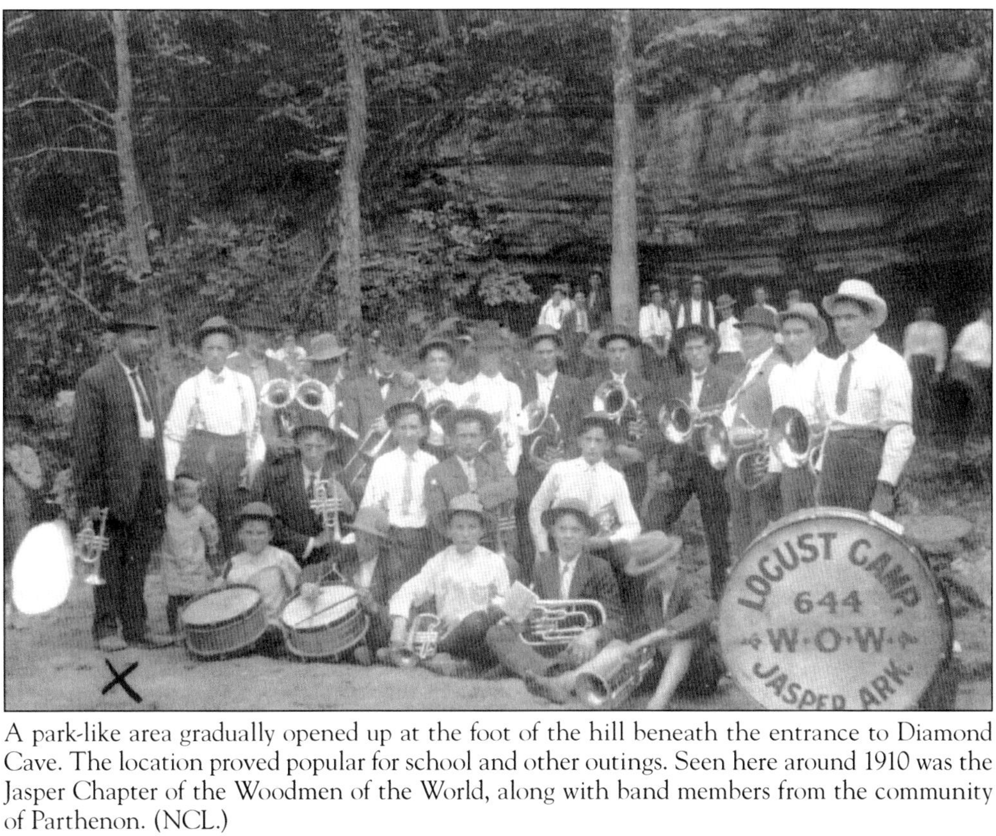

A park-like area gradually opened up at the foot of the hill beneath the entrance to Diamond Cave. The location proved popular for school and other outings. Seen here around 1910 was the Jasper Chapter of the Woodmen of the World, along with band members from the community of Parthenon. (NCL.)

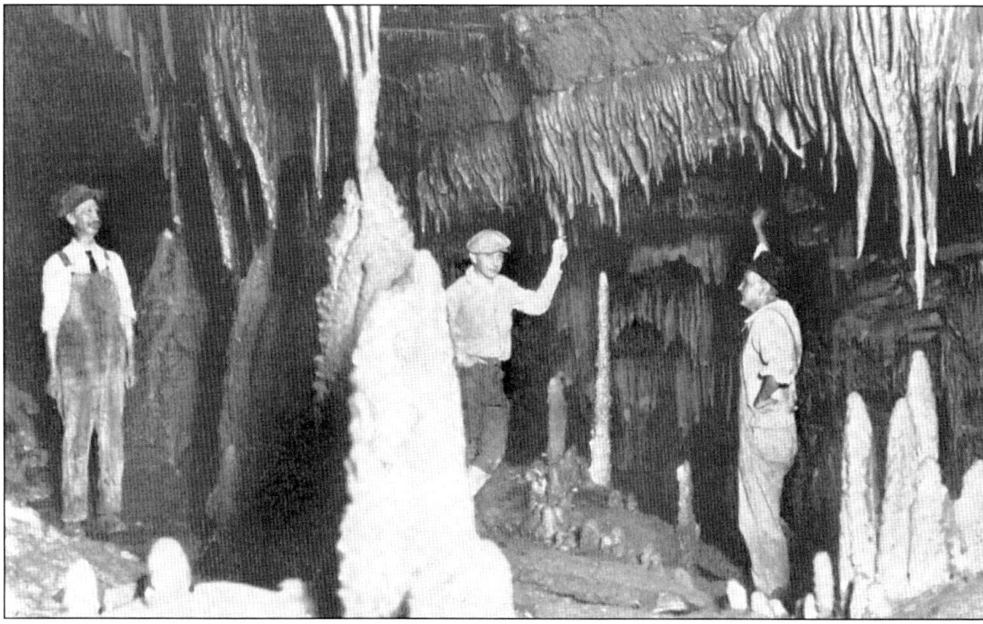

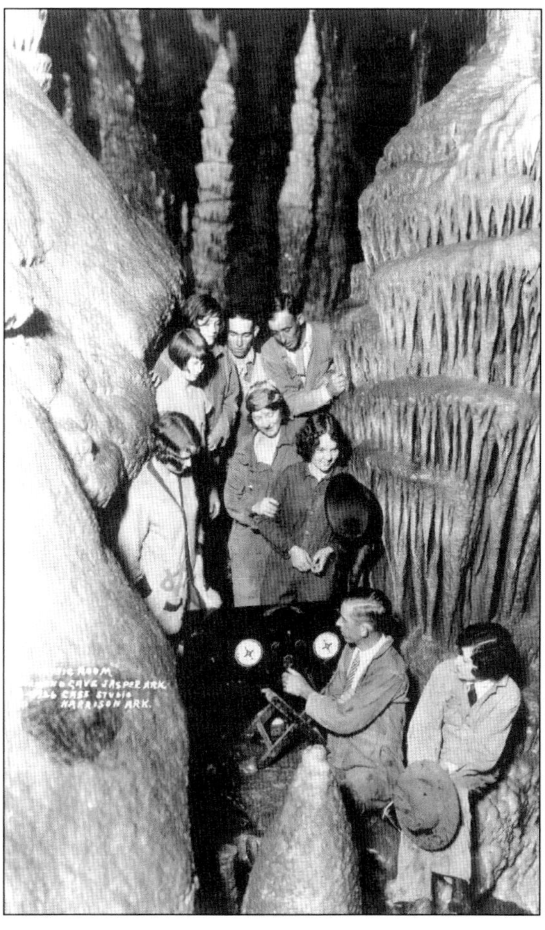

The formations seen here were coined "Snow White and the Seven Dwarfs in the Forest." At the time, around 1930, a brochure billed Diamond Cave as the "Ace of the World's Caverns," proclaiming "this great natural phenomenon stands foremost as the State's most attractive resort."

Set in the "Music Room," this postcard shows sound equipment being used to play off the acoustics of a portion of Diamond Cave. A brochure at the time said, "The formations give out musical tones and you can tap out simple tunes on the 'Grand Piano' in 'Solomon's Temple,' one of the cavern's chambers."

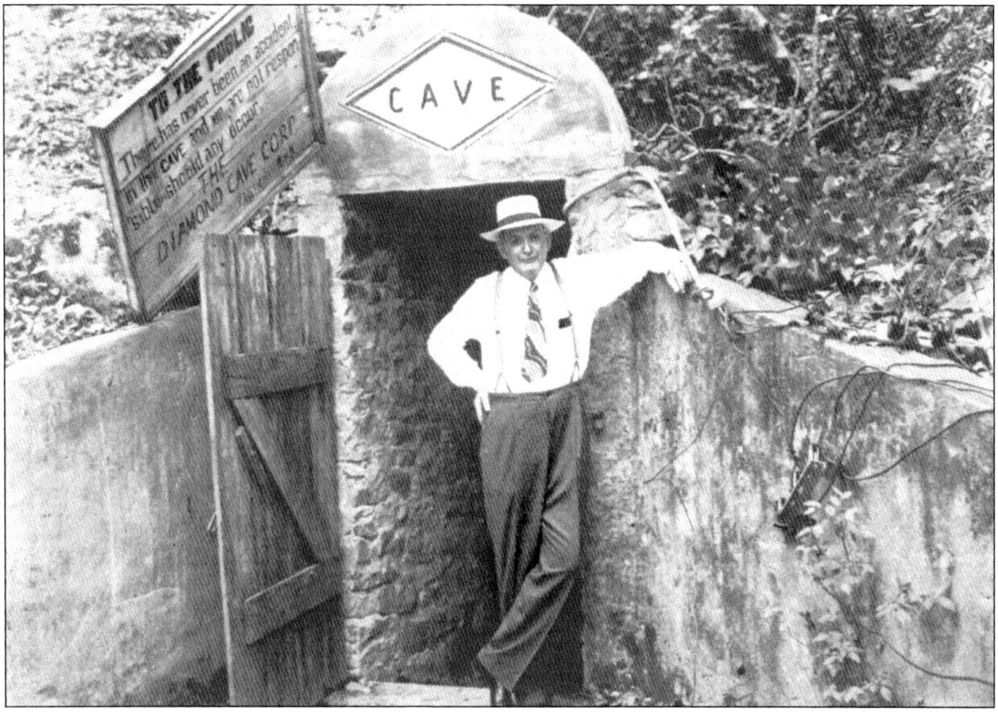

William "Jonah" Pruitt, born in 1872 in the Newton County community of Pruitt, located where today Highway 7 crosses the Buffalo River, owned and managed the cave for many years until his death in 1959. The former Newton County sheriff posed here by the cave's tourist entrance in the 1940s. The "notice to the public" sign to the left says, "There has never been an accident in this cave and we are not responsible should any occur."

As seen here around 1950, area school groups would make field trips to Diamond Cave during the course of the school year. The back of the card reads, "Visit the Most Glamorous and Educational Underground Fairyland—Supreme in Beauty, Size and Mystery. A Profound Emotional Experience Difficult to Put into Words."

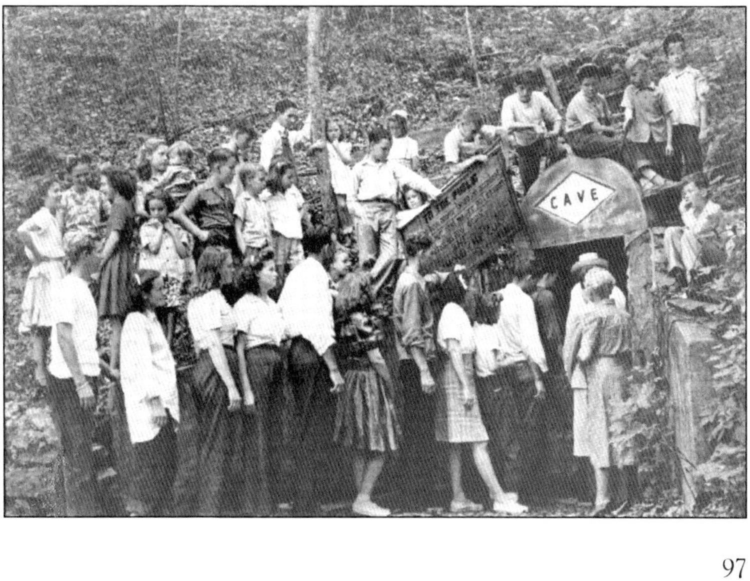

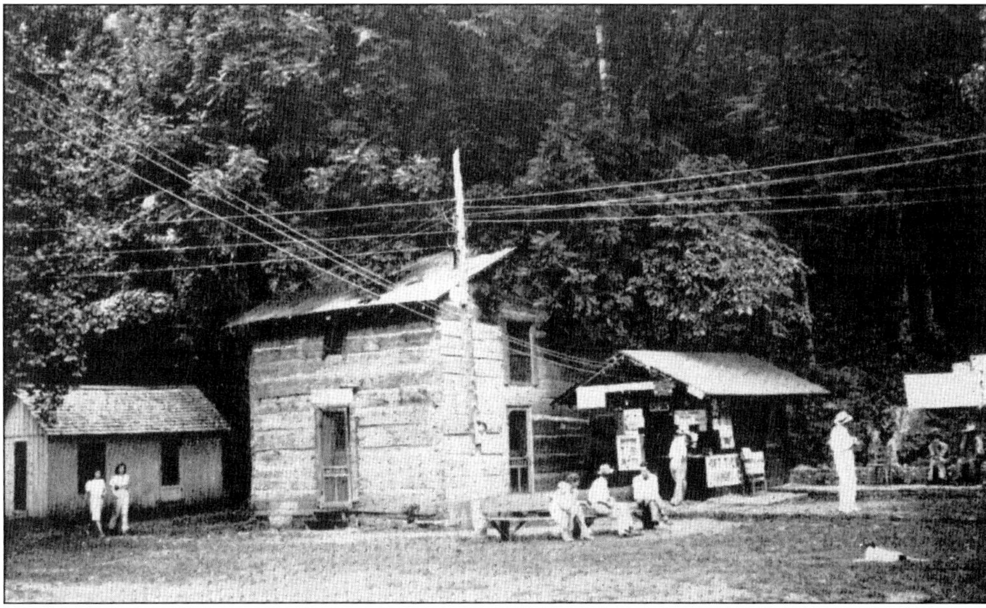

In the 1940s, the century-old cabin of the Hudson family, who discovered and once owned Diamond Cave, was still in use by the operators of the attraction. The cabin had been moved to the site near the cave.

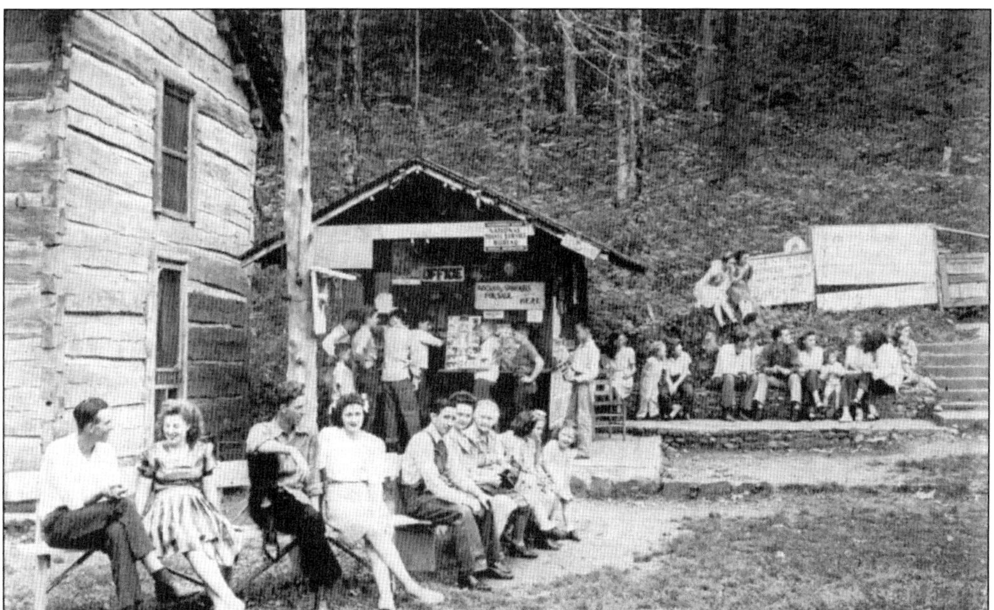

Also around 1950, the ticket office, souvenir, and refreshment stand was located next to the old Hudson log cabin, down the slope from the Diamond Cave entrance. According to the back of the postcard, the cave was open year-round and offered tours at 7:00 and 10:00 a.m. and 1:00, 4:00, and 7:00 p.m.

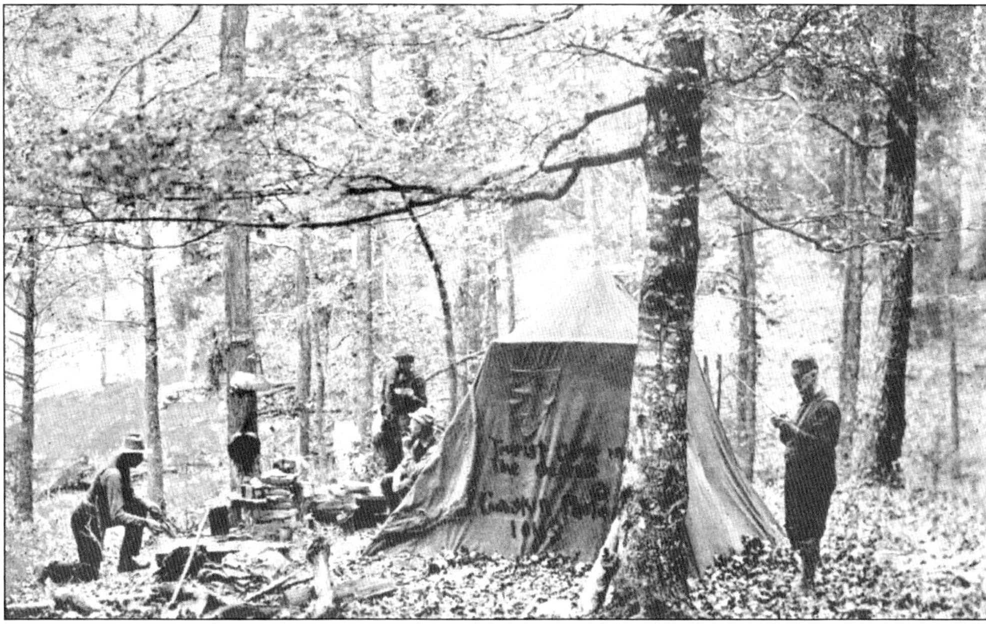

In 1939, a visitor mailed a postcard of one of the rented campsites along Henson Creek near Diamond Cave. The man on the left was cooking on the campfire, while the man on the far right worked on his fishing tackle.

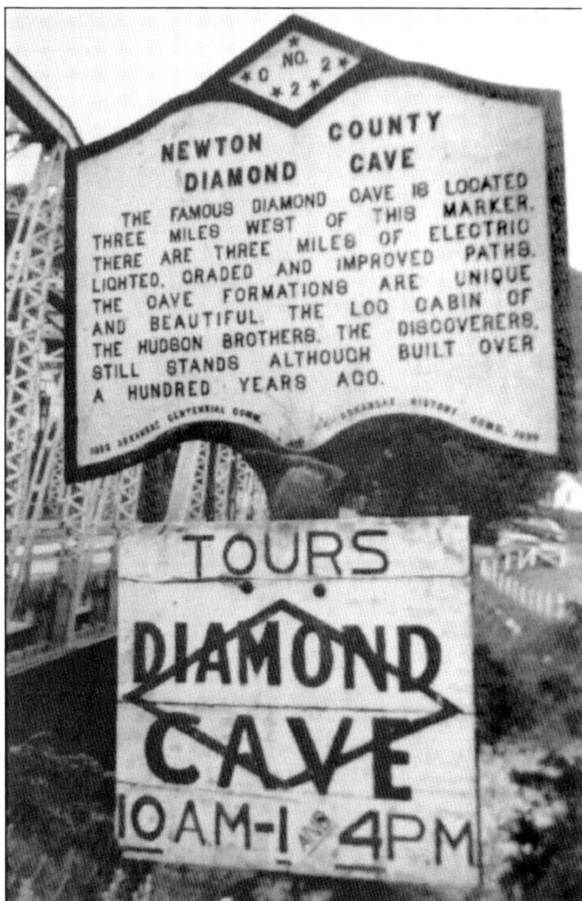

Around 1940, motorists traveling the still unpaved Highway 7 would see Diamond Cave promoted as they crossed the steel bridge spanning the Little Buffalo River on the edge of Jasper. The sign giving the cave story was one of many that had been erected around the state during Arkansas's centennial year of 1936.

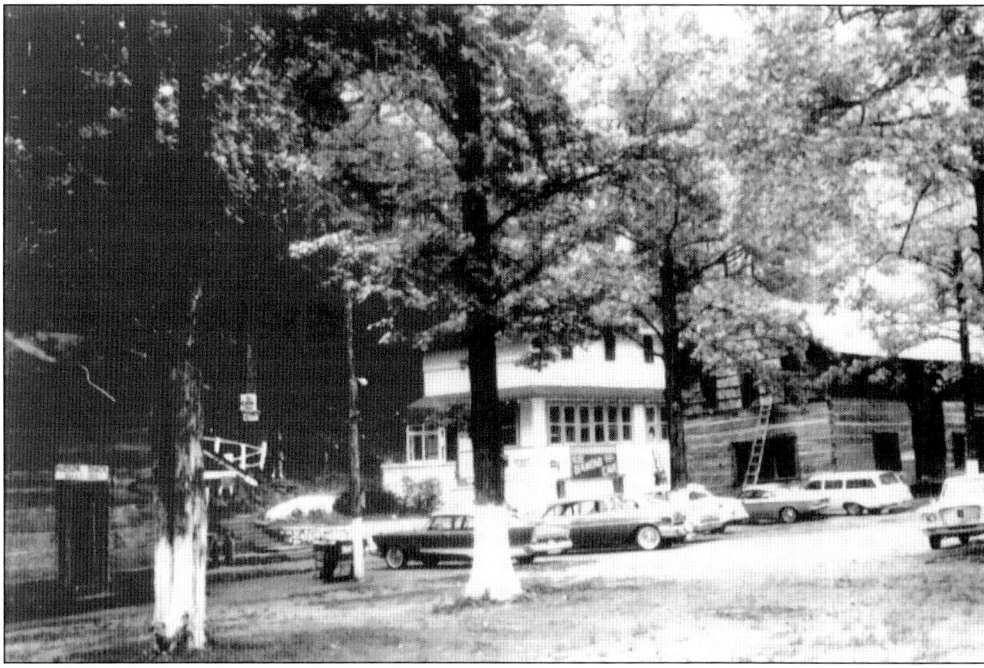

In the 1950s, tourists often stayed in a rustic log hotel at the foot of the slope leading up to the cave; the prominent advertising on Highway 7 perhaps drew some. The site also offered a skating rink, an antique museum, and free camping. (NCHS.)

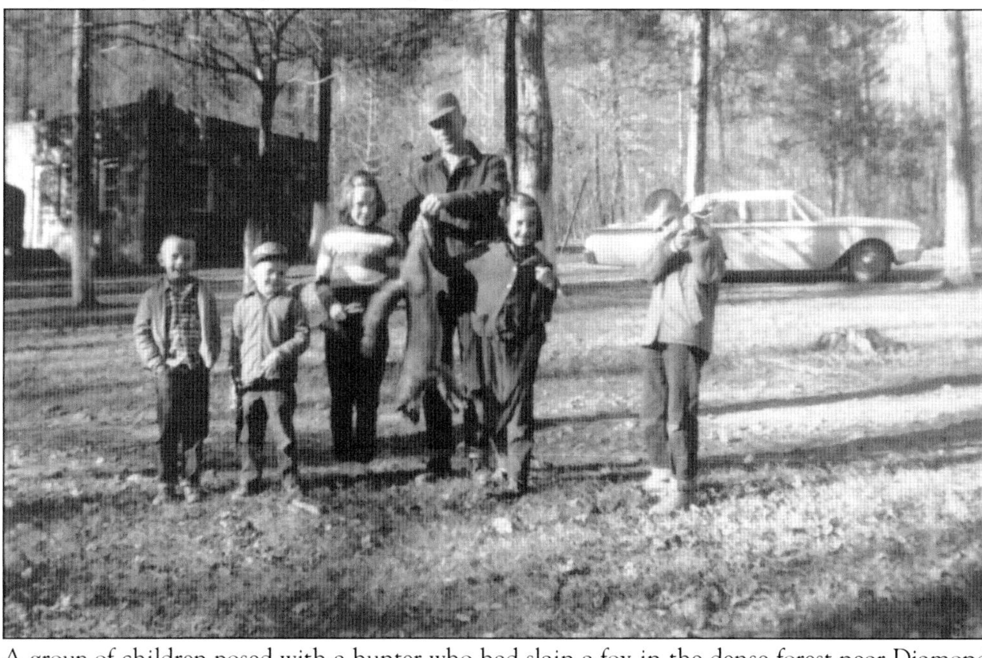

A group of children posed with a hunter who had slain a fox in the dense forest near Diamond Cave, around 1960. The names of the children penciled on the photograph were Kirby Carlton, Gayla Kilgore, Berlin Carlton, Patty Durham, and Randy Kilgore. Diamond Cave closed as a public attraction in the 1990s. However, in 2010, the authors were afforded a private tour of the still wonderful cave. (NCHS.)

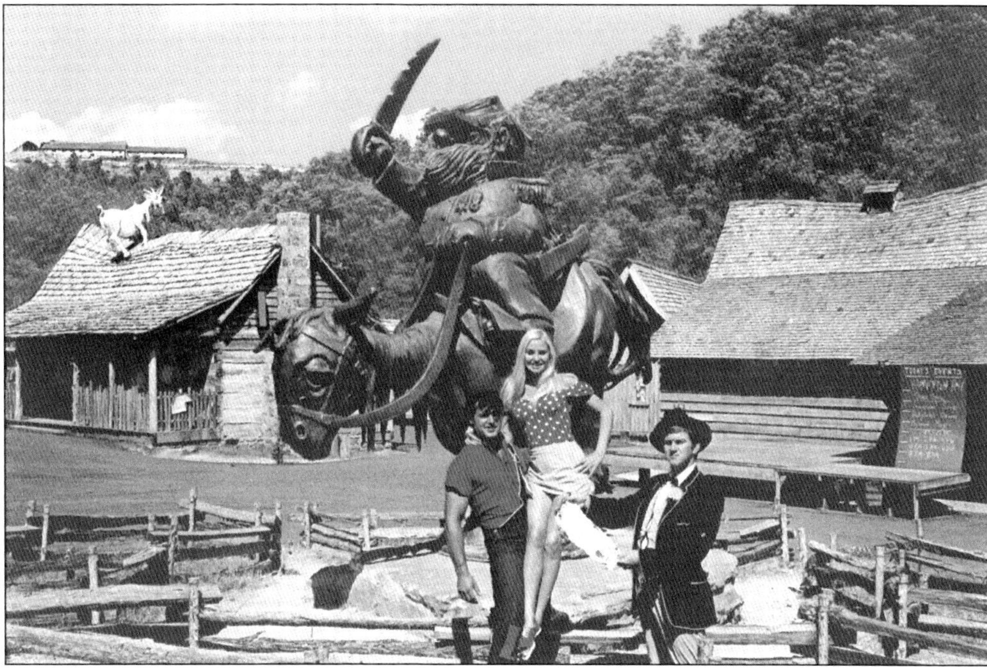

In 1966, the 160 acres surrounding a former Newton County trout farm became a theme park named Dogpatch USA, based on Al Capp's long-running "hillbilly" comic strip. Backed with investment by Capp, the stated goal was to build a theme park to rival Disneyland. At a cost of some $1.3 million, the park opened in May 1968 to a crowd of 8,000 paying the $1.50 adult admission, 75¢ for children. Projections were that annual attendance would top a million within a decade as people flocked to see Li'l Abner, Daisy Mae, Marryin' Sam (seen here), and the other residents of the fictional town made famous in the comics.

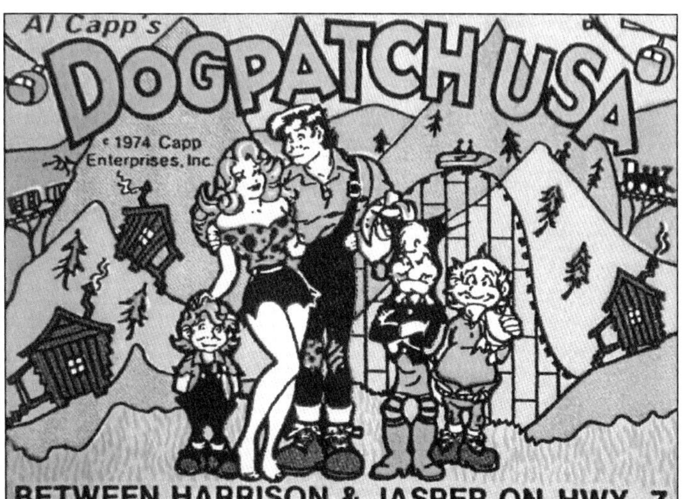

Al Capp chose the name Dogpatch as the fictional setting for the "Li'l Abner" comic strip in 1934. It was populated with characters like Honest Abe Yokum, Li'l Abner, Daisy Mae, and Mammy and Papa Yokum. The strip would run for 43 years, until 1977. Capp had refused offers over the years to lend his creations to a tourist attraction but was drawn to the idea in Newton County; he invested and became a partner in the venture.

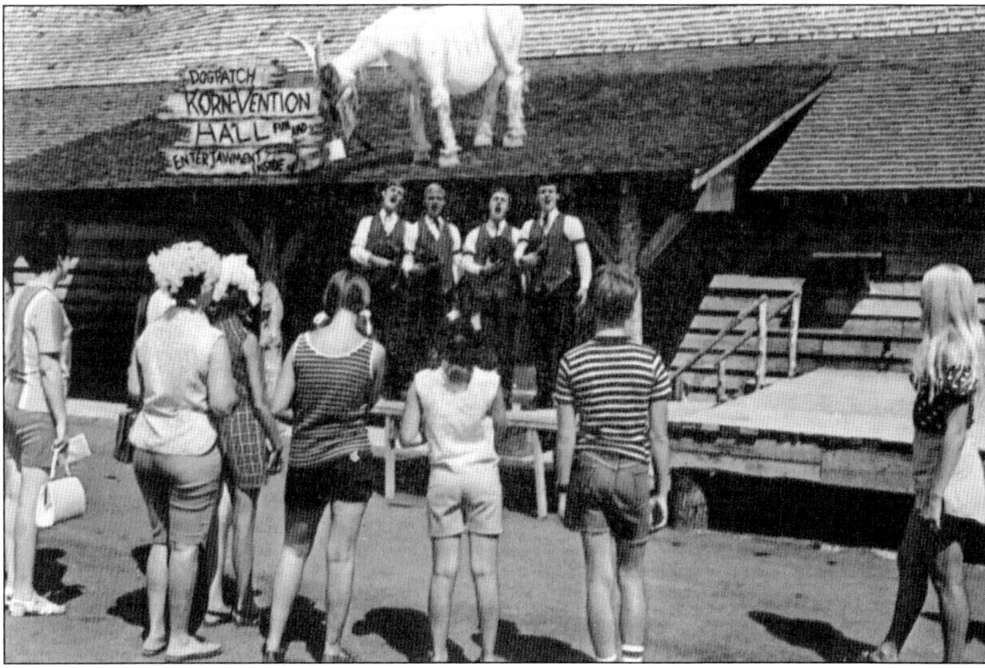

Arkansans, long sensitive to its "hillbilly" image, had reservations about Dogpatch. Still, in the early years, crowds came for the train rides, horseback trips, arts and crafts, and family-oriented theatrical productions. Part of the musical entertainment was set in front of the "KORN-VENTION HALL," with a billy goat on the roof behind a barbershop quartet.

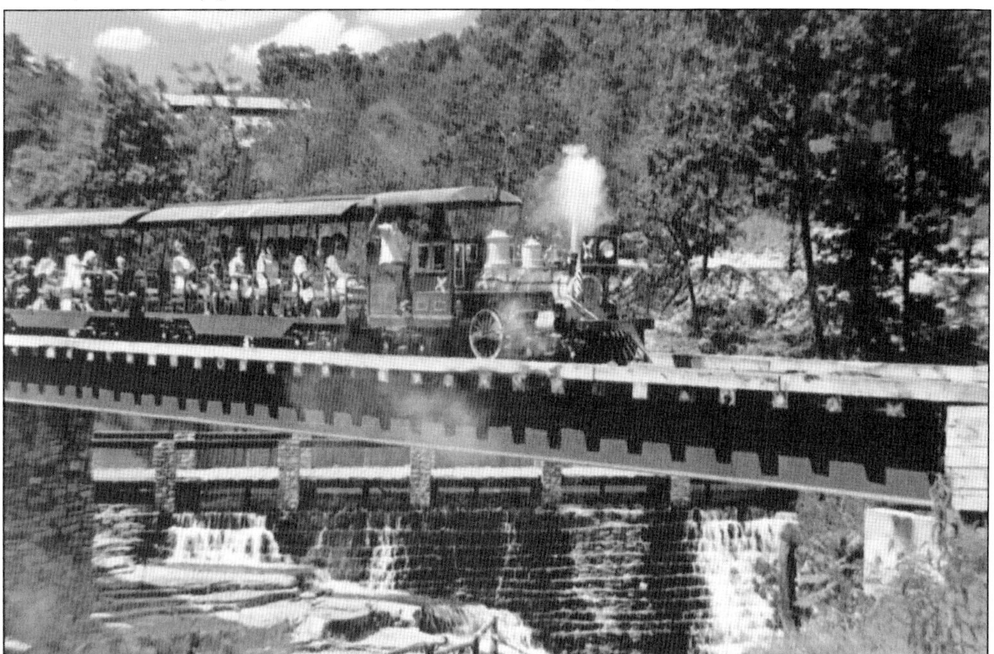

One of the most popular attractions at Dogpatch was the "West Po'k Chop Speshul" railroad around the park. Visible at the top left above the park, a "winter resort" opened with a convention center, ice-skating, and a ski slope that used man-made snow.

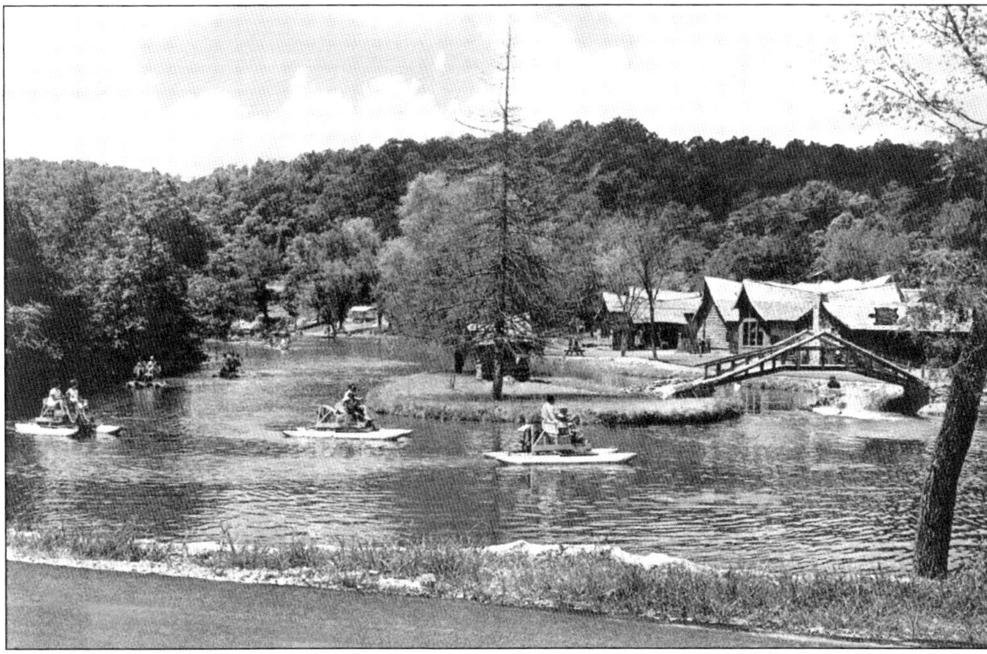

A popular attraction, especially in the heat of a Dogpatch summer, was riding paddle boats around the spring-fed lake, past original log cabins the builders had moved in from Ozark locations and reassembled.

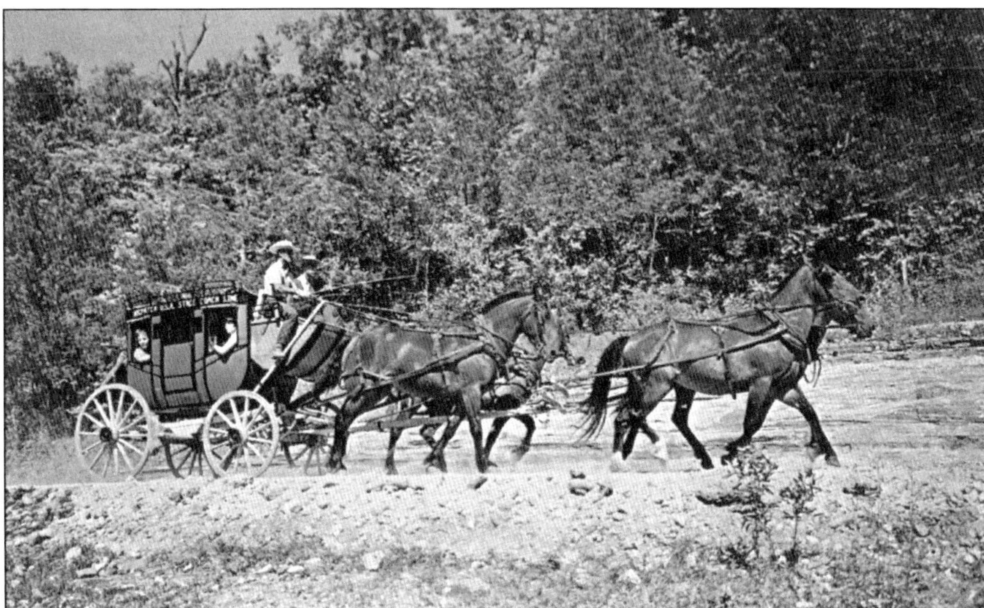

Dogpatch visitors also had a chance to ride a stagecoach through Skunk Hollow. Despite grand opening hoopla, park attendance did not meet expectations in the first year. The principal owner, businessman Jess Odum, hired former Arkansas governor Orval Faubus as general manager for the 1969 season. The well-known former governor was said to have remarked that running the hillbilly-themed park was very similar to running the State of Arkansas, which he had done from 1954 to 1966.

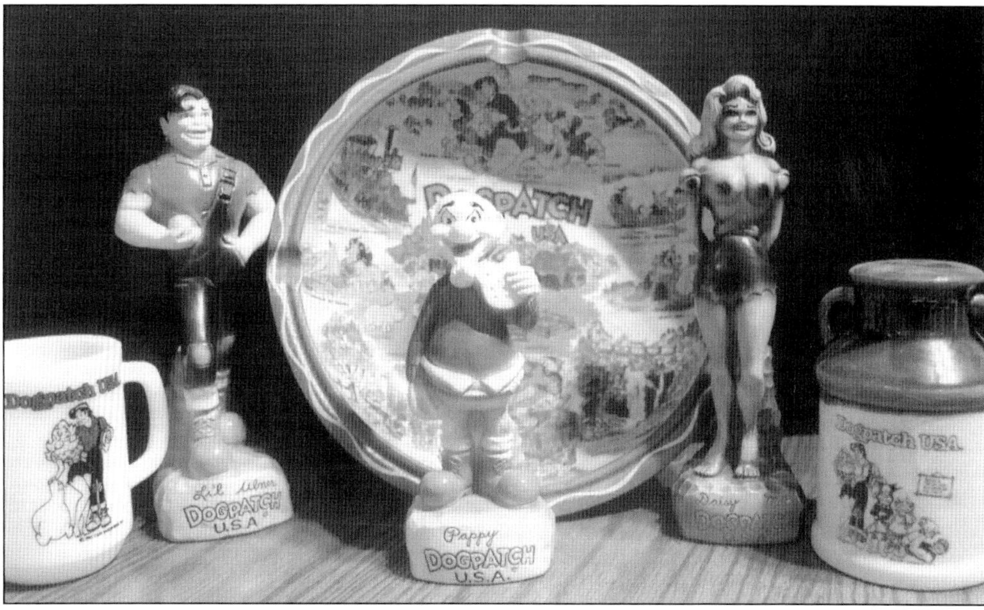

Visitors to Dogpatch could come home with a variety of souvenirs to remind them of their visit to the theme park. These included figurines of characters like Li'l Abner, Pappy, and the voluptuous Daisy Mae, as well as coffee cups, ashtrays, and postcards.

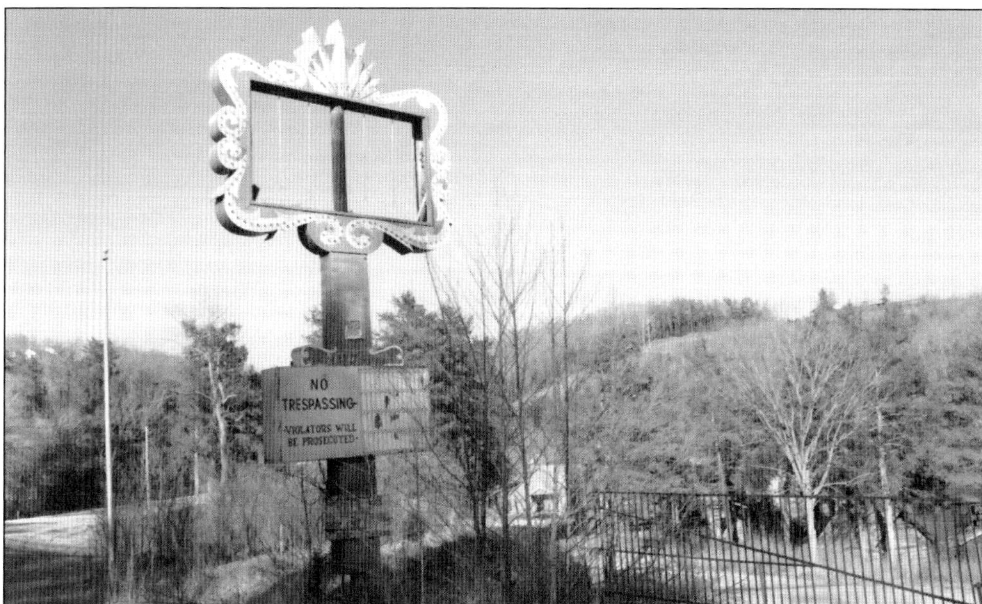

By the mid-1970s, the theme park was beset by debt, declining attendance, and mild winters that closed the ski slopes. Combined with unbeatable competition from the attractions at Branson, Missouri, an hour north, these factors resulted in a death sentence for Dogpatch USA. When the park had first opened, attendance had been projected to rise to 1.2 million by 1977. However, the numbers never topped 200,000 after 1968; after a series of failed ownership changes, the park closed in 1993. Today, it is a decaying ruin off Highway 7 north of Jasper, with its once-welcoming sign now a shell holding a "no trespassing" warning.

Eight

Scenic Highway 7

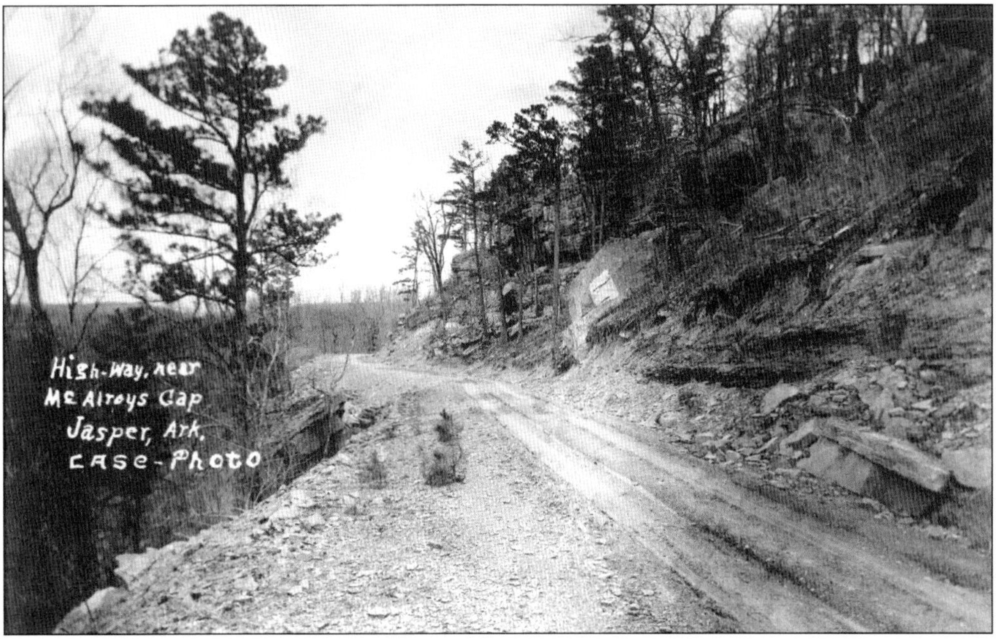

For most of the first half of the 20th century, Highway 7 was primarily a rough dirt road, with occasional sections of gravel surfacing. The section seen above around 1920 passed through McElroy Gap, south of Jasper. The road would be paved in the 1950s, starting with the section between Jasper and Harrison in 1951.

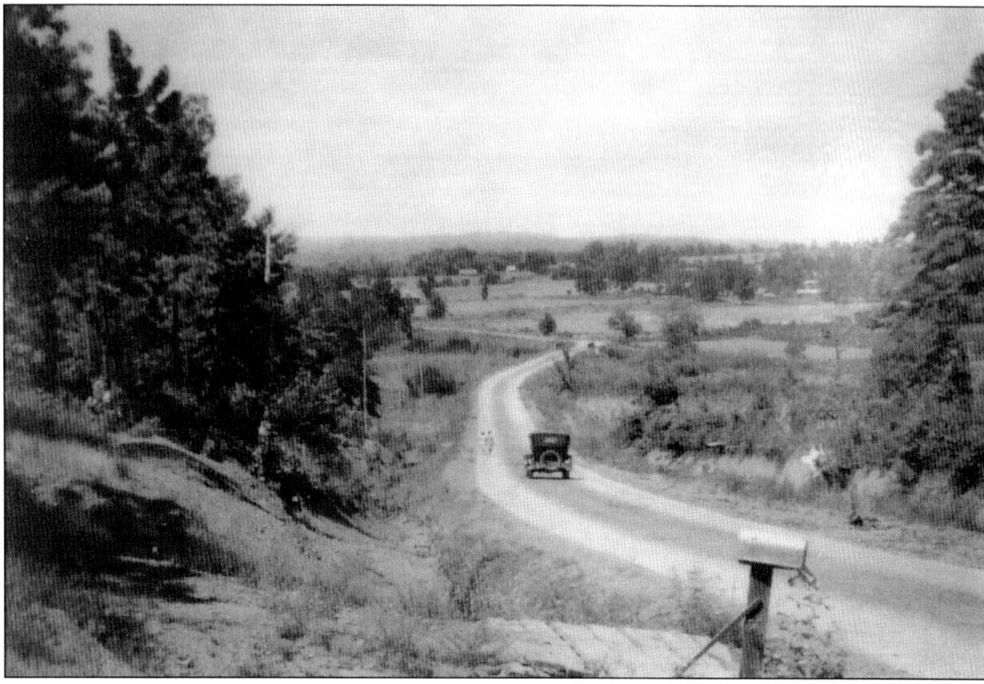

By 1930, the number of automobiles was growing on Highway 7, with the Arkansas Highway Department working to maintain the gravel road to the best of its ability. (Courtesy of the US Forest Service.)

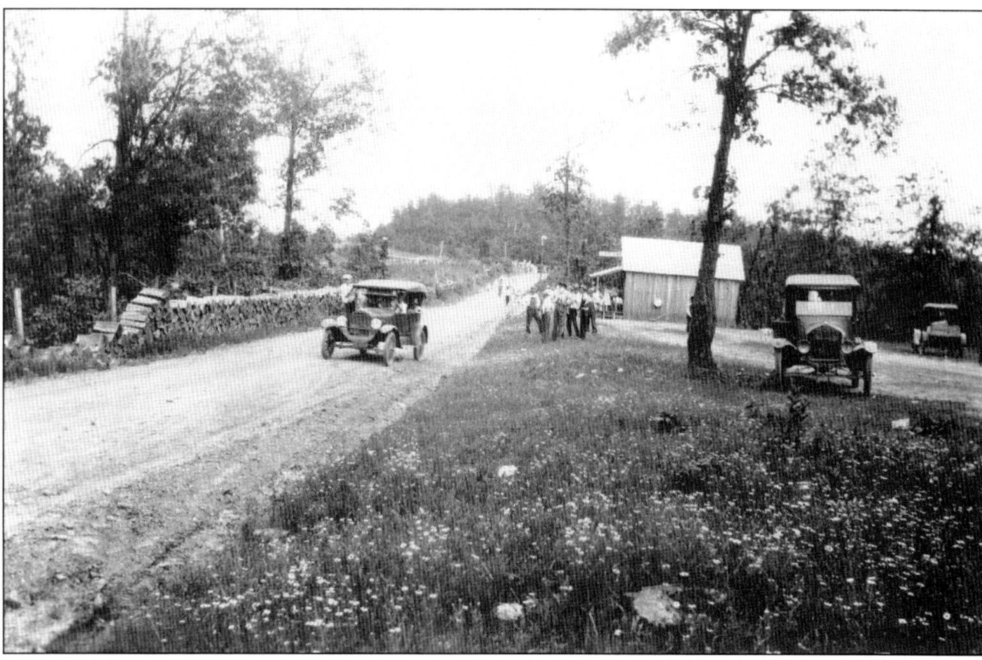

Twenty miles south of Jasper, Highway 7 passed through the tiny community of Cowell, seen here in 1921. Three Model T cars were captured by the camera, while a huge supply of firewood and the community grocery store stand in the distance. Today, motorists zip by the city limit signs on paved Highway 7 without any need to slow down.

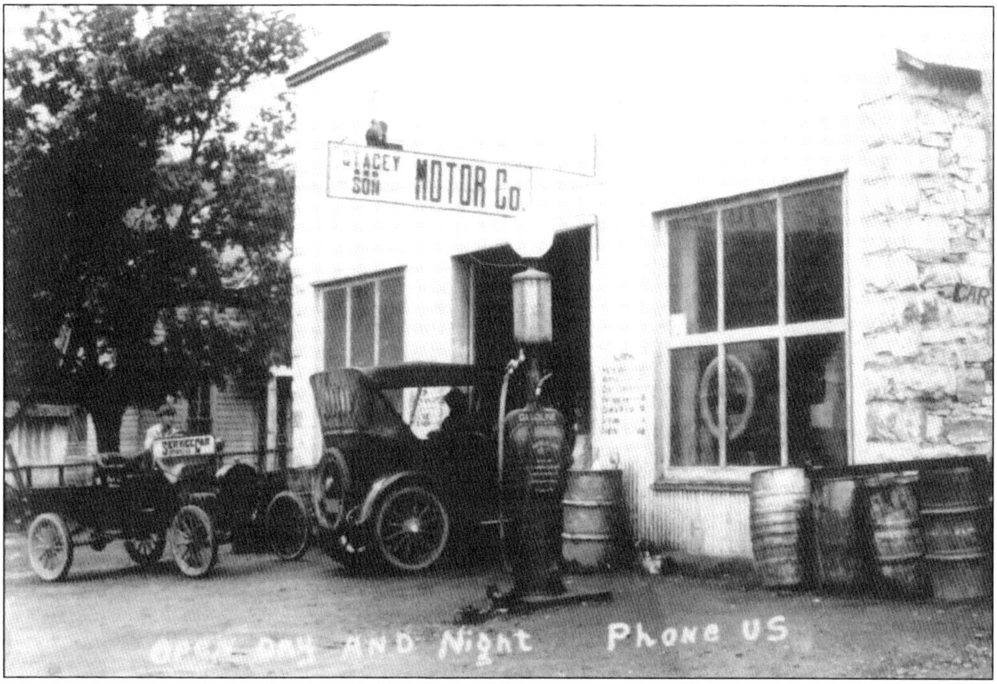

Motorists with repair needs, or perhaps someone shopping for an automobile, would have pulled into Stacey and Son Motor Company in Jasper, seen here around 1918. A gas pump is mounted in the foreground; the average price of gasoline was 8¢ per gallon at the time. (NCL.)

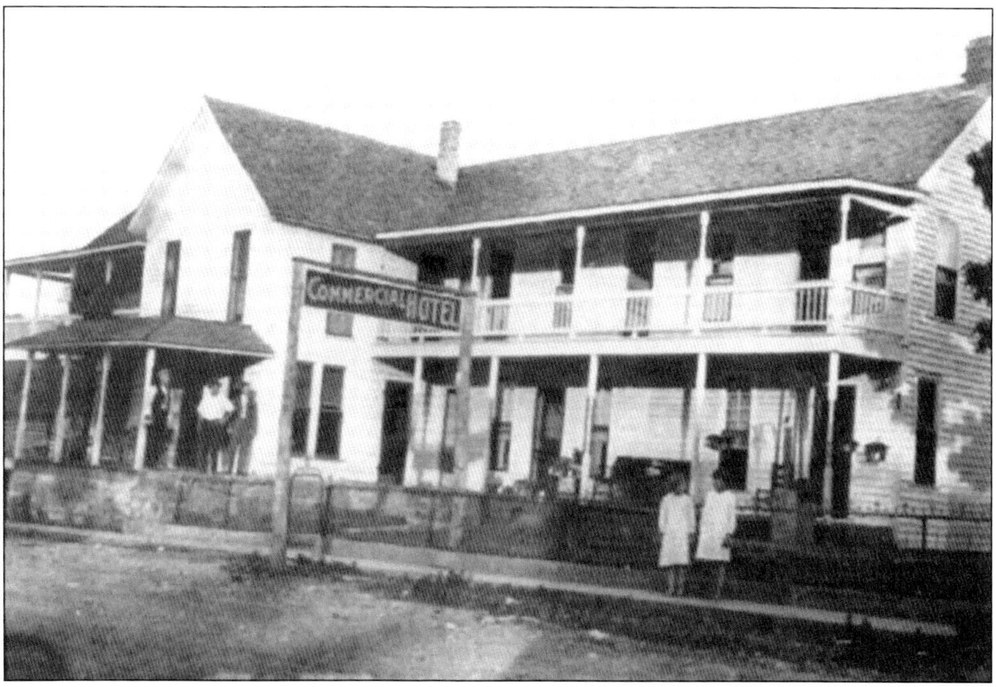

Motorists who drove through Cowell in the 1920s and decided to stop overnight upon reaching Jasper might well have stopped at the Commercial Hotel on the northeast side of the county seat. The hotel had 17 rooms and was a prominent landmark for some 50 years.

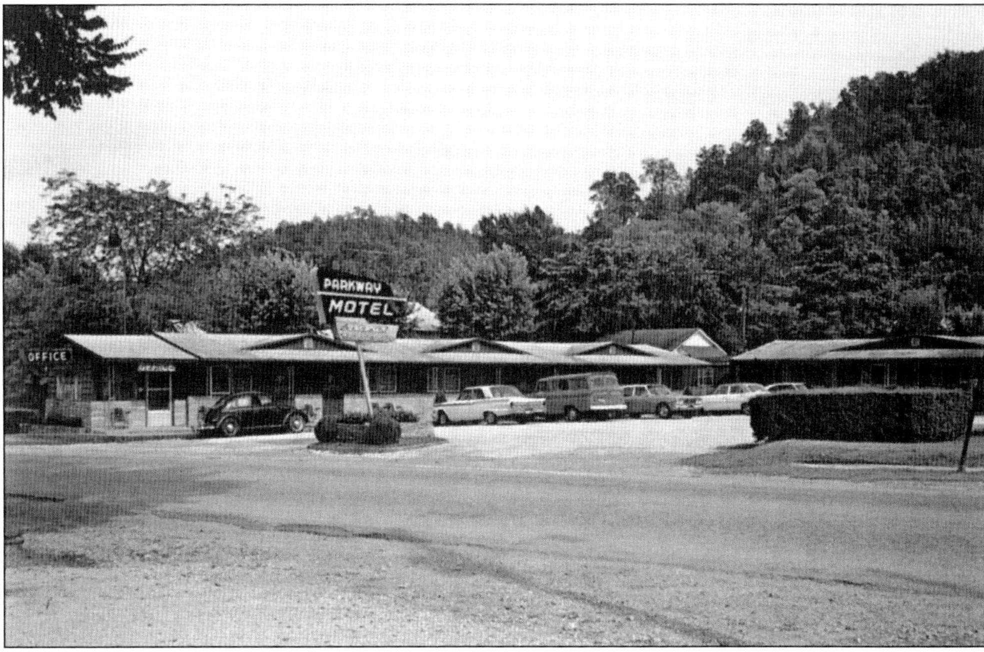

By the time Highway 7 was paved in the late 1950s, the Commercial Hotel was gone. It was torn down in 1956, and the site became home to the Parkway Motel, which still offers lodging to Jasper visitors. (NCL.)

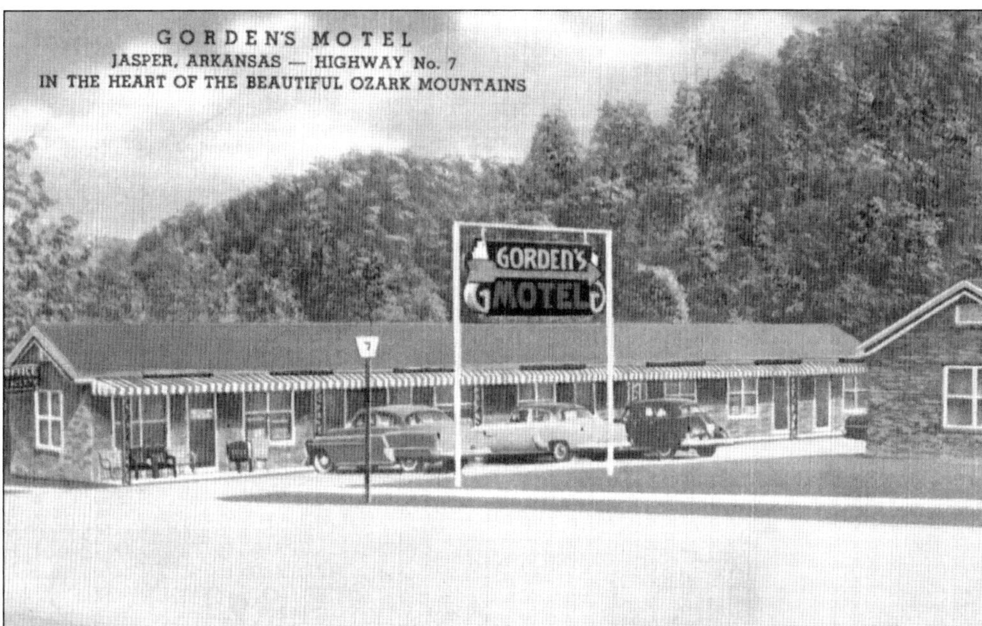

The Parkway competed for guests with its neighbor, Gorden's Motel, which is also still in business in 2012. Gorden's advertised the following: "Tile Baths, Panel Ray Heat, Box Springs & Inner Springs Mattresses. 'Cleanliness' is our motto."

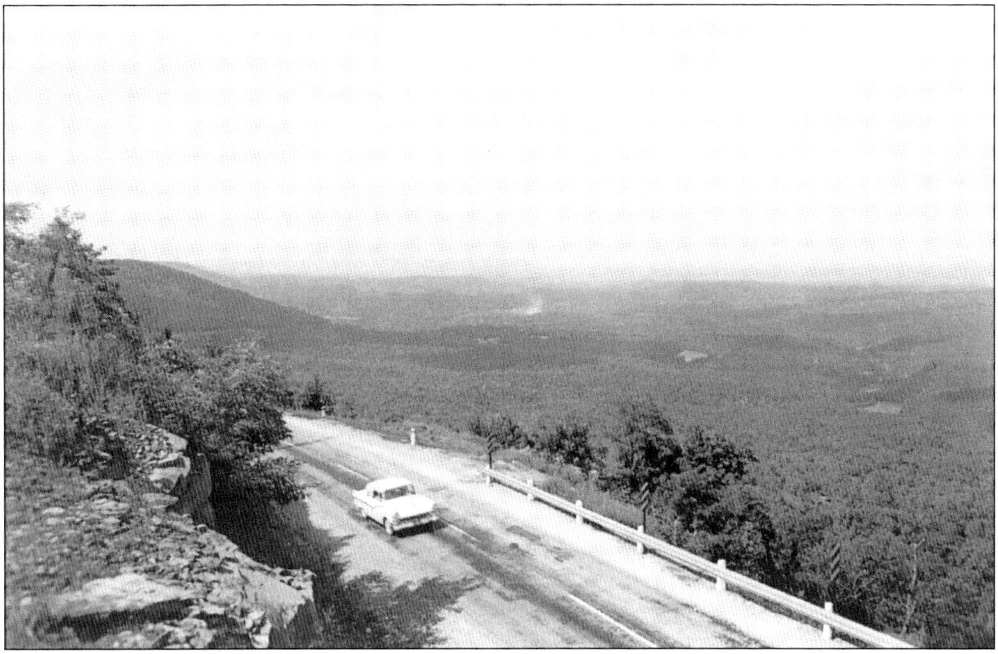

Motorists drawn from across the nation to follow the path of Highway 7 were treated to views of Arkansas's "Grand Canyon" a few miles south of Jasper, as seen here around 1960.

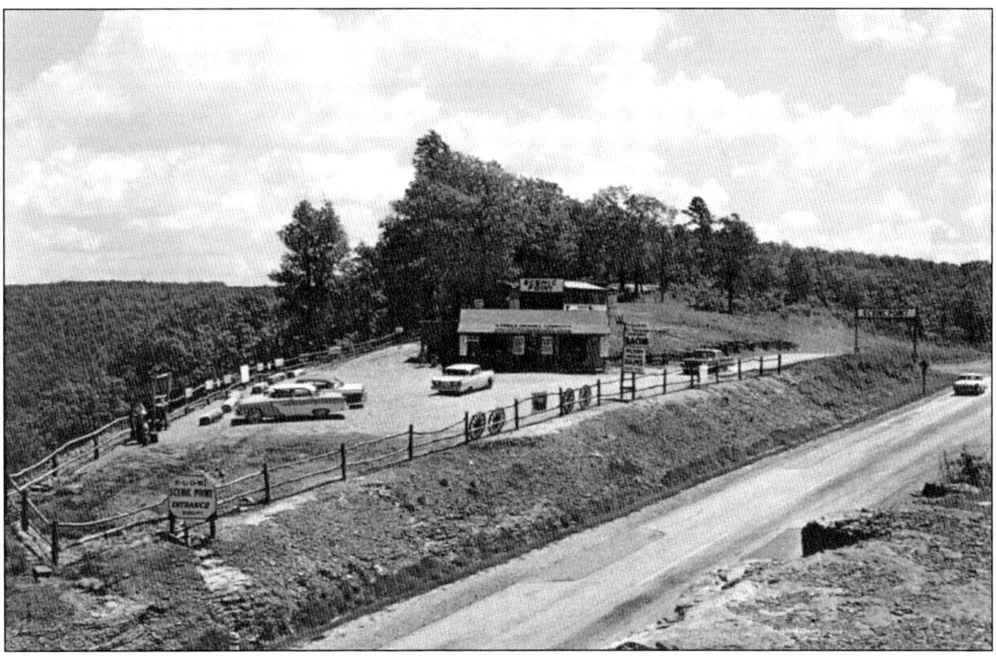

Views of the Buffalo River Valley could be observed with more leisure from Scenic Point, located on Sloan Mountain south of Jasper. The panoramic views are still enjoyed today from the same business, which would later add an observation tower to further entice visitors off Highway 7 to stop and perhaps shop for a souvenir.

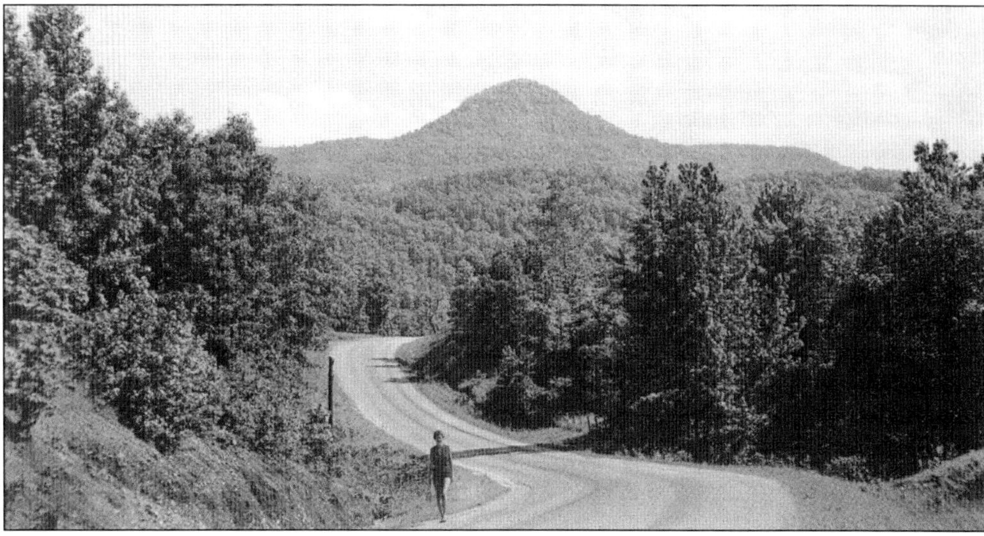

One of the most notable features on Highway 7 south of Jasper is Round Top Mountain, which was the scene of a tragedy on a foggy winter night in 1948. An Army B-25 Mitchell bomber, en route from Wright Field, Ohio, to Little Rock, crashed near the top of the mountain; the five servicemen aboard, all in their 20s, were killed instantly. Today, a hiking trail circles the top of the mountain, with a side trail to the site where part of the plane's wreckage still lays, along with a plaque honoring the men who died.

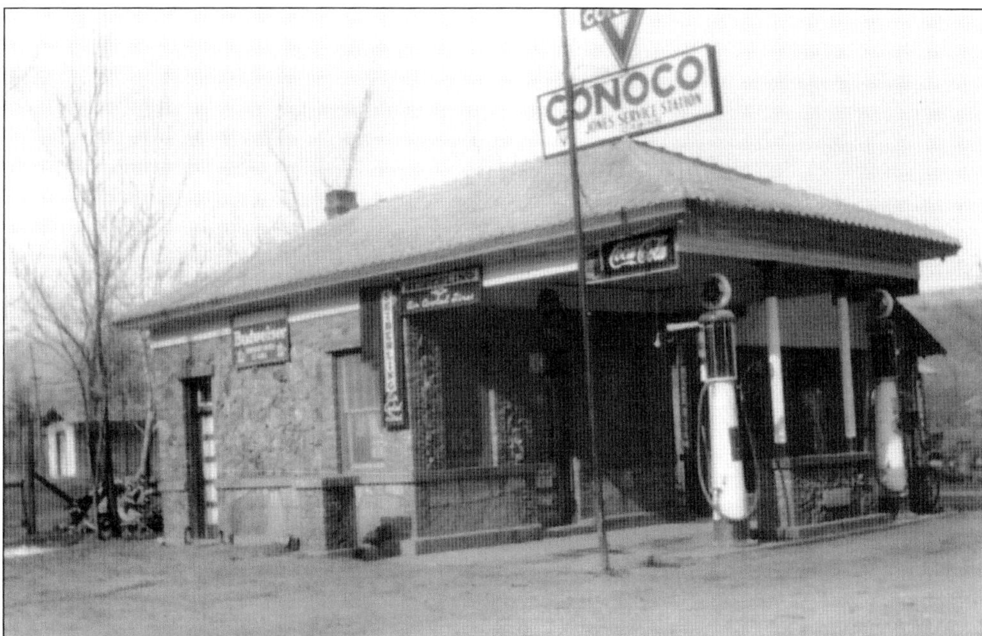

Jones Service Station, located on the southern edge of Jasper on the west side of Highway 7, was housed in a building erected by Gould Jones, a builder who left his mark all over town. When he erected the service station he gave it something no building in Jasper had, which is a tile roof. Seen here around 1940, a Budweiser beer sign was posted on the end of the building, evidence that Newton County was "wet" at the time. The average price of a gallon of gas in 1940 was 18¢. (NCL.)

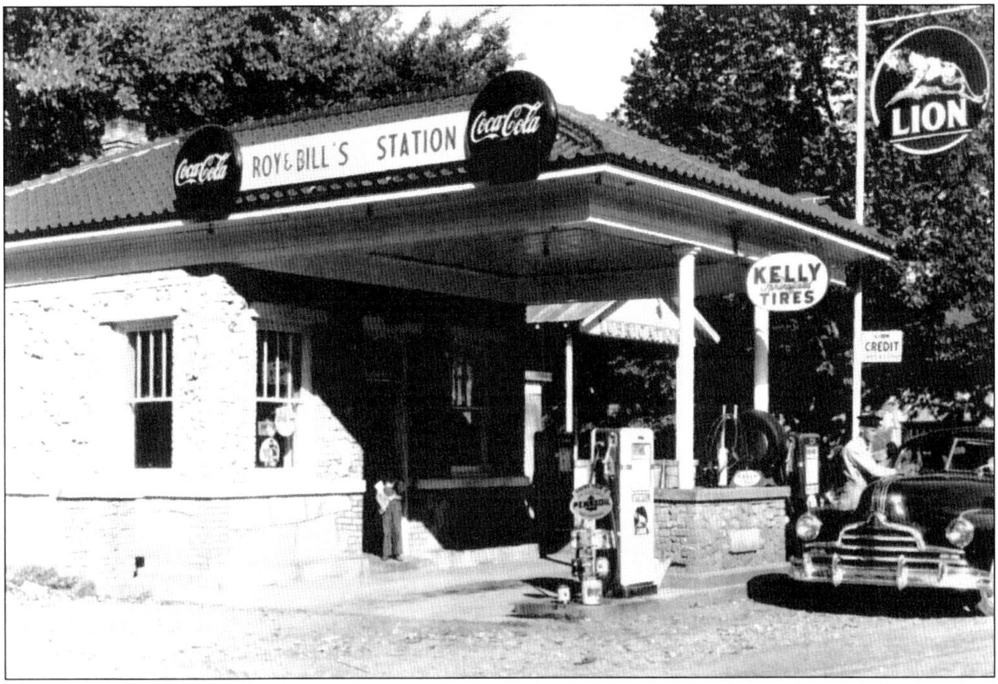

By 1950, what had been Jones Service Station was now Roy & Bill's, its sign anchored by twin Coca-Cola emblems. In 1950, the average cost of a gallon of gas was 27¢. If this was too expensive for one's cash resources, the purchase could be charged on a Lion Oil credit card, according to a sign hanging over the attendant who is busy cleaning the car's windshield. (NCL.)

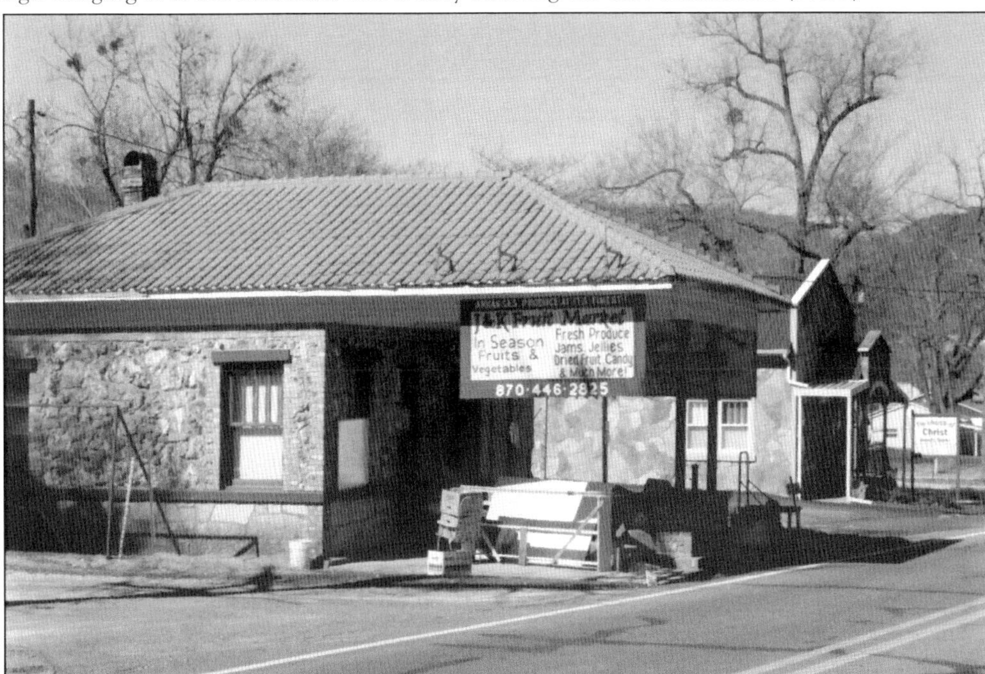

Today, no gas is pumped at what was for many years a service station. The historic building has more recently been home to a fruit market, among other uses. (Photograph by Ray Hanley.)

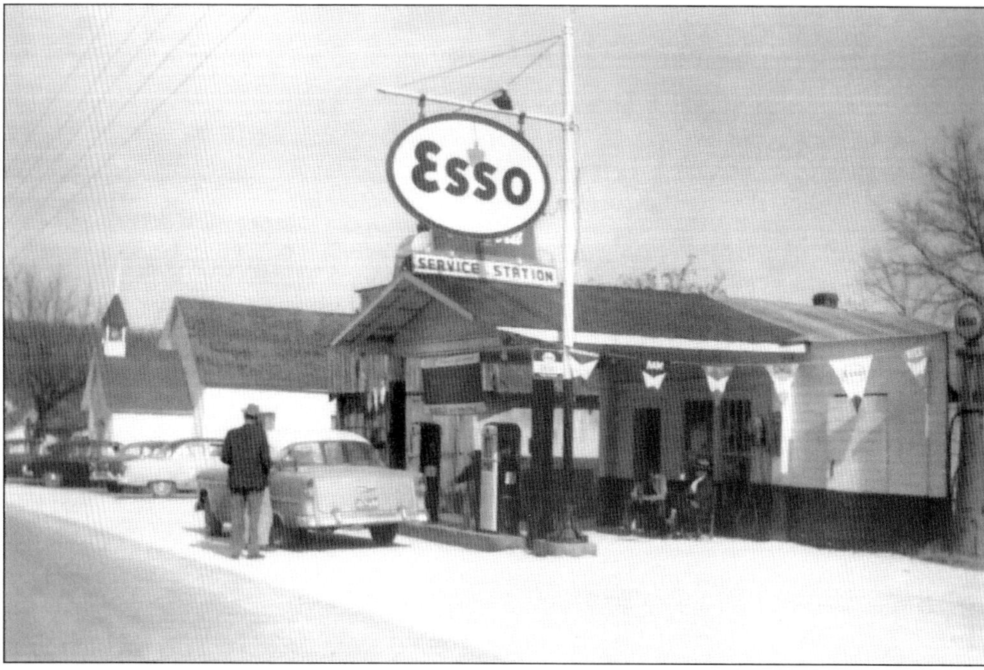

In the 1950s, Roy & Bill's Lion station competed with the Esso station just across the road on the east side of Highway 7 South. The photograph was likely taken on a Sunday morning, based on the full parking lot at the Christian church next-door. (NCL.)

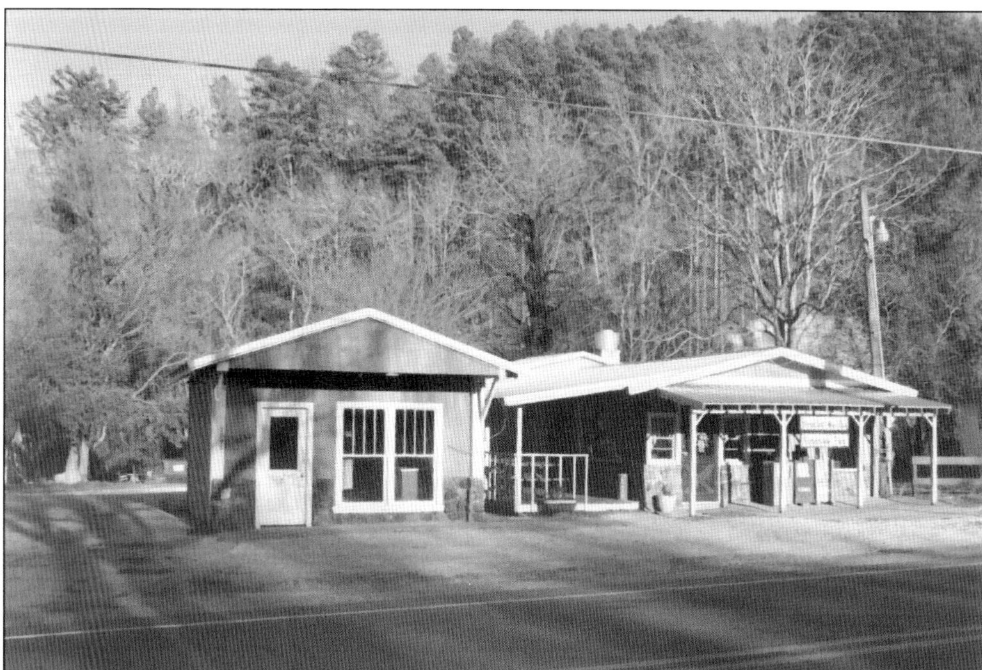

The Esso station is no longer in service, but the building still stands, adjoining Sharon K's Cafe.

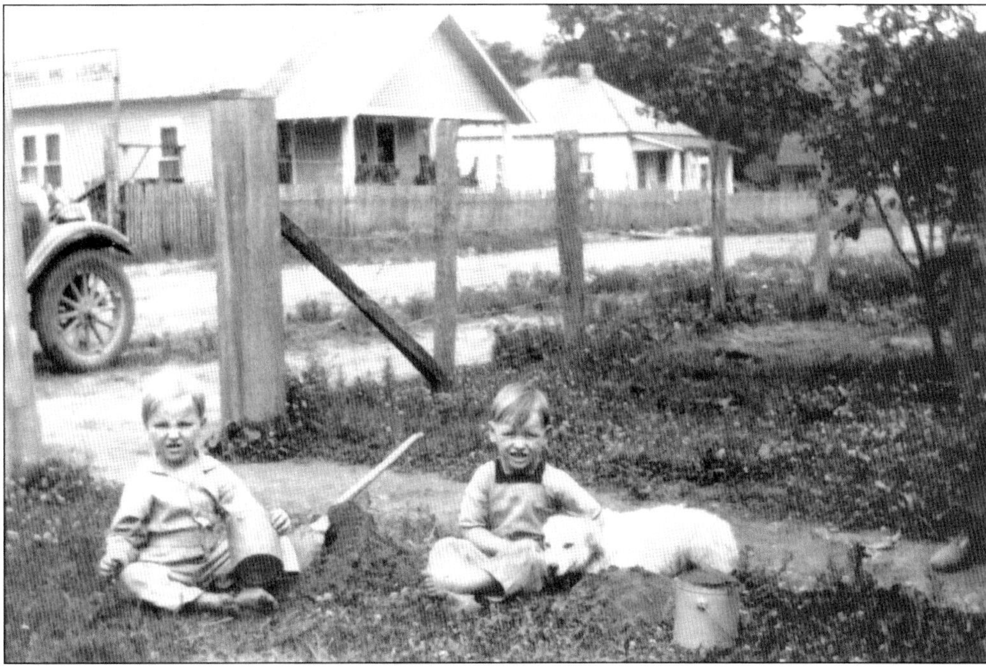

During the 1930s, Jim and Melvin Williard, along with their dog Pinto, spent a lot of time playing in their yard beside the dusty path of Highway 7 on the south side of Jasper. The sign in the upper left corner, across the road, was for a boardinghouse hoping to lure travelers.

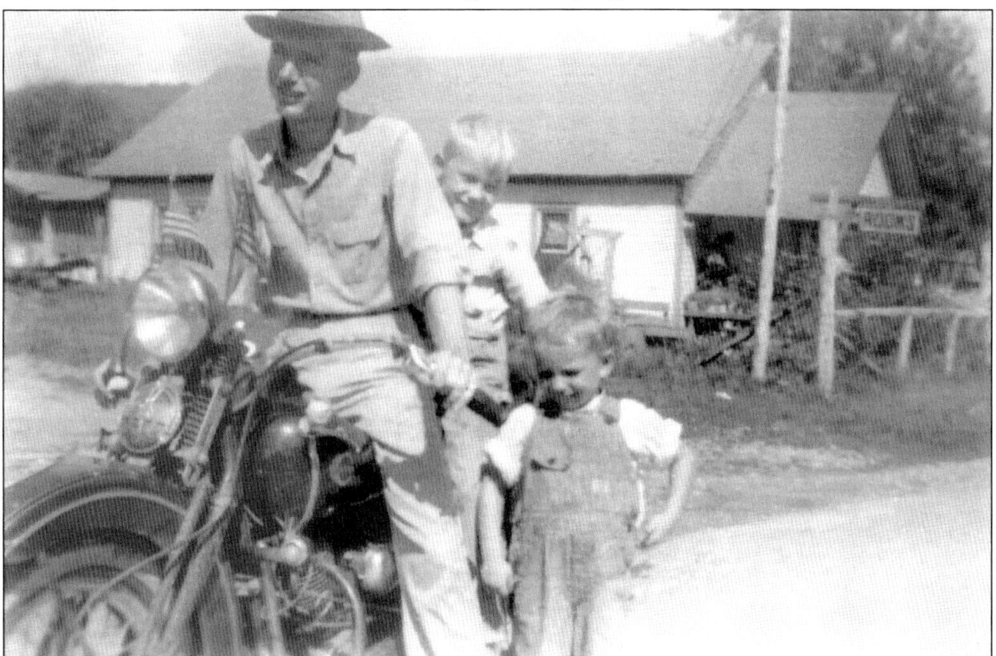

Today, thousands of motorcycle riders come to Newton County to ride twisting Highway 7 and the other mountain roads in the area. Although much more common today, motorcycles are not new to Jasper. Sitting beside Highway 7 on the south side of Jasper in the 1940s was Jerry Dean Vaughan, posing with two children eager for a ride. (NCL.)

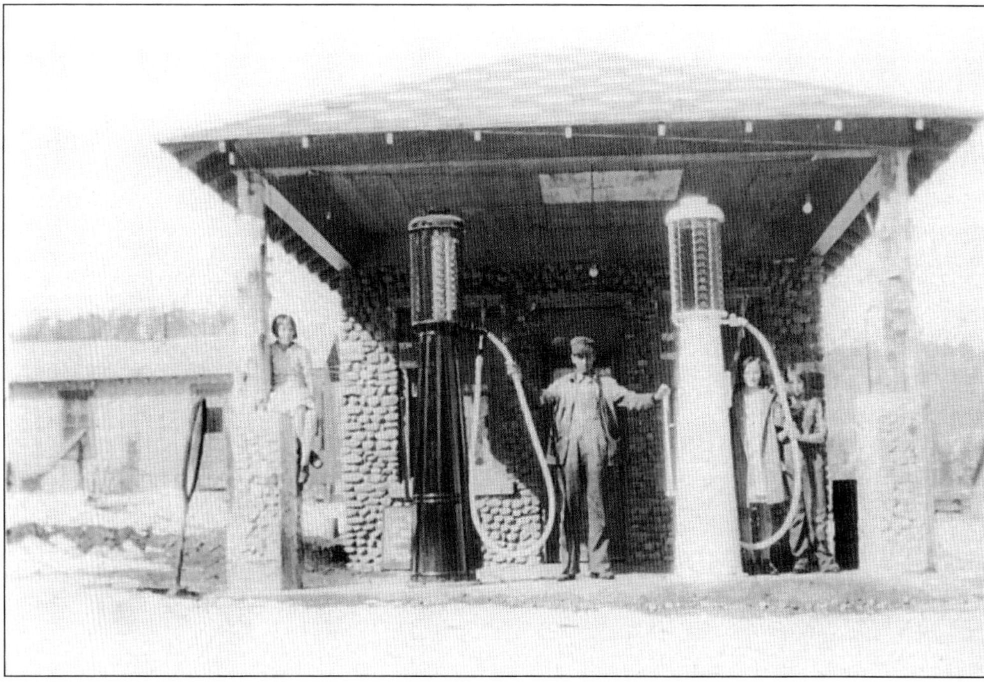

A motorist who bypassed the two gas stations on the south side of Jasper might have filled up at another station, also built by Gould Jones, on the north side of town. The station, with its twin gravity-fed pumps, is seen here in the 1930s. (NCL.)

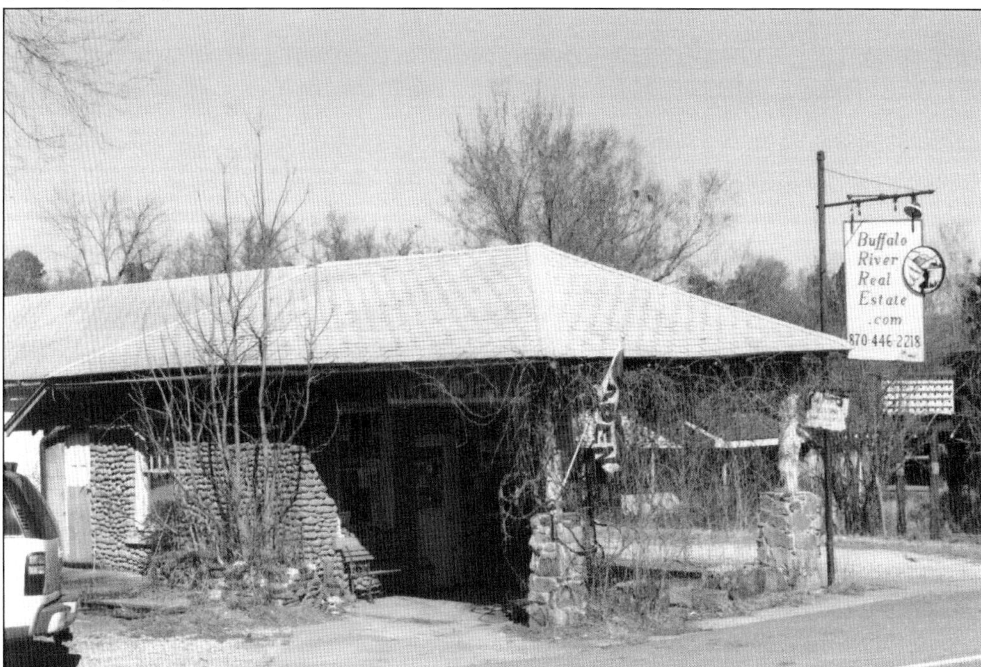

The gas pumps are gone, and the cobblestones are painted gray, but the former gas station still stands on the edge of Highway 7 on the north edge of Jasper. It houses a real estate office today. (Photograph by Ray Hanley.)

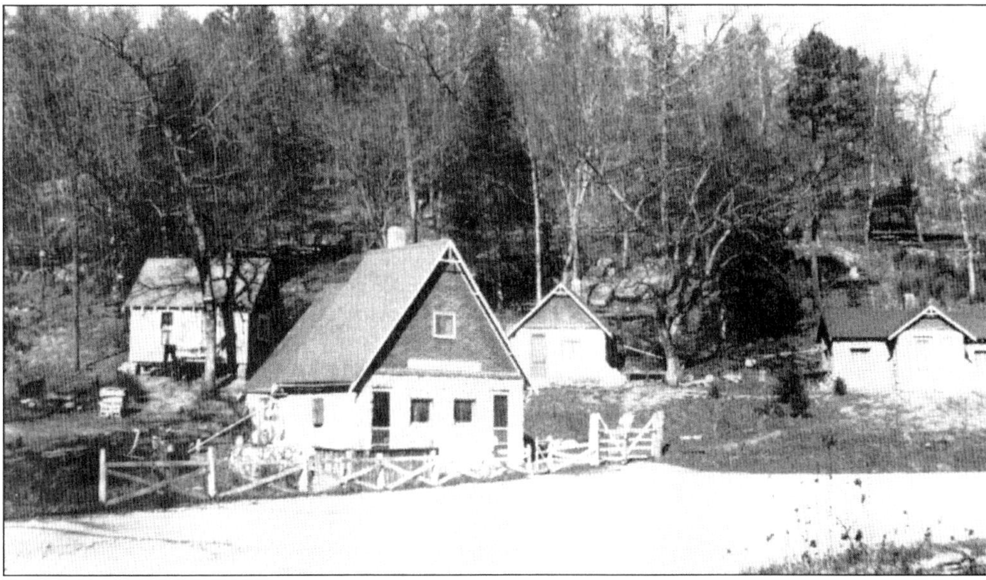

Travelers on Highway 7 north of Jasper looking for a unique lodging experience might have checked into one of the cabins at Little Switzerland. The business has anchored a curve in the highway between Jasper and Pruitt for decades and is still popular today with visiting tourists.

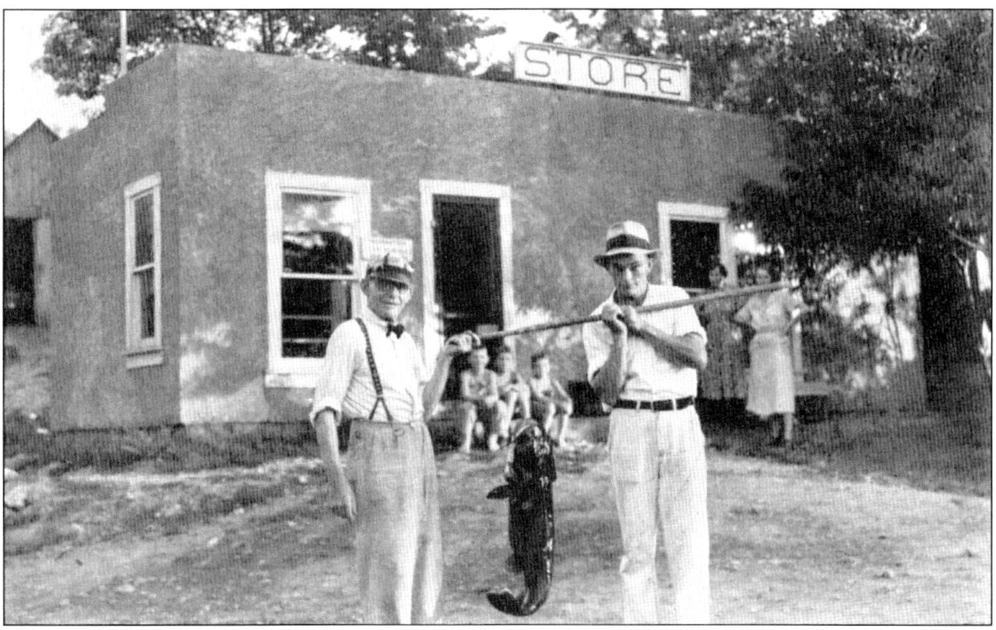

Highway 7 travelers looking for a more rustic outdoor experience might have passed Little Switzerland to check out F.A. Hammon's Shady Grove Camp, beside the Buffalo River Bridge at Pruitt. Within the camp was the grocery store, which served as the backdrop to a freshly caught 20-pound catfish.

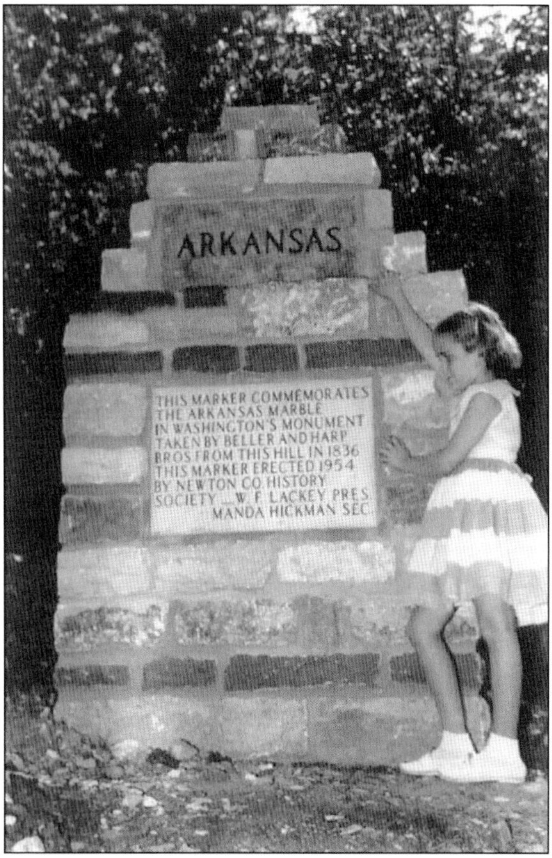

Traveling on Highway 7 south of the Newton and Boone County line, motorists today often speed by a historic monument that was erected next to the road in 1954. Young Mavis Upton posed with the new monument, which denotes that a block of Arkansas marble was quarried nearby about 1836. Shipped by oxcart and then by riverboat, that block of marble was the contribution of the new State of Arkansas to the Washington Monument in Washington DC. (NCL.)

The Arkansas stone contributed to the Washington Monument is visible within the structure, as seen here, likely photographed in the 1960s. The woman pointing is Lillian Rea of Bakersfield, California; she was a great-great-granddaughter of Elijah Bohannon Harp Sr., who helped quarry the stone back in Newton County in the 1830s. (NCHS.)

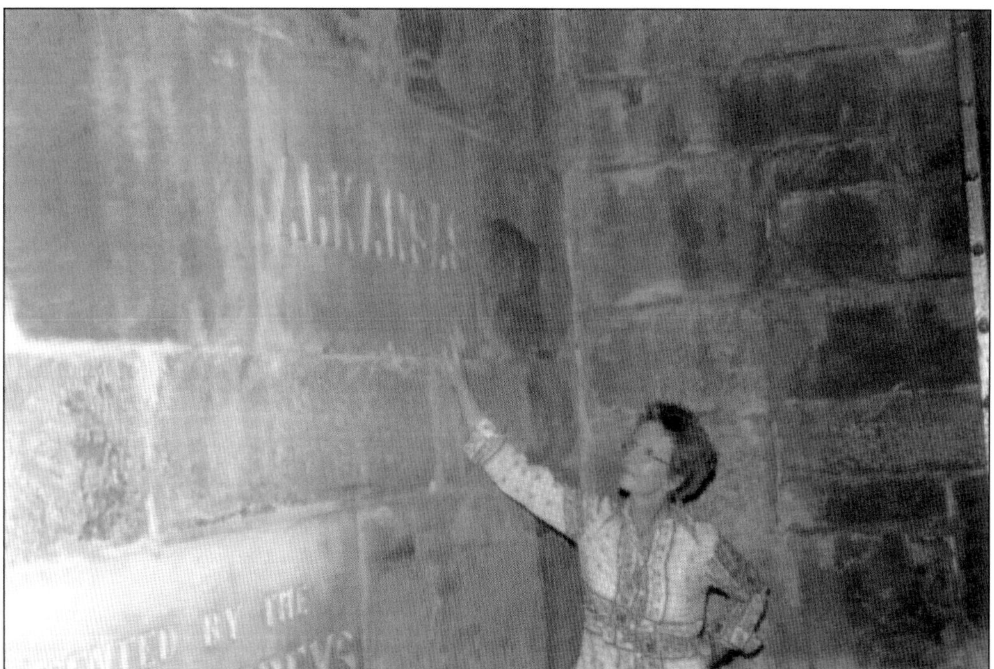

Nine

Faces of Newton County

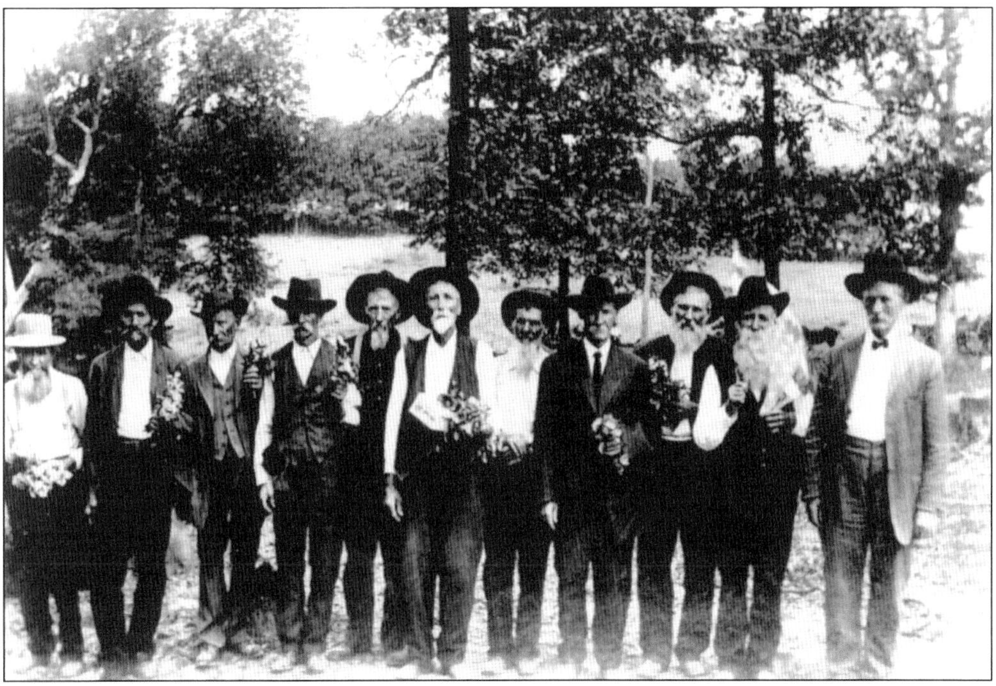

The Civil War started a thousand miles east of Newton County, but the conflict found its way to the remote region. Jasper was burned to the ground during the war in a conflict that saw both sides seeking the nearby ore needed for gunpowder and lead for bullets. In 1910, on Decoration Day, a group of veterans of both sides gathered near Gaither around the Newton and Boone County lines for a reunion to swap memories of the conflict half a century removed from the battles. From left to right are Henry Dart (Union), James K. Polk Jones (Confederate), William Clark (Confederate), Halsford "Tuck" Ratcliff (Confederate), Vach Hickman (Union), Rufus Cone (Confederate), Marion Long (Union), Pete Cook (Union), Rev. J.M. Richardson (Confederate), James Wasson (Confederate), and Ben Estes (Confederate). (NCL.)

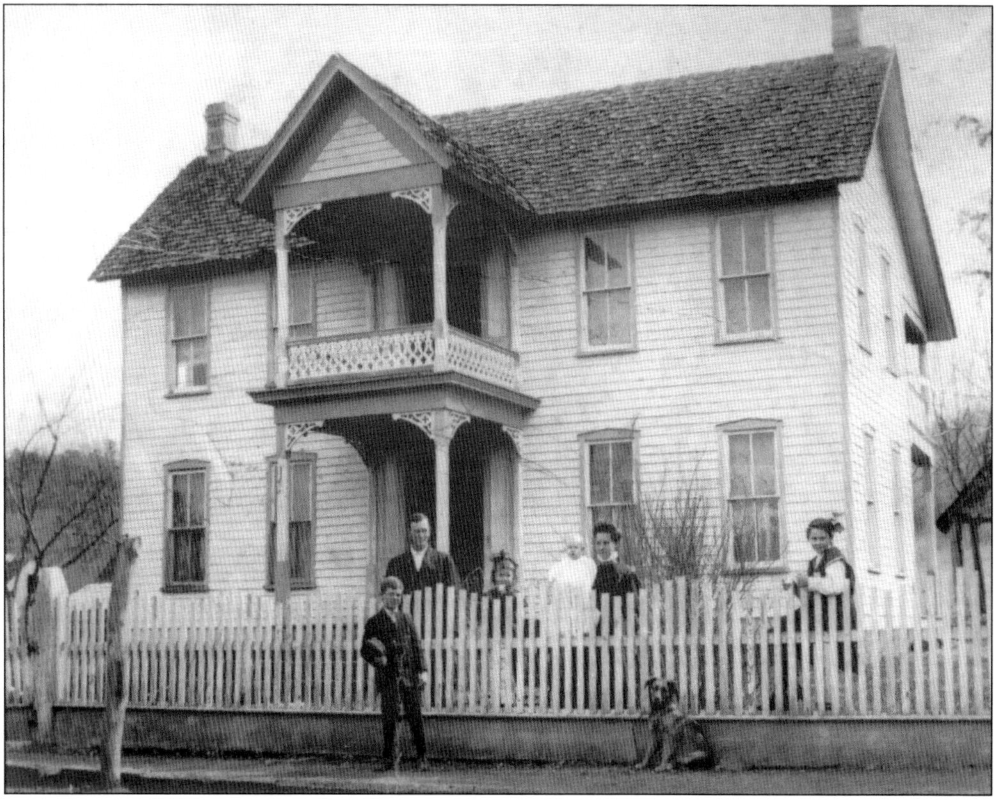

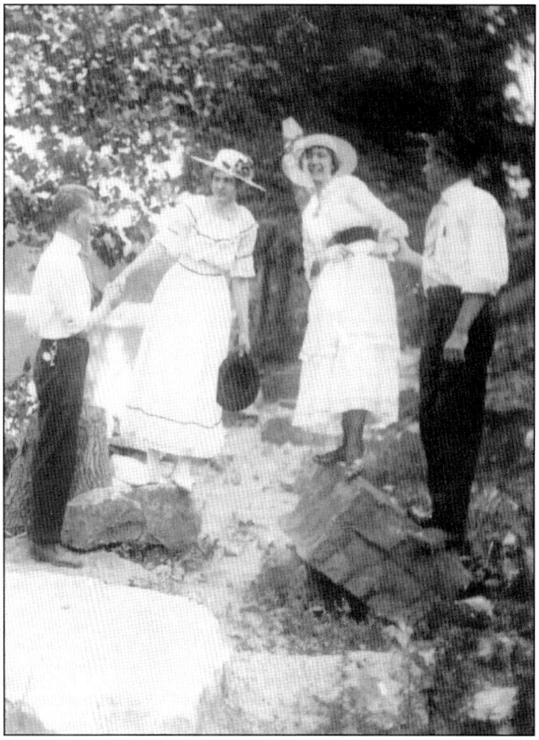

During his lifetime, Dr. W.A. Bradley cared for the health of hundreds of the residents of Newton County. He posed here with his family in front of his home on Clark Street in Jasper in 1912. Today, the restored building houses the Bradley House Museum and the offices of the Newton County Historical Society. (Courtesy of Bradley House Museum.)

Given their dress, it was likely a Sunday when Eliza and Pearl Villines posed while balanced on a pair of rocks. Only one man, Fred Braswell, is identified. (NCL.)

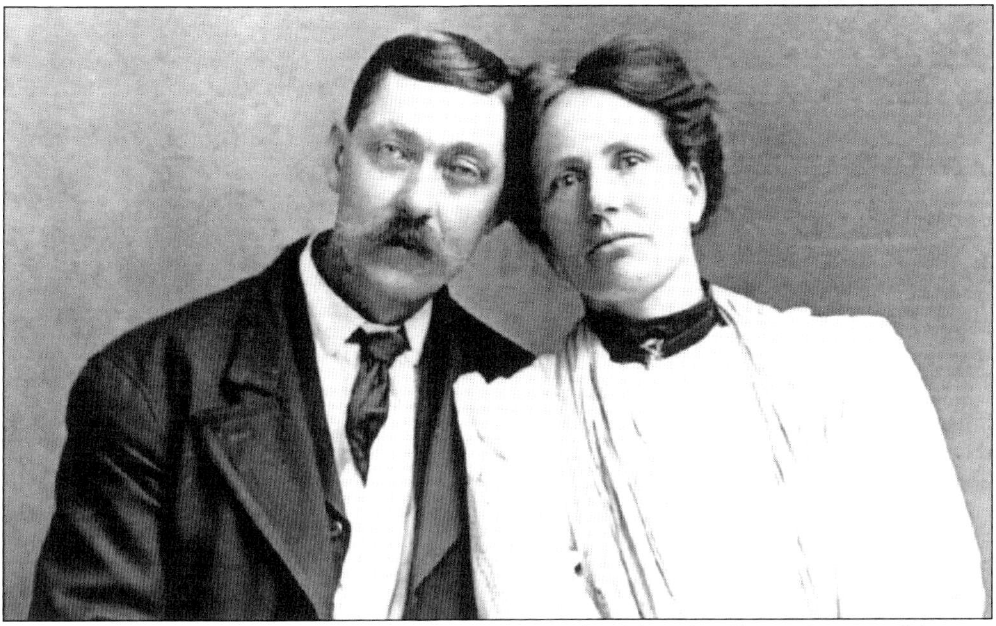

With heads together like a pair of lovebirds, Benton and Adaline (Dial) Meadow posed for a photograph in the early 1900s. It was likely a rare professional studio pose; hence, the couple dressed in their finest attire. (NCL.)

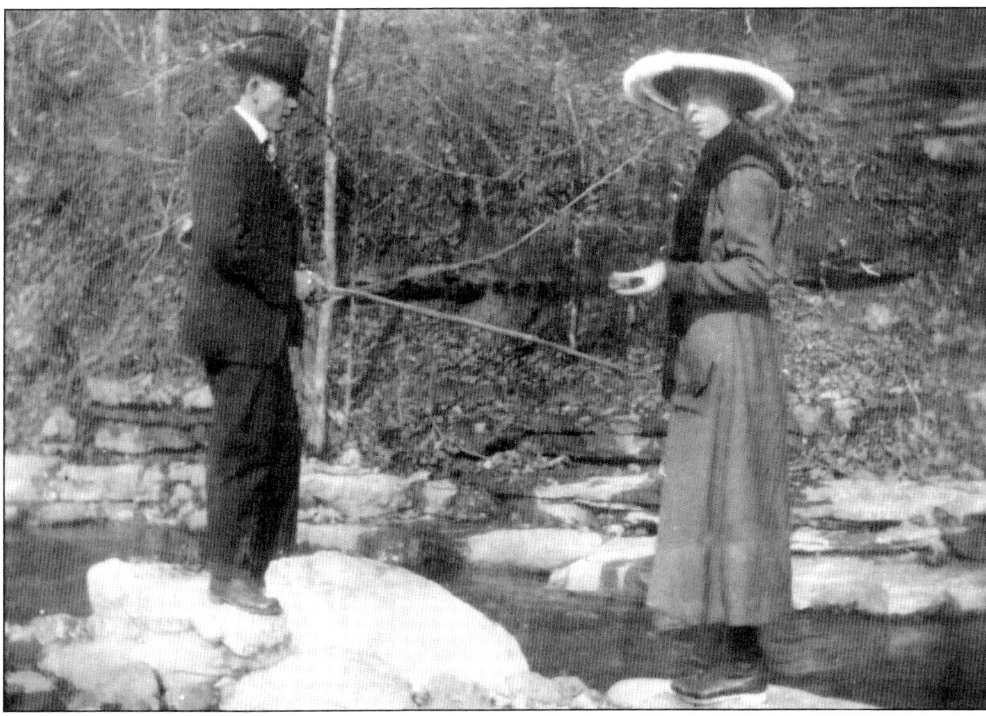

On a winter day almost a century ago, Flora Perky and Jim Vaughn were photographed on the banks of a rocky stream; it appears that he was fishing and she was eating. What they were saying to one another can only be imagined. According to Newton County records, James "Jim" Vaughn was born in 1886 and died in 1971. (NCL.)

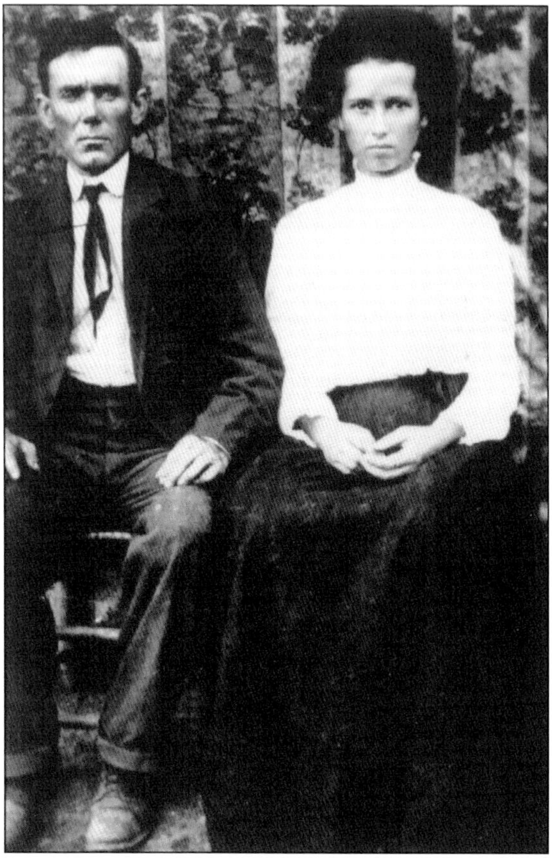

The rather stiff pose and solemn expression on the faces of William and Ellen Cunningham suggested that dressing up for the camera was a departure from the hard workdays that were a normal part of their life. The couple lived in the Smith Mountain community of Newton County. (NCL.)

Joseph Rush was a Union army veteran of the Civil War and one of the first settlers in the Mount Judea area of Newton County. He was photographed with his wife, Sarah, around 1900. (NCL.)

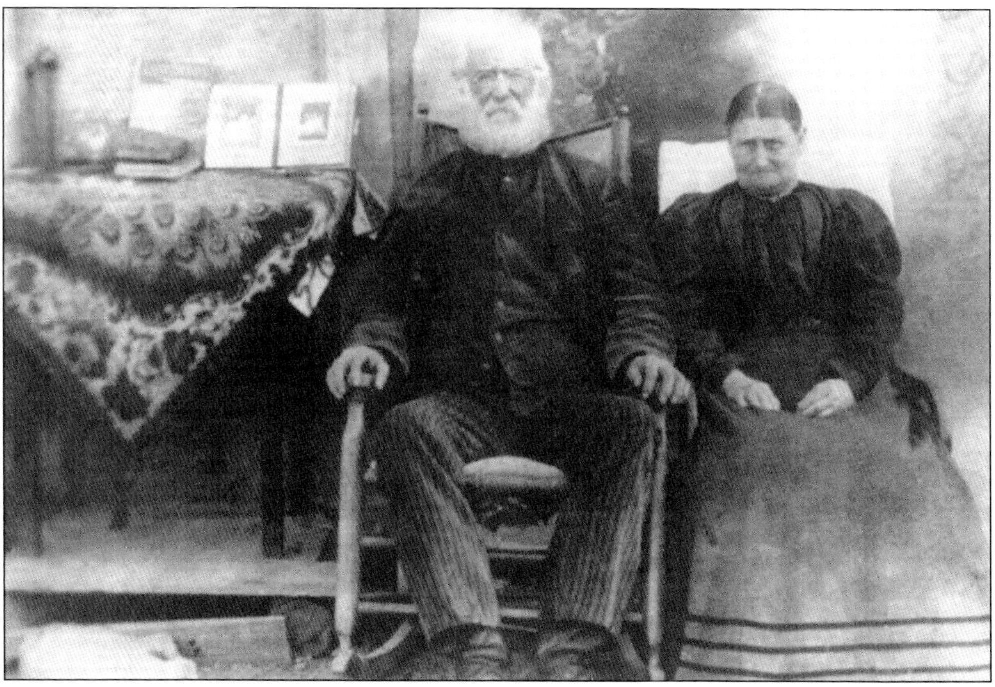

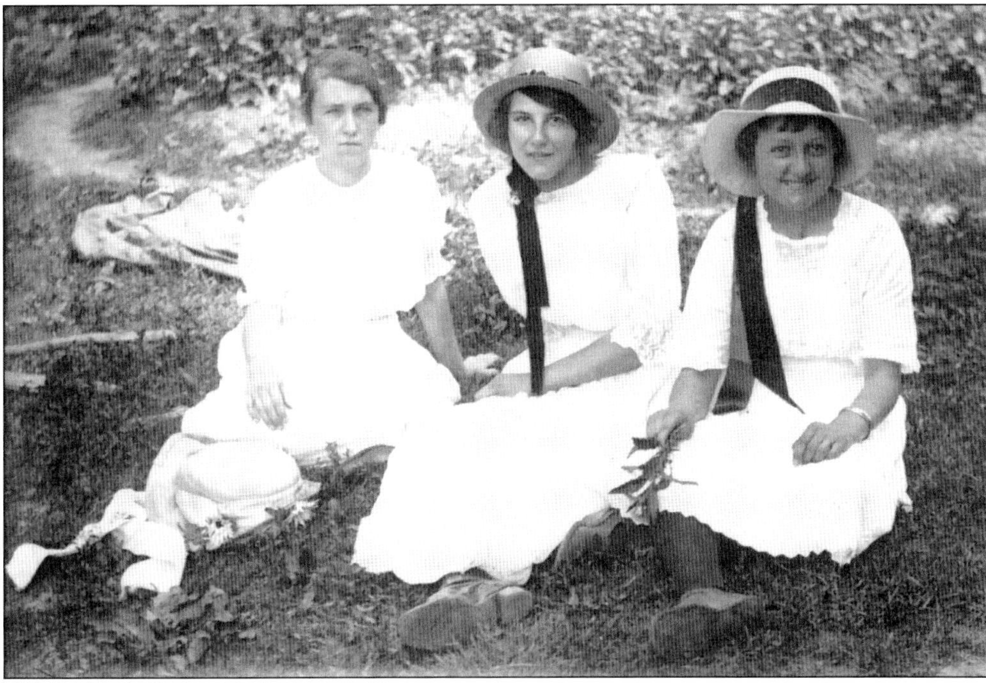

"Those Belles" was the notation on a photograph of Beulah Snow, Frankie Carlton, and Ruth Pruitt, likely taken around 1920. (NCL.)

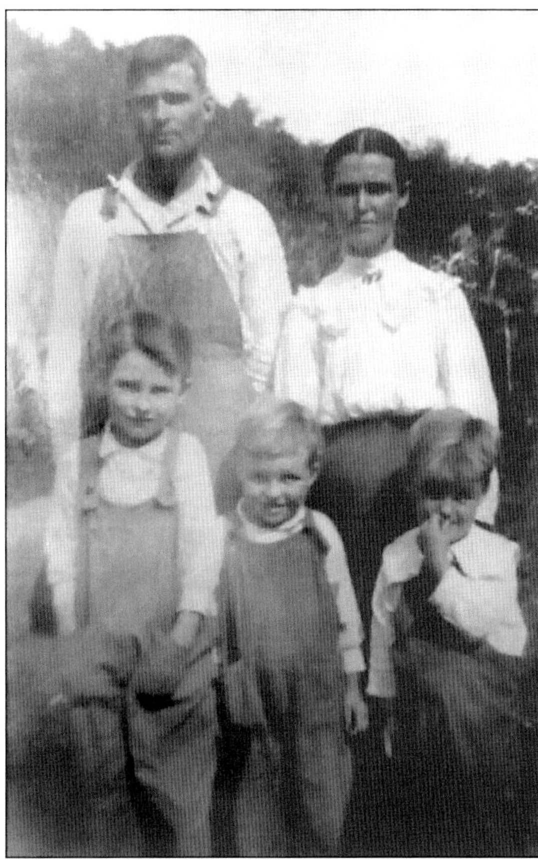

Every family since the invention of photography has captured an image of a boy who chose the snap of the shutter to do the wrong thing, including Ewell Edison Norton, who is picking his nose in this shot. The child, about four, was photographed around 1923 with his family in the Limestone community where his father was a farmer. Josiah Norton and his wife, Liza, had three sons, as pictured here, but later would also have a daughter. Liza Norton died in her late 30s or early 40s. (Courtesy of Dr. Brenda Powell of Hot Springs, daughter of Ewell Norton.)

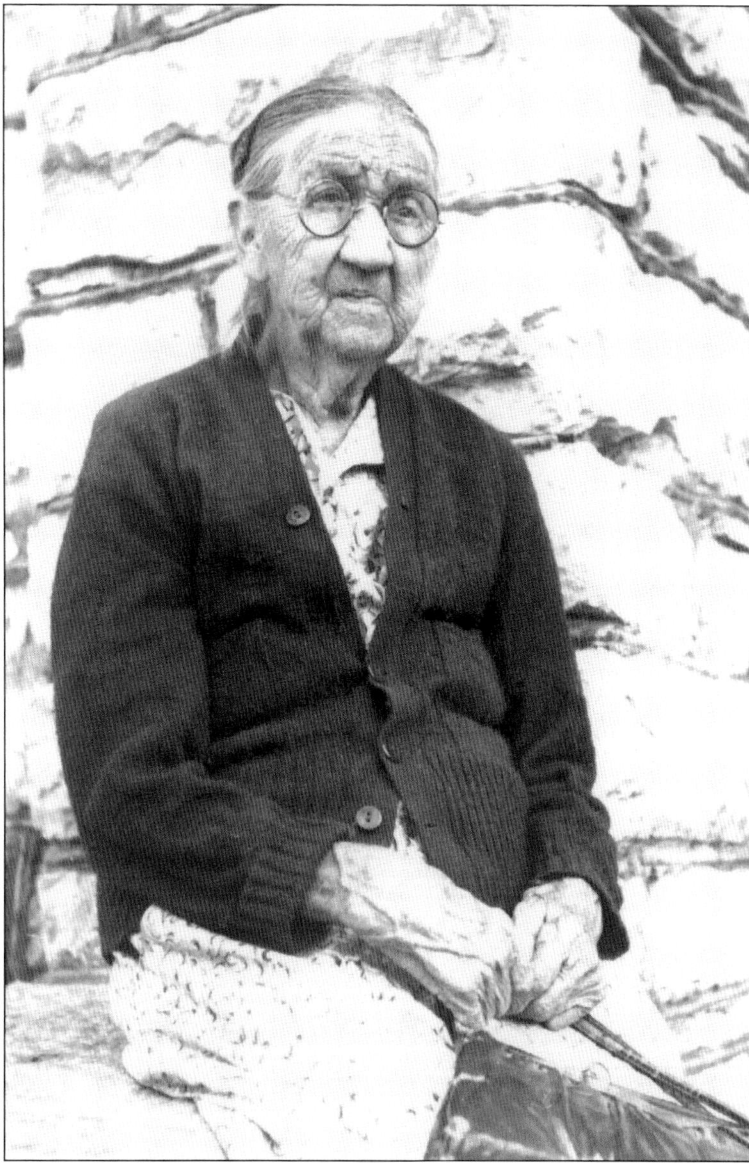

Frances "Fannie" Duck was born in Newton County in 1868 and lived a life of extraordinary service to others. She spent decades as a lay midwife, traveling the remote regions of the county to help bring babies safely into the world. Interviewed toward the end of her long life and asked how many babies she had delivered, she replied, "I never tried to keep a count, but they ran into the hundreds and often I've had two cases in one week." She went on, "I always kept some spicewood and black gum bark on hand, and when I went to deliver a baby I always gave a cup full of black gum bark tea to start the delivery and keep things going right for the baby to be born. I always gave the spicewood tea after the baby came to stop the after-pains, and the women got along well and didn't need any operations. All of them were always stout and healthy." Fannie had married Daniel "Bud" Duck in 1885 on Cave Creek in Newton County; Bud died of pneumonia in 1910. In addition to serving as a midwife, Fannie also mixed cement and made many embellished grave markers around the community of Bass, although she was unable to read or write. She died in 1956 and is buried at the McCutchen Cemetery in Newton County.

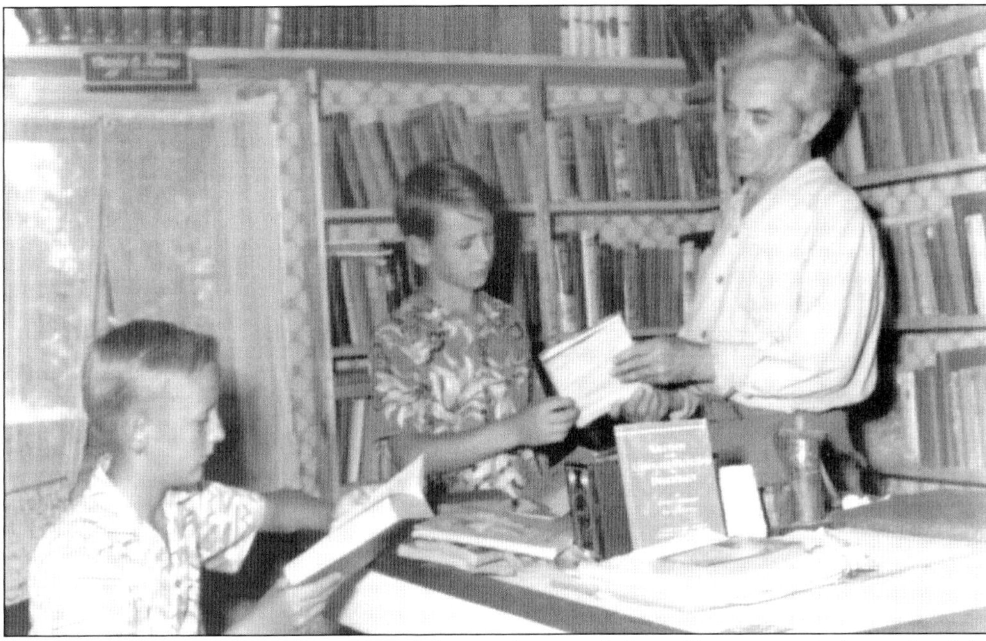

Ted Richmond, after a career as a journalist in places including Chicago, settled outside of the Newton County community of Mount Sherman in 1931. He homesteaded 150 acres and named his new log cabin "Wildcat" after the animal that had followed him as he selected the building site. Recognizing the shortage of books available to area residents, he started a letter-writing campaign to his city friends, requesting book and magazine donations. The Wilderness Library was born from this effort and was housed in Richmond's cabin. Seen here with Richmond are Jether Raney (left) and Don Kilgore, two of the children who patronized the library. (NCL.)

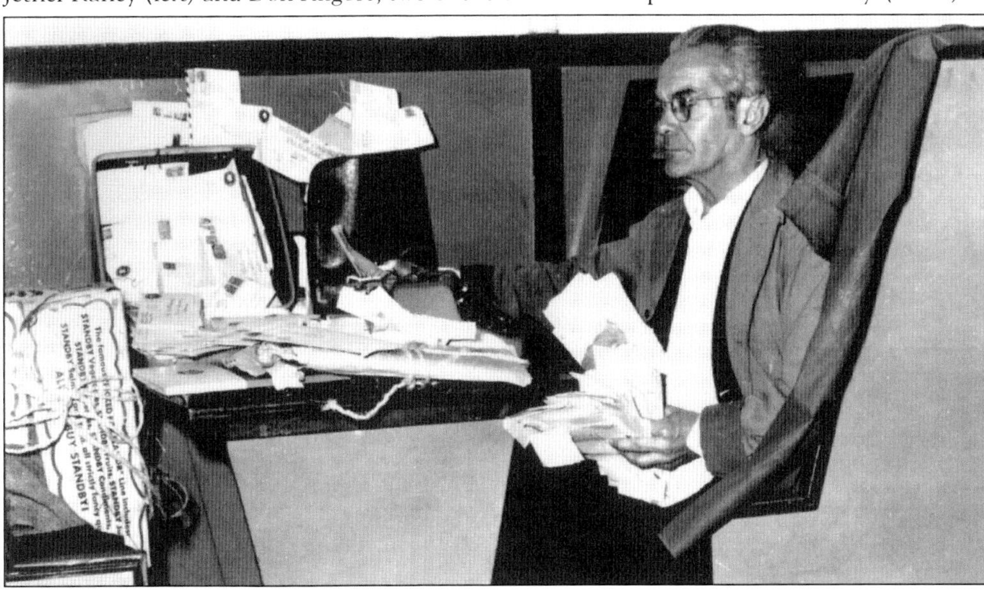

As Ted Richmond and his Wilderness Library grew in fame, he received a flood of fan letters and donated reading materials. He was photographed here in a booth at the Ozark Cafe, reading a portion of his fan mail. Donations of books even came from Eleanor Roosevelt, taken from the library of the late FDR. (NCL.)

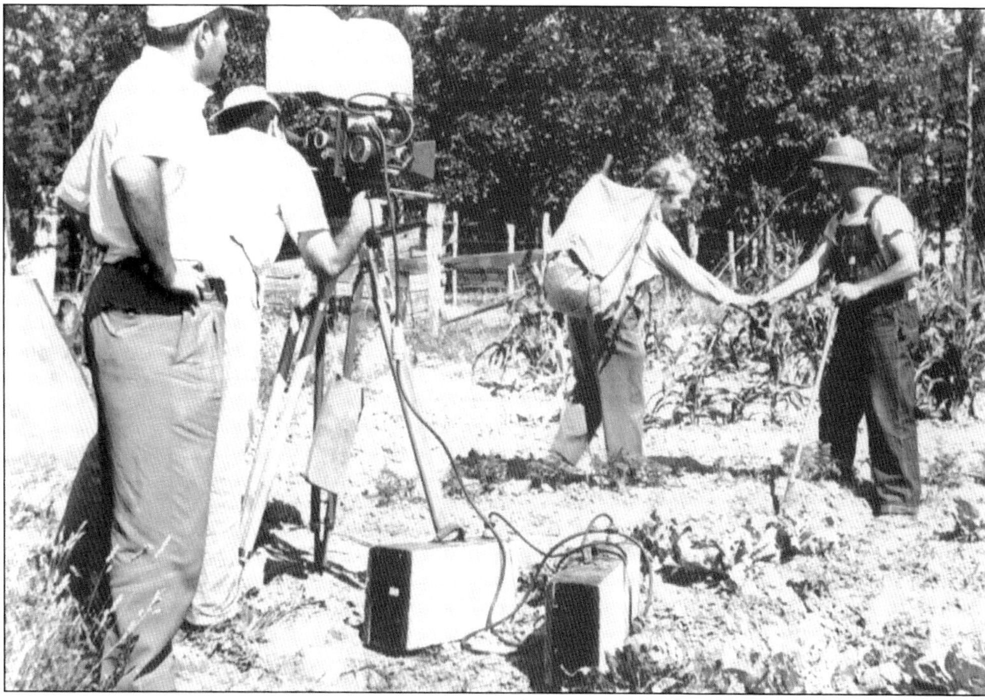

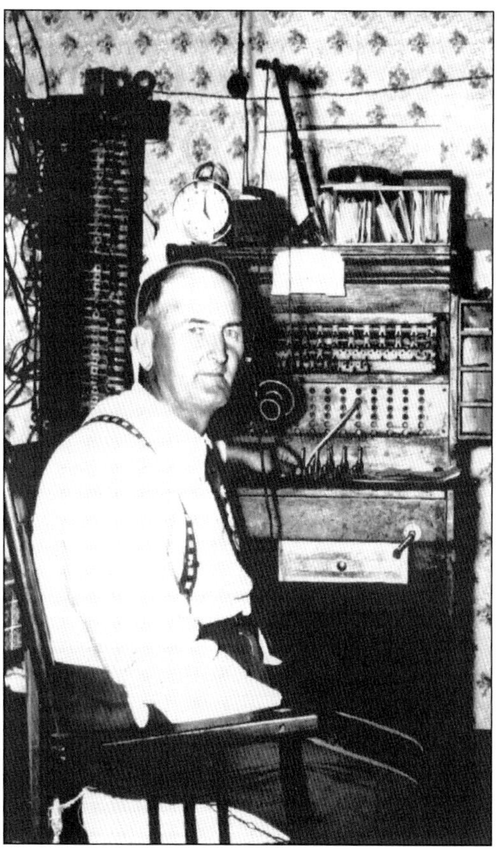

Ted Richmond walked the remote areas of Newton County with a backpack loaded with heavy books, circulating reading material to families who might not have been able to reach his log cabin library near Mount Sherman. The Wilderness Library and its founder became the subject of a film around 1950, funded by the federal government. This photograph shows the crew at work here. Ted Richmond left Newton County in 1956 and died in Texarkana in 1975. Today, Newton County boasts a wonderful public library at Jasper, which has Ted's backpack on display. (NCL.)

Hugh Raney, born in 1892, was a carpenter by trade and minister at the Mount Sherman Assembly of God Church. During the week, Raney took his turn operating Jasper's telephone exchange from this switchboard. Hugh's father, Harvey Raney, started the first Telephone Company in Jasper. Hugh's daughter Nellie took over the operation of the company in 1955 and ran it until 1962, when it was sold to the Tri-County Telephone Company. Though he has long since gone onto his reward, the switchboard is on display at the Bradley House Museum in Jasper. (NCL.)

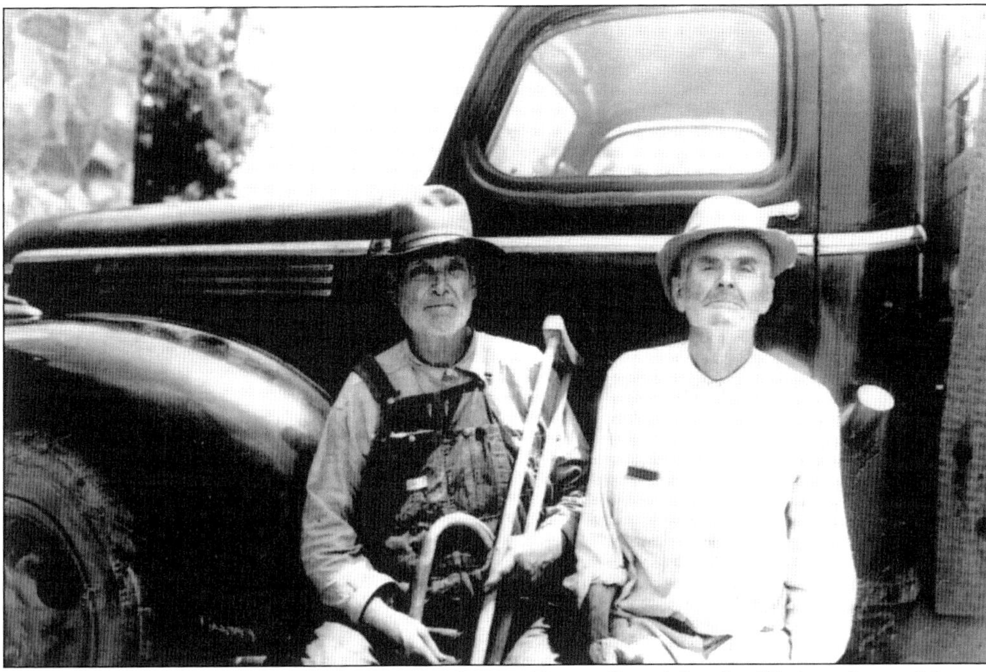

Miles Wishon, born in 1868, was the son of Issac (Conrad) and Sintha Wishon. James Marion Casey was born in 1870 to William Uriah and Mary Casey. The two septuagenarians were pictured sitting on the running board of a truck in the 1940s, doubtless having had many things to reminisce about. Miles Wishon died in 1950, and Marion Casey died in 1955. (NCL.)

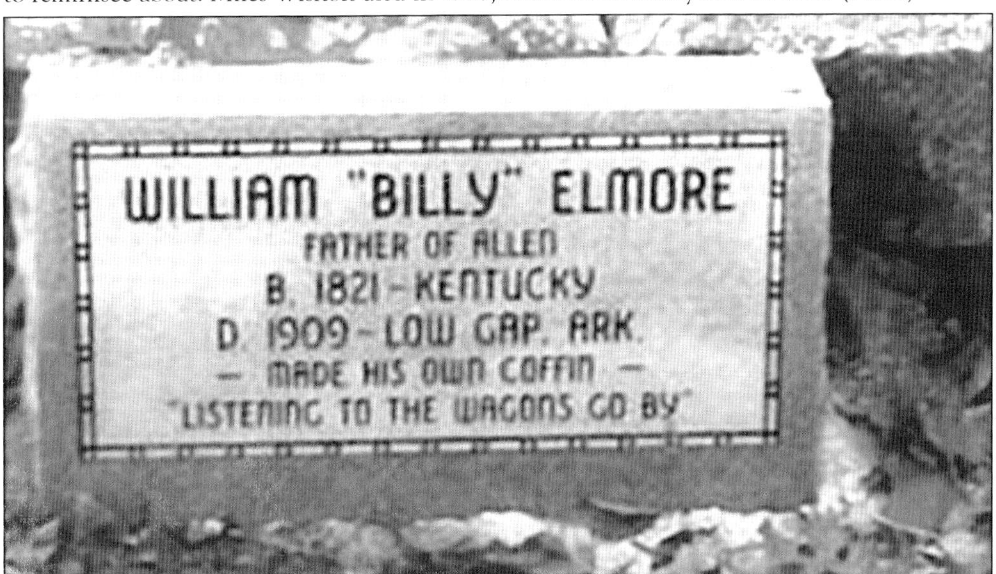

Some of the Newton County pioneers did not leave a photographic image but rather a tale in stone. William Elmore was born in Kentucky in 1821 and died in 1909, at Low Gap, Arkansas. Long before he died, the cabinetmaker had crafted his own coffin of walnut wood. Family stories tell that he often climbed in it to see how it fit, and that in old age, he got stuck and had to be helped out by his grandchildren. When Elmore died, at his request, he was buried three miles south of Low Gap beside the Shiloh Road so that "he could hear the wagons go by."

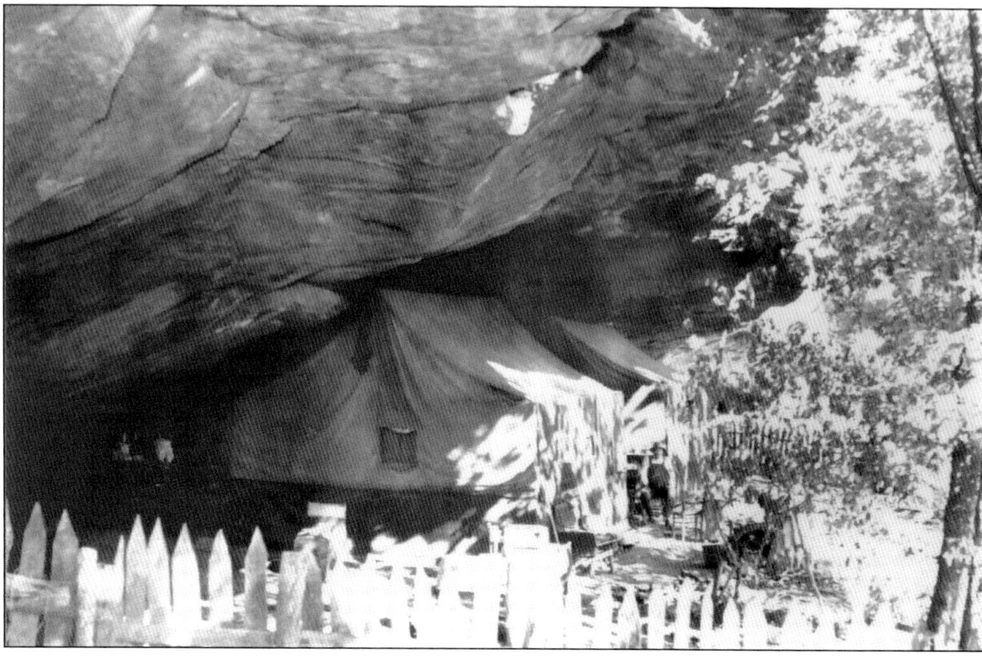

Henry and Bettie Rush lost their home and possessions to a fire; with no insurance, they found the cost of building a new home prohibitive. Their solution was to move into a cave shelter near their old home southeast of Jasper where, with the added protection of two large tents, they installed all the comforts of home. The 100-yard-long cave was portioned off into living space and work areas that included beehives and a profitable herd of angora goats. An adjacent garden helped to make the couple self-sufficient. A cool stream of water in the bottom of the cave even provided running water. (NCL.)

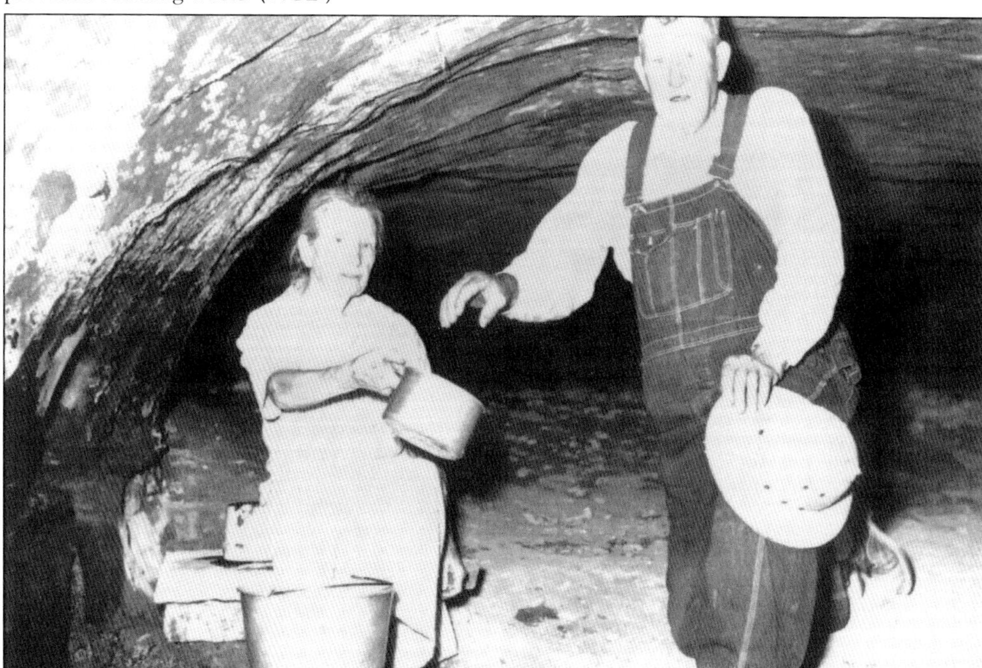

Some images remain as funny after a century as they were to those who had set up the comic pose for the photograph. "The Three Jackasses" at Jasper in 1913 were, from right to left, Daniel Boone Lackey, Jarvis Shinn, and Otto Moten. The message reads, "I hope you are now home from the hospital and feeling like borrowing my hound dogs for a coon hunt."

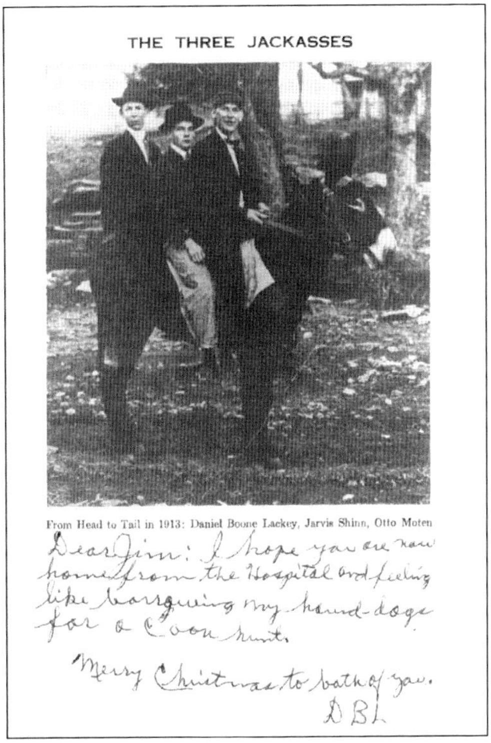

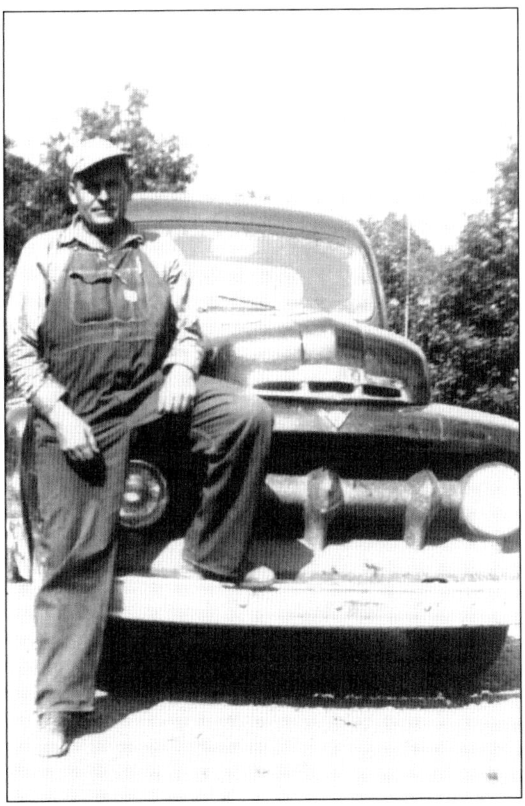

Our remembrances of Newton County close with a classic image of a hardworking resident of the area. Walter C. Christian was born in Cora City, Illinois, in 1905 but moved to Newton County with his family at the age of eight. About 100 years ago, Walter's father, Barlow Christian, and his uncle Walter Christian walked together and led a cow from Illinois to Lurton in southern Newton County, where they selected a homestead in 1912. Their families followed a year later and have been counted among the county's populace ever since. Walter Christian posed with his truck around 1952. (Courtesy of Donna Dodson of Cave Creek.)